BETWEEN
BRITAIN

Also by Alistair Moffat

The Sea Kingdoms: The History of Celtic Britain and Ireland
The Borders: A History of the Borders from Earliest Times
Before Scotland: The Story of Scotland Before History
Tyneside: A History of Newcastle and
Gateshead from Earliest Times
The Reivers: The Story of the Border Reivers
The Wall: Rome's Greatest Frontier
Tuscany: A History
The Highland Clans
The Faded Map: The Lost Kingdoms of Scotland
The Scots: A Genetic Journey
Britain's Last Frontier: A Journey Along the Highland Line
The British: A Genetic Journey
Hawick: A History from Earliest Times
Bannockburn: The Battle for a Nation
Scotland: A History from Earliest Times
The Hidden Ways: Scotland's Forgotten Roads
To the Island of Tides: A Journey to Lindisfarne
The Secret History of Here: A Year in the Valley

BETWEEN BRITAIN

BRITAIN

WALKING THE HISTORY OF ENGLAND AND SCOTLAND

ALISTAIR MOFFAT

CANONGATE

First published in Great Britain, the USA and Canada in 2024
by Canongate Books Ltd, 14 High Street, Edinburgh EHI ITE

Distributed in the USA by Publishers Group West
and in Canada by Publishers Group Canada

canongate.co.uk

1

British Library Cataloguing-in-Publication Data
A catalogue record for this book is available on
request from the British Library

ISBN 978 1 83885 438 6

Typeset in Dante MT Std by Palimpsest Book Production Ltd,
Falkirk, Stirlingshire

Printed and bound in Great Britain by Clays Ltd, Elcograf S.p.A.

To Barbara and Marjie,
with love and thanks for a lifetime's kindness.

Contents

Map of Route

Day One

The Berwick Bounds

This is a history of histories, a tangled tale of versions of half-forgotten truths, of contradictions and complexities, and of enduring misunderstandings. But perhaps most of all, it is an account of a hundred-mile journey between the once-known; an exploration of profound change, of the rediscovery of territory long thought of as familiar, comfortably comprehensible.

It began on a March morning when a red dawn lit the eastern sky and the crumpled clouds on the horizon were briefly burnished gold before they quickly cleared. The sun would shine as I set out and perhaps more enlightenment would follow my footsteps. A Scotsman born, bred and educated – and more than that, a Scottish Borderer – I planned to travel along a thick black line, the border between England and Scotland. I had grown up in the shadow of England and long believed that I understood, or was at least familiar with, Englishness. But over the last two decades, and perhaps unnoticed before that, England had begun to change, sometimes visibly. Out of nowhere, it seemed, thousands of St George's flags had begun to flutter from taxi and car windows, in front gardens and from upstairs bedroom windows, and not just on sporting occasions. Instead of the irritating and lazy use of England to mean Britain, Down South was becoming more obviously aware of itself, restlessly searching for a more sharply defined identity. Was England still Elgar and Benson's 'Land of Hope and Glory', the mother of the free? Or were its wider still and wider bounds narrowing, beginning to turn inwards? England voted to withdraw from the European Union. That seemed to me to signal a process of redefinition, or perhaps a rebellion against globalisation, the homogenisation of high streets with international chains rather than local shops, the control exercised by supra-national companies no one elected and whose phone lines were constantly experiencing a high volume of calls. We seemed to be living in a world of faceless transactions. Who were we any more? Algorithms?

And England now seems diffident about the continuation of the British union. Perhaps parliaments in Edinburgh, Cardiff and Belfast have altered England's sense of itself, induced a process of reflection? Would a Scot, an outsider, be able to detect that transformation, discover detail and difference as the myths of empire unravelled to reveal another England, defined by older glories, ancient identities and newer hopes? I wanted to understand better the stories England was now telling itself.

I also wanted to look over my shoulder at the Scotland that lies to the north of me, a place whose history I have written about, a place I thought I knew well. No longer. Scotland looks different; sounds different, too. Was a similar rebellion against globalisation going on? And instead of withdrawing from the European Union, did Scotland want to leave the British union? Were we re-inventing a sense of ourselves by embracing much that is unquestionably un-English, that could only be Scottish? In the last thirty years or so, the iconography of the Highlands has come to represent the whole country. When I was young, kilts were worn in the Lowlands by marching soldiers, eccentrics and men my dad called 'professional Scotsmen'. Now no wedding would be complete without the groom, the best man and most of the male guests tricked out in kilts, plaids and a knife stuck in the top of their socks. Instead of leading a battalion of the Black Watch, pipers play the bride and her kilted father into the church. What has happened to Scotland's sense of herself? Why has the Tartan Army mustered at about the same time as the crosses of St George have been unfurled?

It seemed to me that the best vantage point, a place where I could look in each direction, might be the border between England and Scotland as it runs up into the Cheviot Hills from the Tweed at Berwick before descending to Gretna Green and the Solway Firth in the west. And to see the turns of history more clearly, I needed not to sit behind the windscreen of a car or the glass window of a railway carriage or a bus; I needed to walk and feel on my face which way the winds of change were blowing.

Having packed a rucksack with a change of clothes, I turned my attention to the vital business of pockets. While women tend to pack their travelling possessions into bags of one sort and another, men like pockets. One of the main reasons for the enduring popularity of the jacket and trousers (or jeans – less so the suit these days) is that between them most have nine pockets: four in the trousers, front and back (three in cheap pairs), and five in the jacket. Like most mildly obsessional older men, certain items can only go in certain pockets: hankie in the left-hand trouser pocket, keys and change in the right, wallet in the inside-left jacket pocket (for those who are right-handed), mobile phone in the right-hand outer pocket of the jacket, and comb (you never know) in the top pocket. I smiled when I discovered that one of my literary heroines, Daphne du Maurier, often went walking and she never failed to put make-up in her rucksack. You never know.

While I toyed with the notion of a warm Harris Tweed jacket for my journey, I needed something that was more waterproof and could also accommodate a map. This involved a careful rethink of the use and distribution of pockets. Trousers were as usual, but the three zipped pockets of a bodywarmer could safely hold a wallet and other spare items such as sunglasses, a hat and a spare hankie that did not have to be immediately to hand. My waterproof needed pockets that were large enough for my notebook, a map and my mobile phone (for taking photographs – I most certainly did not want to speak to anybody or check my emails) – and it took a good deal of rummaging around to find a light anorak with a hood. This rigmarole may seem petty but it is most assuredly essential for someone about to undertake a long walk, often over rough country, sometimes in terra incognita and miles from home. If something were dropped unnoticed, it would be lost and gone forever, and I could carry only essentials.

I had gone into Edinburgh a few weeks before to splash out on something that would repel splashes. My old boots had ceased to be waterproof and I needed a new pair that would take me through the puddles, dubs and mires of the Cheviots. A confident young man sold me boots that were very comfortable and light but an unfortunate shade of beige. Not only did he invite me to walk on an area of the shop floor embedded with rocks, real ones, and walk up an uphill slope to test flexion, the salesman also showed me how to tie the laces in knots that would not come undone.

Sensibly shod, pockets sorted, I drove down the Tweed Valley on that sunny March morning bound for the strange stretch of the border known as the Berwick Bounds. About twelve square miles north and west of the town on the Scottish bank of the great river, it is a strong memory of England's power over Scotland. Once the town had finally been torn out of its hinterland of Berwickshire (the only county named after a place that is not in it) in 1482, land was demanded so that the citizens could conveniently pasture their cows and sheep, and farmers could cut hay and cultivate crops to feed them. It seemed to me that the English bear had stretched a paw over the Tweed to claim what is known as the Liberties of Berwick. An enormous and dangerous English bear that had snarled often at Scotland.

I had also decided to walk the border from east to west, from morning to evening. I'm not certain what prompted that decision – certainly not common sense. The prevailing wind is from the west or south-west and there would inevitably be more than a breeze once I'd gained some elevation. Berwick is the only large town on the border, and maybe I had thought it would be good to walk from its ancient streets and bloody history into the peace of the hills and long views to the south and the north.

Cast adrift from history, denying its geography, Berwick-upon-Tweed is now a place apart. Often described as the most northerly town in England, it is in any sensible reality nothing of the kind. Lying on latitudes further north than Lanark, Kilmarnock, the Isle of Arran and much of Islay, its early development owed everything to what is now Scotland and nothing to England. The commercial hub of the medieval Tweed Valley, its gaze was directed westwards to the great wool and cattle producers of the Scottish Borders and east-wards to Europe and the textile industries of Flanders and northern Italy. Berwick only looked south when the English bear growled and armies marched north.

Now entirely effaced, not one stone left standing upon another, the great inland market town of Roxburgh was Berwick's business partner. Nestled in the river peninsula formed by the junction of the Teviot and the Tweed near Kelso, the town once boasted four churches, a grammar school and a mint, all protected by a mighty royal castle on the riverbank. But Roxburgh has completely disappeared, a blank testament to the sweeping power of history. Since childhood, the haunted, silent, empty grass parks where the town once stood have fascinated me. Wondering what secrets lay beneath the turf, imagining the bustle, smell and excitement of the markets, I walked there often, and on that spring morning when I drove down to Berwick I stopped for a few minutes to look at the place where urban life had begun in Scotland.

In the early twelfth century, David I of Scotland and his incoming, innovative Anglo-Norman lords had endowed four sprawling monastic foundations in the Borders at Kelso, Melrose, Dryburgh and Jedburgh. Great entrepreneurs, the abbeys were the engines of the medieval economy of Scotland, as they developed vast sheep ranches in the Cheviot Hills and the Lammermuirs. On the fertile flood plains, the abbots and their tenants raised cattle and created a lucrative export business in hides. Melrose even pioneered the sale of futures, borrowing against the wool crops to come, in order to rebuild and embellish their great church. When merchants bought leather and woolpacks at Roxburgh's markets, they moved their goods down the Tweed, probably on barges or rafts, to load them into ships tied up at the Berwick quays that were bound for southern England or Europe.

Behind the town walls and also protected by royal statute were established communities of Flemish and German merchants in their halls and warehouses. Craft guilds were formed and the Scottish Laws of the Burghs, which regulated trade and tolls, were almost certainly formulated at Berwick in the later twelfth century for application throughout the realm. The annual value of the town's customs, the taxes levied on outbound and inbound trade, was enormous. In 1286, the revenue from

Berwick to the Scottish Crown was £2,190 compared to £8,800 for the whole of England, including London. Business was booming and, in most senses that mattered, Berwick was the capital place of Scotland.

On the night of 19 March, in that same year of high customs revenues, everything changed for the town, and for the whole kingdom of Scotland. Alexander III was feasting with his cronies in the Great Hall of Edinburgh Castle, and drinking too much. Perhaps unsteadily, the king rose from the table and roared that he had had enough of male company. Where was his young and beautiful new queen, Yolande de Dreux? The kingdom needed an heir and that very night, by God's blood, he would make one!

The immediate difficulty was that the queen was not in Edinburgh but across the Firth of Forth in Fife, at the royal manor at Kinghorn. And outside, a late winter rainstorm was raging on a moonless night. No matter! Horses were saddled, and the royal party clattered across the cobbles of the castle gatehouse and galloped hard for the ferry. High winds were whipping spindrift off the firth, but, no doubt flushed with wine and his desire not dampened, the king insisted on crossing.

Once on the Fife shore, fresh horses were found and Alexander III rode into the darkness, spurring his horse, taking the fate of his realm with him. On the cliff path at Pettycur, only a mile from the warm embrace of Queen Yolande, the king's horse may have spooked in the wind. It certainly lost its footing and plunged itself and its rider to their death, dashed on the rocks two hundred feet below. When Alexander's body was found the following morning, the long line of macMalcolm kings had failed and Scotland's sudden vulnerability woke the English bear. For three centuries afterwards, intermittent warfare crackled across the border, devastating the farms and villages of the Tweed Valley, as English dynasts tried and often succeeded in subjugating Scotland. Commerce broke down, merchants fled, few ships sailed from the Berwick quays, and behind its crumbling walls Roxburgh began to wither and die.

The great and immensely valuable Scottish port was assaulted again and again. Perhaps the most savage English siege was laid in the summer of 1333 when the army of Edward III arrived under Berwick's walls. A truce was arranged. In return for a pledge that the town would surrender if a relieving army did not appear in a matter of days, the governor, Sir Alexander Seton, gave up a number of hostages, including his sons, Thomas and Alexander. With no regard for the agreed terms, King Edward ordered a gallows to be set up across the Tweed from the town walls, just out of bowshot but in full view of the town's defenders. Seton's sons were brought forward, their hands bound behind their backs, and they were stood on stools with nooses around their necks. Edward then demanded the immediate surrender of Berwick – or not only would Thomas and Alexander die, but with each day that passed two more hostages would wriggle on the end of an English rope in front of their parents and friends. It is said that Lady Seton turned her husband away from the battlements, as the stools were kicked from under their children's feet and they slowly choked to death. On the southern end of Old Berwick Bridge there is a place known as Hang-a-Dyke Neuk.

Even further north than the town is the little hamlet of Marshall Meadows, the most northerly inhabited settlement in England, five hundred and fifty-six miles from Land's End, four hundred and twenty-six by crow. It is three hundred and thirty-five miles from Marshall Meadows to John O' Groats and it is nearer to Edinburgh than Newcastle. Far from help or reinforcement from the south, Berwick lost its role as a commercial port and became instead a garrison town. Roxburgh was deserted, the dressed stone of its ruined buildings robbed out as the streets and gardens sank beneath the weeds and grass, and the ancient clamour of its markets died away into silence.

Royal orders from London in 1560 established the office of High Marshall as deputy to the military Governor of Berwick. And on that sunny, still morning in early March I found myself in the Marshall's meadows, sitting on a bench outside a handsome country house hotel, checking my pockets, unfolding a map, about to take the first steps on a long journey that would take me from England's northernmost outpost along the length of the border, as far as the western coasts and the Solway Firth.

But first, I wanted to walk the Berwick Bounds. I planned to make my way along the line of the Scotland–England border inland from the Marshall Meadows before turning south towards the Tweed and the riverside pasture known as the Coroner's Meadow. Fortified by Scott's Porage Oats and strong coffee, I reckoned that the five- or six-mile journey would take me about two hours. Once I reached the great river, where the border turns west to follow its midstream, I would then walk along its northern bank to begin my journey west.

I had crossed the border countless times but never walked around it. Of course I knew that the fields on either side looked the same and that the people were familiar. But important cultural differences had developed since 1482, when English and Scottish borderers began to turn their backs on each other. Accent is one of the most obvious. A version of Northumbrian, a country cousin of Tyneside's Geordie accent, the speech of Berwickers, is very different from what is heard on the Scottish side. Probably a consequence of divergent national churches and their control of separate education systems, the fact that accent switches so abruptly when an artificial line is crossed is still a jolting surprise. People who live no more than a hundred yards apart, but on either side of the thick black line, speak dialects that only just sound like derivatives of the same language.

Different jurisdictions and political arrangements, and other formal distinctions, feed a divide that began to widen with the passing of the centuries since the occupation of Berwick by an English garrison. But in 2008 old perceptions were suddenly upended. The results of a poll showed that a staggering 79 per cent of Berwick residents would prefer the town to be returned to Scotland. Cynics saw the Scottish Parliament's provision of free care for the elderly and the payment of tuition fees for students as the main motives to move the border, and there was certainly some truth in that. But the council leader at the time, Isabel Hunter, said, 'The

Scottish Parliament is less than sixty miles away from us, while Westminster is more than three hundred miles away. Berwick feels like a wee little block nobody wants.' Another prominent local figure added, 'Berwick is just a lost town.'

These findings and comments should not be so surprising, given all of the history that has rumbled up to the town's formidable walls. Berwick had been torn out of its cultural and geographical context in 1482, and for five centuries the town had been searching for a different identity.

Where England reluctantly begins seemed a good place to start. Like a piece of history's driftwood washed up by the ebb and flow of war and stranded far above the high-tide mark, Berwick has long seemed to me to exist in a version of eternal limbo: not England, or Scotland, but suspended somewhere between Britain. Uncertainty and provisional history would set a good tone for a journey of rediscovery.

Through a gap in the hedge behind the hotel at Marshall Meadows, I could see and hear the dual carriageway of the A1 and two sets of three flags marking the moment when cars and trucks crossed from Scotland into England. I reckoned it lay less than a mile to the north. Down a tidy tarmac lane lay Marshall Meadows Caravan Park. Perched on the high cliffs above a small bay were many static caravans, all of them with a sea view of sorts and very few of them occupied. The site seemed bleak to me, less like a jolly holiday camp, more like an army camp, the corrugated sides of the caravans resembling Nissen huts. Perhaps it was only in the summer that a border guard of English OAPs mustered, ready to repel raids from the north.

The only activity I came across was at the foot of a huge hole, like a bomb crater. A crane was lifting very large Lego-like blocks of white concrete and slotting them on the sides of a small, square housing. Fifteen years ago, I had come to this caravan park (when there were far fewer pitches) to look at a curious tunnel cut out of the rock. It led under the original line of the Great North Road out of Berwick and, later, the old line of the railway. The steep tunnel took workmen and -women to an outlet about halfway down the sheer cliffs of Marshall Meadows Bay. In the nineteenth century, the brown seaweed known as kelp was much valued for the production of chemicals such as sodium, magnesium and potassium, essential ingredients in the manufacture of glass, soap and fertiliser. Kelp prices were high, fetching more than £20 a ton.

The semi-circular shape of Marshall Meadows Bay was perfect for the gathering of this valuable seaweed. Collecting began in the winter, when it was hoped that storms over the North Sea would have loosened large quantities and the powerful tides driven it inshore. Kelpers were lowered from the end of the tunnel through the cliff to begin what must have been miserable, soaking, shivering work, as they gathered up bundles at low tide. They used toothed sickles to cut it. The kelp was then pulled up, loaded onto bogies and dragged up a track to the tunnel entrance. Where the rows of empty caravans now stand, it was burned in kilns, coffin-shaped ditches. Best was red wrack, sometimes also called yellow, black and prickly tang. The kilns burned for a long time: more than twenty tons of kelp were needed to produce a ton of chemical-rich ash, and it had to be left for weeks before it was cool enough to be lifted out.

Chemicals of a different sort supplied the reason why the entrance to the old tunnel was now being excavated and secured. One of the workmen told me that it had become a handy hidden rendezvous for drug dealers from both sides of the border, and the separate jurisdictions and police forces on either side. A locked iron gate would be installed and the key held at the office of the caravan park.

Around the bay ran a securely fenced coastal path. As a late-winter sun glistened on the flat calm of the North Sea, I made my way north to the line of the border. Just below the sheer cliffs a small boat chugged along in step with me. On the left of a latched field gate a large blue sign with part of a white saltire announced, 'Welcome to Scotland', and in case anyone doubted that a different country was ahead, there was also *Fàilte gu Alba*, the Scots Gaelic version. It seemed out of scale and melodramatic, like a fanfare of trumpets introducing a solo harmonica. I heard the distant echo of bombast, of an old lack of self-confidence. The fields on either side looked identical and the sheep were the same colour. Not for the last time, I wondered who made these decisions about signs. On the other side of the fence, there was no equivalent, nothing announcing England to those travelling south. What did that say about national self-confidence?

In fact, there was something much more interesting

on the fence. Below the first and only sign for something called the English Border Cuddy Trail was a small information board that spoke of the time when this was an international frontier. In July 1503, the slow process of union between the two kingdoms began when Margaret Tudor landed with her retinue on a beach a mile or so to the north, known as Meg's Dub. Clearly, deference to royalty lay in the future, at least in Scotland. The daughter of Henry VII of England, young Meg met the representatives of James IV of Scotland at Lamberton, a hamlet close to the coast. In its church the English princess had contracted a proxy marriage and it was celebrated on the moor with a knightly tournament. Quite why the king did not turn up in person is not clear, but in due course this dynastic union led to the succession of Meg's great-grandson, James VI, to the English throne when the kingdoms were united a century later and the frontier began to lose its meaning and its sharpness.

As the sun climbed and warmed, and I began to walk up the Scottish side of the border, its line now less than impressive – only a post and wire stock-fence – I noticed the first of the spring lambs. Lying on its side in the lee of the longer grass by the fence, one seemed abandoned, immobile. But when I looked more closely, it was panting, enjoying the warmth of the sun's rays along its flank. At the end of this first hundred yards of the border a deep canyon cut through it and leviathans roared in its depths. The main railway line from Edinburgh to London is impressive just north of Berwick, as it runs very close to the coastal cliffs, slicing through the landscape.

I looked over the dyke and realised that there was

no way I could cross it and keep to the line of the border, as I had hoped. Not only would scrambling down the steep bank and up the other side be dangerous, it was also almost certainly illegal. But further north, about half a mile away, I thought I could make out a bridge. Looking down into the cutting, I saw that a version of history had been marked. Impossible to see from a speeding train for more than a nanosecond stood an elaborate sign headlined 'Across the Border', with 'England' and a St George's cross to the south and 'Scotland' and a saltire to the north. Below was a cartoonish painting of an English lion with its tongue sticking out and beside it a Scottish unicorn that seemed to have broken a tether rope secured around its neck. And below all of this was a yellow sign prosaically announcing 'Zone Boundary', its position extending Scotland southwards by an extra yard. Beyond the railway cutting the borderline climbed a low hill towards the main road, the A1, again only a post and wire stock-fence.

Safely across the bridge over the railway line, I crossed another over the dual carriageway and walked up the verge to where the six flags marked the border. On the England side, welcoming those driving south, there were three different standards: the cross of St George, the Union Jack and a banner that is probably very ancient. The red and gold bands of the device of the Percy family, the Earls of Northumberland, has been adopted by the local authority but its origins may stretch much further back to an older identity. In his *Ecclesiastical History of the English People* of the early eighth century, Bede of

Jarrow wrote that after his death in 642, King Oswald of Northumbria was venerated as a saint. His relics were preserved and 'to furnish a lasting memorial of the royal saint, they hung the king's banner of purple and gold over his tomb'. It may have been an expression of *romanitas*, an imitation of the Roman imperial purple.

Almost certainly the ancestor of the Percy flag, Oswald's banner was emblematic of Bernicia, the name given to the northern part of his kingdom. It encompassed modern Northumbria and the Scottish Borders. The first of many contradictions, the flag of an ancient kingdom was fluttering over a frontier that divided it and forgot an ancient identity.

On the Scottish side, welcoming drivers travelling north, there was uniformity and history of a kind mixed up with modern politics. All three flags were identical, the white saltire on a blue background. Also known as the St Andrew's cross, it has been used as an emblem of Scottishness since at least the early fourteenth century, when soldiers were advised to wear patches with the cross on them 'before and behind' so that they could be identified in the ruck and chaos of battle. It was believed that St Andrew was crucified on a *crux decussata*, a cross of two diagonals, and after the building of the vast cathedral at St Andrews in the fourteenth century he finally supplanted Columba as the nation's patron saint.

What struck me was the absence of the Union Jack on the Scottish side. Whatever politics persuades people to believe, Scotland remains in the United Kingdom, for now. But again, I wondered about change and who made these decisions about symbolism. Was some sort of political statement being made on the roadside, as cars and trucks rumbled between England and Scotland, and was history being rewritten or, worse, ignored?

Subsequent research revealed that my instincts were by no means idle musings. In 2014 residents of eastern Berwickshire and local politicians questioned the flying of three saltires at the border on the A1, the place known as Lamberton Toll. It turned out to be Transport Scotland, an agency reporting directly to the Scottish Government, that had made the decision on the flags. It was proposed that there should instead be a Berwickshire banner on one of the poles to mirror the Percy colours across the road and that a Union Jack should replace another of the saltires.

The immediate difficulty was that no such thing as a Berwickshire flag existed. A frivolous design involved a bear and a wych elm tree, but thankfully nothing came of that. It would have been much mocked. The derivation of the place name of Berwick has nothing to do with bears or trees; it comes from *bere*, an old term for barley, and *wic*, Old English for a farmstead. Nevertheless, the campaigners pressed on and in 2015 Councillor Michael Cook wrote to Transport Scotland: 'people want to emphasise their local identity. To show that they're proud to be from the Borders, proud to be Scottish and proud to be part of the UK'.

Nothing has happened. Three saltires still fly at Lamberton Toll and it seemed to me that history and local identity were indeed being ignored, even denied. All of us were being shoehorned into something pan-Scottish, something uniform, someone else's idea of how we should be seen north of the border and how we should see ourselves.

The snack van in the layby was at least ecumenical. It advertised Stottie Cake, a large, round, flat loaf about twelve inches across that is a speciality in the north-east of England. Traditionally, the dough is heavy and lightly baked in the bottom of the oven. Fillings ranged from Bad Boy Bacon to a Belly Buster with four slices of black pudding. Below was a list of smaller fillings for Scottish morning rolls of more modest dimensions. Big England, Little Scotland.

Not tempted, and anxious to get on, as my diversions to cross the railway and the A1 had taken an hour, I walked through a gap in the hedge behind the snack van and over a mound of plastic debris to follow the line of the border up to the higher ground. Rather than a stock-fence, a drystane dyke snaked westwards into the heart of the Berwick Bounds. Electric fencing on both sides made it even more of a barrier. Its stones speckled with white lichen; I reckoned it had been a dyke for a long time.

Halfway up to the summit of the ridge, I crossed a ghost road, and my own tracks. In the summer of 2016, I had walked the Great North Road from Berwick up to the village of Cockburnspath. Its line lay to the west and then crossed to the east of the A1. History also travelled its length. I could hear the echo of hoofbeats. Sir Robert Carey galloped past me on his epic, four hundred-mile ride from London to Edinburgh in March 1603 to tell James VI of Scotland that he had become James I of

England. He carried a ring from the dead Queen Elizabeth's finger as proof. I stopped at a rackety tangle of old gates, barbed wire and electric fencing to look for the baggage train of the new king coming in the opposite direction, as it moved south to Berwick a few weeks later and into his new realm of England.

On the horizon the motionless silhouette of a surprise was waiting. I could make out the shape of a very large pig, watching me, standing very still. When I reached the top of the ridge, I saw that the sow was not alone. Stretching far into the distance on every side for at least a mile and more was a huge pig farm. Thousands were rootling in the mud of a barren landscape relieved only by several silver-coloured corrugated-iron shelters and bounded by low electric fences. Pigs are not to be trifled with and at first I could see no way forward. The dappled border dyke was to my right, but its electric fencing discouraged me from clambering over it. To repel very large animals like pigs, there would be a substantial current running through it. Perhaps I would have to abandon this journey almost as soon as it had started.

However, I could see that between the knee-height inner electric fence and the dyke, there was just enough space to walk. So long as I did not hurry or slip sideways in the mud, and the pigs respected the fence, maybe I could make progress.

Some of the sows lolloped off at my approach, but others, probably the older, more dominant ones, were inquisitive, coming close as I passed quickly by. With very human eyes, these vast creatures seem intelligent. I wondered if George Orwell had found it easier to imagine the characters of Napoleon, Snowball and Squealer as individuals for that reason. Perhaps in this vast army of pigs there were generals, Stalins and Trotskys, guarding the gateway to England, a bulwark of belligerent, bad boy bacon. Instead of the peace of the countryside after the roar of road and rail traffic, I found myself in a border zone patrolled by an army of twenty-five-stone sows. I walked on carefully, not wanting to share the fate of Farmer Jones.

The die-back grass along the margins of the pig farm was long and it turned out to be home and cover for some elegant and all-too-rare creatures. I gasped when I started a large hare. It suddenly bounded over the electric fence, but like me went nowhere near the pigs, skedaddling along the line of the hot wire. Its long legs seemed to unfold like a card table, as it sprinted away at an astonishing speed, before making a handbrake turn back into the long grass. These beautiful creatures look like a collection of articulated angles. Unlike rounder, smaller rabbits, their heads are sculptural, their ears longer, and when they run, their bodies rise up high off the ground.

I saw four hares that morning and one of them crossed the border, jumping the dyke like a frightened deer, springing off its long hind legs. I remembered it was March, time for March hare madness, which is really display, mating activity. Perhaps the jumping hare was in search of a Scottish bride. Having seen the first lambs and so many hares racing around the landscape, perhaps spring was arriving early.

At last I came to a turning point, and could leave

behind the no-man's-land of the pig farm. Having clambered over a well-fastened field gate, I found myself on the tarmacked road where the line of the border begins to run south to the Tweed. The faded white line in the middle seemed like the only time geography looked like the map. Walking was much easier. When I got to the road that leads west to Duns, the substitute county town of Berwickshire, the signs for England and Scotland were much more muted and everyday. No flags or fanfares and no Belly Buster stottie cakes. When I quickly reached the farm at High Cocklaw, I realised that it was the only place in England where it was possible to look south into Scotland. Far in the distance rose the foothills of the Cheviots and the fertile ridges that shelved down to the Tweed. To my left I could see the highest point of the Berwick Bounds, and one of the lowest moments in Scotland's history.

On 19 July 1333, a Scottish army was slaughtered on the slopes of Halidon Hill as death rained down from the skies. A substantial force did eventually arrive to relieve Edward III's ruthless siege of Berwick, but it was badly led and far less well-equipped than the ranks of Englishmen who had taken up position on the hill. In front of squadrons of dismounted knights, the ground being unsuitable for cavalry, and men-at-arms were companies of archers. They carried the lethal English longbow and sheaves of deadly, bodkin-tipped arrows, cast-iron points that could pierce shields and all but the best armour.

Edward III's captains had set the archers in what was known as the harrow formation in front of all the other soldiers. Rather than a series of straight ranks, they stood in shallow chevrons, so that they could fire arrows to the side in a crossfire, as well as ahead. They 'laid their bodies into the bow', according to a sixteenth-century handbook. It meant that the draw-weight or power of a six-foot yew longbow was achieved not only by pulling back the bowstring with the right arm, but also by leaning and pushing with the left arm so that body weight bent the bow, not just biceps. Volleys of arrows were not fired directly at enemy soldiers but into the sky above them, as high as possible, so that gravity helped create a deadly hail of bodkin points.

Sir Archibald Douglas commanded an army of thirteen thousand Scots, considerably larger than Edward III's nine thousand, but the English position on Halidon Hill was dominant. From the lane at High Cocklaw, I could see clear gradients on all sides. Douglas should have refused battle, even if it meant the loss of Berwick and the surrender of the dogged Sir Alexander Seton. But instead he formed his troops into three schiltrons, close-packed formations bristling with spears, and advanced uphill across boggy ground. The dense deployments of the Scots presented unmissable targets for the English archers, and the chevrons of the harrow formation meant that arrows fell from at least two directions, making shields much less effective. With their sheaves of arrows planted in the ground at their feet, longbowmen could fire up to ten or twelve arrows every minute and, according to one chronicler, they fell 'like sleet' in the faces of the advancing Scots. A fourteenth-century version of the machine-gun fire across the no-man's-land of Flanders, the bodkin tips mowed down many and the schiltrons began to splinter. Douglas's army was barely able to engage Edward III's dismounted knights and men-at-arms. Only the Earl of Ross and his Highlanders, swinging their Lochaber axes, fought fiercely, and that was in a rearguard action.

Scots casualties were very severe, but the English king did not follow up his crushing victory. Edward's attention was elsewhere, focused on France as the Hundred Years War began to ignite. In 1346 at Crécy, the archers deployed once more in the harrow formation and destroyed a huge French army. Techniques developed throughout the fourteenth century. By Agincourt in 1415, a thousand English arrows were fired into the air every second.

South of High Cocklaw, I encountered a considerable obstacle. Before it reaches the Tweed, the border crosses the Whiteadder Water. There is no bridge there and I was forced to divert along its banks to the B646. At that point, I could get over the river and rejoin the line. My detour turned out to be even more awkward than passing the pigs. In woodland above the Whiteadder, a much wider river than I had thought, paths kept running out or becoming muddy and treacherous. Eventually, I crossed a sluice gate over an old mill lade and found a road that led to the bridge. The last lap took me to Paxton Toll House, a very rutted lane down to the Tweed and to the first day's journey's end.

Swollen by winter rains and a high tide, the great river wound its way to Berwick and on its banks I could see two salmon shiels. There are the remains of many more up and downriver, relics of an ancient industry now almost completely withered. Sheils were small, cottage-like buildings where fishermen could shelter and sleep as they waited for the returning Atlantic salmon to swim up their home river to spawn. High wooden watchtowers were manned day and night, as the sharp-eyed gazed downstream for the moment when the fish entered the river. Salmon swim near the surface and these men searched for a V-shaped wake. It can clearly be made out, even on moonlit nights, where the water is calm and shallow.

Once the salmon wake was seen, the watchers rang a bell and, like firemen or fighter pilots, the fishermen in the sheil scrambled into their rowing boats to haul a net across the river. They all hoped that 'a head of fish', a small shoal of salmon, was moving upstream.

Once the fish were caught, they were laid into a cool store dug into the riverbank before being taken down the river to Berwick. There, they were boiled, pickled, smoked or sold fresh at a daily fish market. As the fisheries multiplied, live Berwick salmon were taken down to London in smacks, vessels that let seawater into their holds. Huge ice-houses were built in Berwick to store fish and these were paid for by coopers, the barrel-makers who controlled the trade.

Now, the salmon fishing at Berwick has virtually vanished. Stocks have become so depleted that only one boat is allowed to net fish at the mouth of the river, just below the old bridge. The industry is also remembered in an annual festival at Tweedmouth, when a young lass is made Salmon Queen for a year.

Before I returned to my walk along the Tweed and

the border, I decided to visit Mr Corvi in West Street to have an early supper. My walk around the Bounds had worked up an appetite for his excellent fish and chips, with a pot of tea and a slice of white buttered bread, served on a Formica table, with only salt and vinegar as condiments. Even the crockery was the right colour: 1950s pale green, classic Utility cups and plates. Perfect.

★   ★   ★

History made the Berwick Bounds and the clash of battle formed much of the border. Geography did the rest, with the windy wastes of the Cheviot watershed ridge as formidable a barrier as any wall, moat or wide river. The Scots slowly became the Scots and the intermittent attention of the English wandered elsewhere, eventually reaching across the oceans to make a vast empire.

In the way that those who dominate think only of their dominance and how it sprang from exceptional qualities, few at that time considered what Englishness might actually be. Apart from a good thing, a blessing. As the great empire-builder Cecil Rhodes boasted, 'Remember that you are an Englishman, and have consequently won first prize in the lottery of life.' William Blake even attempted to hijack the origins of Christianity and make it part of Englishness:

> And did those feet in ancient time
> Walk upon England's mountains green:
> And was the holy Lamb of God,
> On England's pleasant pastures seen?

Now that the empire has vanished into the darkness of the past and Britain has ceased to be Great, we on these islands appear to have entered a period of introspection. The fires of Scottish and Welsh nationalism have flickered on the far horizons, and Irishness, and what it means, has cost too many lives. When Britain and England were constantly, casually conflated, even in the lengthening shadows of the lost empire, Englishness seemed not to be much thought about: hard to describe or define. How was it different from Britishness? And now that the British Empire was no more than a scatter of tiny islands and tax havens, what did it mean? But now the old bear is stirring, and the red and white banners of the cross of St George have spilled out of sports stadia into front gardens or are clipped to the windows of London taxis. It seems that when the Welsh dragon breathed a little fire and the Scottish lion rampant roared, they awoke an English sense of self. And the English have three lions.

A drowsy nostalgia for the greatness of the past has roused itself and become a force that has quickly found political expression. Fringe parties with no policies past what they don't like have begun to attract protest votes in England that number in the millions in the last few years. However, the antiquated first-past-the-post voting system denied these people a parliamentary voice, unlike the Scottish and Welsh nationalists, who sent MPs to a parliament they wanted to abolish. But a catastrophic, thoughtless miscalculation by a Conservative prime minister presented the disenfranchised millions with an opportunity. When a referendum on Britain's member-ship of the European Union was announced in 2015, a momentum shift began to rumble. All of the post-imperial, post-war frustration felt in England coalesced around a visceral dislike for Britain's role in Europe, and even of Europeans themselves. The binary nature of a referendum made 'LEAVE' into an inchoate, inarticulate policy, a magnet for those who harked back to a glorious past and wallowed in a grieving nostalgia for a Britain, and an England, that never was.

Even though the nation's manifest post-imperial destiny clearly lay with France, Germany, Italy and the rest of the European Union, voters decided that Europe was somehow to blame. And not only for the loss of empire but also for the disappointments after the Second World War. While Europe had meekly succumbed to the tyranny of Nazi Germany only Britain stood alone against Hitler. That made the British exceptional, different from the Europeans. And it made that lot across the Channel an ungrateful bunch, rubbing salt in the wounds of history by rebuilding, by doing well economically, better than Britain. There was even a grudging acceptance that they made much better cars, something that became impossible to argue with when successive governments allowed our car manufacturing to all but disappear.

The vote to leave the European Union has been followed by political chaos. As the Labour Party lurched to a prehistoric version of left-wing ideologies, themselves a form of nostalgia, the Conservatives tried in vain to clean up the mess they had made. At the same time the Scottish and Irish nationalists complained that their nations had been dragged out of the European Union against their will: 62 per cent of Scots and 58 per cent of Northern Irish voted to remain. The border on the Cheviots seemed to be widening into a political chasm, with the old neighbours on either side growing much less interested in each other.

And now nationalism in Eastern Europe has risen like a monster from a Cold War swamp. Events in Ukraine and Russia are changing the world utterly and are every bit as significant as the French Revolution of 1789, the Congress of Vienna of 1815, the Treaty of Versailles in 1919, Yalta in 1945 and the fall of the Berlin Wall in 1989. The smoke over Kyiv will take a long time to clear, if it ever does, and the consequences are very difficult to predict. What the unfolding tragedy of Ukraine does throw into sharp relief is how remarkable Britain's exit from the European Union was.

What is clear is that Britain, along with the other democracies, must be part of making a new world order, a better order, a safer order that not only saves lives but saves the planet too. But before we can understand how that might be done, we first need to understand ourselves.

Scottish, Welsh and Irish nationalists have attracted many headlines and much analysis, but by far the most powerful and most enigmatic political force at work in Britain is English nationalism. It is what lay behind the vote to leave the European Union, and its agonies and contradictions may become the unstoppable political force that breaks the British union.

I have lived between Britain for most of my life, close to the border between England and Scotland. Northumberland, Tyneside, Durham, Carlisle and

Cumbria are familiar territory. Or so I thought until recently. In the last few years England has ceased to be terra cognita and seems to be in the process of becoming elsewhere.

Walking between Scotland and England, looking occasionally north as well as south, I planned to spend a great deal of time on my own: time to think about Englishness. I am not a politician or a political theorist or a philosopher but a Borderer, and someone who has written a great deal about Scotland's history and often about the border, both sides. I understand and will try to continue to explain how the border came to be where it is and what it meant and means. At the same time, I want to remember how ideas of Englishness began to present themselves, and not only in the pages of history books.

*　　*　　*

Growing up in Kelso (five miles from England) in the 1950s, I was taken by my mother to the Carnegie Library, an imposing building with large windows and a grand, brass-plated swing door that swished as we entered the hushed silence behind it. We passed the Reading Room, where old men stood at large lecterns quietly turning the pages of newspapers that seemed to have been bound to long sticks. There was an atmosphere, a faint smell of paper, of pages and the worlds they would unfold. Mr Bird, the librarian, wore small, National Health spectacles that made him look like a kindly owl. He peered over them and his polished mahogany counter at me, leaning on his elbows, pausing for a moment before saying to my mother, 'Richmal Crompton, I think.'

So began my understanding of Englishness. Having devoured the Just William stories, marvelling at the besting of Hubert Lane and wondering about the strange nature of the creature called Violet Elizabeth Bott, I moved quickly on to the Famous Five and the Secret Seven. England seemed to me exciting, sunny, settled, well-off, very tidy (except for William Brown) and safe. These enormously popular children's books, more than anything, established my sense of what Englishness was.

Fiction, it has appeared to me long since those early days, forms an enormously important component of Englishness – at least as important as history and politics. Perhaps even more so. The Vote Leave campaign of 2015–16 was founded on a series of more or less explicit fictions that persuaded many millions to listen to their hearts and instincts and not to their heads. Nationalism, in general, seems to me to be much more about stories than facts or economics. Perhaps as a Scot, an outsider with a few miles of distance, I might be able to stand back and find perspective. From the border fence deep in the Cheviot Hills on a clear day, I am certain I can see Casterbridge, Manderley, Nutwood, The Shire, St Mary Mead and Walmington-on-Sea.

Day Two

St Mary Mead on Tweed

There was April snow high on the pillowy Cheviots. Down in the Tweed Valley it had fallen overnight as hail, and along the furrows of freshly ploughed fields it lay like white ribbons in the rich chocolate soil. The sun had begun to burn off the mist floating over the great river as I crossed it just below Berwick. Having made my circuit of the Bounds, I wanted to walk west, back into Scotland for a few miles. The border follows the midstream line of the Tweed and I planned to skirt around the Scottish bank before re-crossing and returning to England.

My trusty Pathfinder map fitted well into the back pocket of my jeans; it had been an invaluable companion as I navigated my way around the army of pigs before finding my way down to Paxton Toll and the river. These little maps are so beautifully made, delightfully detailed, accurate and easy to read. And of course they are no longer updated or published by the Ordnance Survey. Instead we are forced to use the huge, unwieldy Explorer series. Almost a metre square, they are difficult to unfold out of doors in any sort of breeze. Even worse are the so-called Outdoor Leisure series. These are double-sided and almost impossible to re-fold in a such a way that you can refer to the bit that maps the ground you are standing on. Utterly useless. Whoever decided to discontinue the lovely Pathfinders and substitute them with these huge paper sails needs to get out more. Maps are the language of the Earth and it is maddening to see them badly made.

Mercifully, some years ago I bought a series of these beautiful little Pathfinder maps, the set that covered the Tweed Valley, North Northumberland and North Cumbria, and allowing for the fact that they are at least thirty years out of date I reckoned they would be a reliable, user-friendly guide on my journey along the hundred-mile length of the border. Nothing much would have changed along the Cheviot tops, except perhaps the clear-felling of commercial forestry and its replanting.

I was walking west along the B6461 towards Paxton village, and from there I'd turn south to Paxton House, a stately mansion set in wooded policies close to the riverbank. Then I would make my way along the Scottish side of the Tweed and cross back into England over the Union Bridge. When my dad drove us down to the sea in the early 1960s, to Berwick and sunny Sunday picnics on the sweeping, deserted beaches at Scremerston, he always diverted so that he could frighten us by crossing the Rumbling Bridge. In those days the road deck across the wide river seemed to consist of thick wooden beams, like long railway sleepers, laid cross-wise. The rumbling was caused, I think, by their slight movement as the car wheels bumped along, and when we squealed in the back my dad laughed.

Villages rather than bridges were on my mind as I walked to Paxton. From there I wanted to make my way first to the English village of Horncliffe, and then on to Norham. When I graduated from Richmal Crompton and Enid Blyton, my older sister, Barbara, passed on her love of Agatha Christie, Miss Marple and the warm, sunlit, polite, comfortable world of the village of St Mary Mead . . . where people were regularly murdered, poisoned or burgled.

Many years later, my big sister told me that she was so gripped by Christie's mysteries that when Mum had come into her bedroom and told her to switch off the bedside light and not switch it back on, she had tiptoed out onto the lit landing to sit shivering, still reading. That way she'd done what she had been told, but risked hypothermia.

Perhaps because the Just William stories were for children and concerned the escapades of the scruffy hero's gang, the Outlaws, the village where they all lived seems now like a blurry background for adventures and scrapes. St Mary Mead is much more sharply drawn, much more than a setting for a series of whodunnits or the home of the unlikely detective who worked out who dun it. It is also a recurring collection of images, atmospheres, themes, versions, I have come to believe, of a quintessential aspect of Englishness, one that has entirely fled. If it ever existed. None of which matters.

As I walked westwards to Paxton, I found I could effortlessly call up the geography of Agatha Christie's

English Brigadoon, a place that came alive when Miss Marple opened her front door. She lived in Danemead, one of three houses belonging to three elderly spinsters in Old Pasture Lane. They looked onto the village green – vaguely triangular it was, I think. On one side stood the Vicarage, an imposing detached building, maybe Georgian like the spinsters' houses. But not thatched, definitely slates. Around the corner were the gates of Gossington Hall, the rather grand home of Colonel and Mrs Dolly Bantry, the latter being Miss Marple's close friend and confidante. Near the gates to the policies the High Street ran towards the little railway station, and along its length were shops – the butcher, baker, grocer and, I'm certain, a solicitor's office. The village church must have been close to the vicarage, and somewhere close to the village was the Old Hall, a large estate belonging to Colonel Protheroe.

I am almost sure that is right. I wrote it all down from memory, from sixty years ago, without picking up a copy of *The Murder at the Vicarage*. As if I had any chance of finding it in the chaos of my office.

What does that demonstrate? It may be little more than the ancient residue of a period of binge-reading at an impressionable age, but I think not. (I checked my recollection later and found I had forgotten the church was opposite the gates of Gossington Hall, but otherwise it was pretty much as Christie described the core of St Mary Mead.) The village seems to me to be central to a nostalgia for an ideal England that has never had to compete with reality, and has never faded. Scale is important in this central image. Just as I could, people can hold in their imaginations somewhere the size of St Mary Mead. Cities are far too large. The village is also picturesque, old and unchanging (although in fact it did change as the series of Miss Marple mysteries grew), and it plays to the 'roses round the door' romanticism of a happy, contented life. Even though St Mary Mead was clearly a very dangerous place to live.

Stability seems to ooze from the warm stone walls tumbled over with climbing roses or covered with Virginia creeper, from the quirky, irregular street plan, or lane plan, and the fact that the villagers are creatures of regular habits. In 1993, the then prime minister, John Major, made a famous speech about Englishness. His much quoted line about 'old maids bicycling to Holy Communion through the morning mist' could have been witnessed by Miss Marple, even though his speech writers lifted it from an essay by George Orwell. Major was attacked for talking outdated tosh, but that didn't matter. People wanted to believe in this tosh, these old sepia images of a lost past. They offer reassurance, however bogus.

That reassurance is intimately bound up with the social architecture of St Mary Mead. Miss Marple's community had pillars. The Bantrys at Gossington Hall and Col. Protheroe at Old Hall were something like squires in their halls – definitely halls, not houses. And all was well with the world. The vicar, his vicarage and the church I forgot about are there to be bicycled to in the morning mist and to minister to the people, all the people, of the village. On the High Street, a solicitor, a doctor and a butcher, a baker and a candlestick-maker are all a warm and welcoming presence, shopkeepers who will wrap purchases in brown paper parcels and put them in your wicker shopping basket for you, a soothing far cry from supermarkets, malls and online emporia. As they worshipped, got married, were christened, stood on the corner of the High Street to gossip and went about their daily business, the people of St Mary Mead knew where they were, who they were and what their station in life was. And more than that, they themselves seemed to me to be quintessentially English, white and not at all diverse. Agatha Christie's village could be nowhere else but in deepest England, Angleterre Profonde, completely unlike Clochemerle or Don Camillo's Ponteratto.

Nostalgia is certainly at work here, and a world created by a novelist whose heyday is long past (although TV versions of her stories are constantly made and remade, with a new Miss Marple for every generation – Joan Hickson being the best of a very good bunch). But the icon of the English village endures, from ITV's knock-off of the Christie settings, the dreadful *Midsomer Murders*, twenty-two series and still running, to the enduring popularity of *Emmerdale Farm*, now *Emmerdale*, to say nothing of *The Archers*' Ambridge. Villages and their dramas are still enormously popular because they resonate. But are the contents of that wicker shopping basket of images, even clichés, peculiarly English, or just a little bit different from Scotland?

When I turned inland from the river towards Paxton, I saw something that forced a change of plan. A yellow sign by the side of the road told me that the Union

Bridge was still closed for repairs. I'd thought it would be passable for pedestrians, if not cars, but now I'd need to find another way into England, and I'm no swimmer. But first to Paxton.

The sun had climbed above the horizon clouds and the frozen droplets of overnight rain glistened in the leafless hedgerows. On the back lane to the village the puddles in the potholes sparkled with the zig-zag geometry of ice. Like small stained-glass windows designed by Picasso, their triangles, pentagons and parallelograms were framed by a pattern of precisely straight shafts of thicker ice. A memory flickered, a passage of stop-frame filming of ice forming, perhaps a sequence on 'winter is coming' in a 1950s Disney wildlife film, the sort of cinema short where they used to give the bears names and human emotions. 'C'mon now, little one,' says Mom, 'no time to play in the snow. We gotta find someplace cosy and warm to hibernate.' As the early morning sun glinted off them, I stepped around the fragile beauty of the frozen puddles and headed towards the cluster of houses surrounded by fields.

There is always a barely perceptible shift in early spring, when rain and sun combine to make the new grass begin to flush. It's not obvious growth that signals change, but colour. The tired, washed-out, muddy fields of the late winter begin to brighten and green, and I noticed the ewes newly out of the sheds with their spindly lambs were grazing vigorously at the tiny, sweet shoots full of sugars, making nourishing milk for their little ones.

Paxton seemed to huddle, the houses turning their

backs on the beautiful farmland that surrounds them. Perhaps the snell, scourging winter winds whipping off the North Sea have turned the village in on itself. Despite a sprinkling of new bungalows and a small street of recently built, identical houses (judging by their gardens, for the style of architecture was not new and it featured stone cut by machines to look like it had been chiselled by dusty old masons of the old school), the settlement is ancient. It lies in the old Anglian kingdom of Bernicia that is inadvertently remembered by the red and gold Percy flag I'd seen where the A1 crosses the border.

Bernicia began to emerge in the second half of the sixth century. The dramatic seaside rock on which Bamburgh Castle now stands was the site of a fortress built sometime before 547, when a king called Ida ruled there, feasting with his warriors in a timber hall behind the stockade on the summit. The Anglian king appears to have named his stronghold after his queen, Bebba, and the earliest form of the name was written as Bebbanburh.

Toponymy, the study of place names, fascinates me. Familiarity can overlook the rich store of history hidden inside them, and how they can be read together to tell a story. Paxton is a simple Anglian name. It means the settlement or farm belonging to a minor lord called Pace or Paccus, and over time Paccustun was rubbed smooth into Paxton. This man was not a native but an incomer, his people being originally Angles from Angeln in Northern Denmark, a place that ultimately gave England its name. Perhaps he fought in the warband of Ida or one of the short-lived kings who followed him and ruled from the rock at Bebbanburh. That's possible, because Paxton might have been a reward. Paccus or his immediate ancestor took the farm and its land from someone else, from a defeated native lord.

The sixth and seventh centuries were a time of seismic change all over what is now England and southern Scotland, as fertile land was fought over. The Germanic incomers in the north, probably fanning out from what had originally been a pirate base at Bebbanburh, quickly took over the old Celtic kingdom of Bryneich, a place name that morphed into Bernicia. The natives spoke dialects of Old Welsh and their kings fought hard against the Angles who had sailed across the North Sea. The clash and din of their battles are only echoes now, the places where the shield walls faced each other a matter of conjecture. Winners not only write history, they draw the map, re-make the geography and only a very few Old Welsh place names have survived the defeats and eventual takeover. Kelso is originally from *Calchvynydd*, Old Welsh for the Chalk Hill, and, further up the Tweed, Peebles is from *Pybyll*, a group of shielings.

The Anglian kingdom of Bernicia reached as far north as the Lammermuirs and when it joined with Deira, modern Durham and Yorkshire, to form the great kingdom of Northumbria, it stretched to the shores of the Forth and west to the Solway. The red and gold standard I saw on the A1 fluttered over a vast area of what is now Scotland.

Paxton has no village green and no shops that I could see. Houses lined three roads that led into it and the winding lanes behind them. Front doors and windows mainly looked at each other and not the sweeping views over the rich, undulating fields of fertile Berwickshire. There seemed to be little or no public space. Nevertheless, Paxton had what my grannie called innerliness, a warm, neighbourly – even cosy – feel. If the village has a centre, perhaps it is the Cross Inn, fashionably labelled as a pub and kitchen.

A plaque on an old wall nearby spoke of recent history. It marked the birthplace of Mary Jane Reddin, on a house next to the long-gone smiddy. The wall was all that remained of either. She travelled to China as a missionary in 1899 and married James Dunlop Liddell in Shanghai Cathedral. Three years later, Mary Jane gave birth to a famous son. Eric Liddell won a gold medal in the 400 metres at the Paris Olympic Games of 1924. A devout Christian, he had withdrawn from the 100 metres heats because they were to be held on a Sunday. Eric would almost certainly have won another gold medal at what was considered to be his best distance, but that went to his British team-mate, Harold Abrahams. His and Liddell's achievements were celebrated in the Oscar-winning film *Chariots of Fire*. When fellow Scot Allan Wells won gold in the Olympic 100 metres in 1980, he was asked if he had run the race in memory of the last British winner, Abrahams. 'No,' said Wells, 'I would prefer to dedicate this to Eric Liddell.'

That strikes me as a quintessentially Scottish story, one of many that complete circles and remember a very particular history. Before the film made him famous across the rest of the world, Allan Wells knew what Eric Liddell had achieved and what he had given up. His sporting reputation had never dimmed north of the border. Not only did Eric win Olympic glory, he also played rugby for Scotland while he studied at Edinburgh University, scoring four tries on the wing in only seven appearances. But none of that made him unique. It was the strength and power of his beliefs that anchored his place in Scotland's story. Raised in the credo of what was known in the Reformation as the priesthood of all believers, the notion that every Christian was responsible for their own salvation (and should therefore be able to read the word of God, the Bible, themselves rather than depending on priests to interpret it for them), and the son of missionaries in China, his faith absolute, Eric disdained further sporting fame. Even though he had won his gold medal at the age of twenty-two, he returned to work in China a year after the Paris Olympics. After seven years as a missionary and a teacher, he was ordained a minister in the Congregational Union of Scotland. One of many small groups who broke away from the mainstream of the Church of Scotland, its focus was on missionary work. And it was also inde-pendent, each congregation being absolutely autono-mous, answering only to God. In 1928 the Church appointed Vera Finlay as the first woman to be ordained a minister in Scotland, something that would not happen in the Church of Scotland for another forty years. And not until 1994 did the Church of England ordain a woman as a priest.

The reputations and achievements of the men and women who went to China, Africa and elsewhere on missions of conversion have suffered recently as attitudes to history have altered. The appalling, inhumane brutalities of the slave trade, the ruthless exploitation of natural resources and native peoples across the British Empire and the racism that informed virtually all the exchanges between Britain and her colonies are to be excused in no way. Those who sailed the slave ships where people were packed below decks like sardines as part of the infamous triangular trade, or profited from other sorts of suffering, must have been aware of the evil they did. I am certain of that. No defence of different times, different mores can be entered. They knew what they were doing and that what they were doing caused immeasurable suffering. But these are not the only stories to be told of the interaction of the British with native peoples in Africa and the Far East.

Eric Liddell and his family brought more than the word of God to China. Education, albeit framed by the teachings of the Bible, was central to what he and others did. Some missionaries had medical skills. All of them profited in no way and many made tremendous personal sacrifices. Five months before the end of the Second World War Liddell died very young, at the age of forty-three, in a Japanese-run internment camp.

Although I am no Christian, I admire these men and women enormously, but I confess I have a personal connection, one I should disclose. Robert Moffat, too, was a missionary. He was born at Ormiston in East Lothian. His parents were farm labourers who had regularly moved around the county and neighbouring Berwickshire on year-long contracts known as fees at different places. My ancestors, as far back as I can reliably trace them, were Moffats from Berwickshire and I am almost certain that Robert was a distant relative. The link is John Moffat (my father's name and one that occurs often in my genealogy), who was beadle at Fogo Kirk near Duns in the late eighteenth century. One of his many sons moved away to work on farms in East Lothian, and while I can't make an absolutely secure link, I think it very likely that Robert Moffat was my ancestor.

Moffat is not a common name. Some are to be found in Scotland, with a particular concentration in Berwickshire and East Lothian. But the country where most people bear the surname is not Britain but Malawi in Central Africa. Robert Moffat is the reason for that.

In 1820, he and his wife, Mary, went to Griquatown in the north of South Africa as Congregational missionaries. They stayed for almost fifty years, and on his travels across deserts and into the upcountry Robert suffered great privation, often so thirsty he could not speak and starving so badly that he tied a cord around his waist to try to ease the pain. They nevertheless raised ten children and Robert laboured mightily to translate the whole of the Bible into the Setswana language. And of course he spent a great deal of time teaching native people to read, and also the skills needed to print their own devotional reading material. The belief in the priesthood of all believers was still strong. Robert passed on all he knew about carpentry, building techniques, water supply and blacksmith work. He tried not only to convert the native peoples to Christianity, but also to improve their lives. His grandson, Howard Moffat, became prime minister of Southern Rhodesia from 1927 to 1933. David Livingstone, also a Congregationalist, married Mary Moffat, Robert and Mary's eldest daughter. At first she was much more widely known in southern Africa than Livingstone, and she greatly facilitated and supported his early expeditions.

I'm proud of these links with the colonial, evangelical past – despite recent, powerful and wholesale rejections of these legacies. Proud because instead of personal profit, or material gain of any kind, Robert and Mary Moffat suffered great hardships in their attempt to bring Christianity to Africa. Mary died when she was only forty-one. Even though it was an alien creed, it was nevertheless a creed of love, forgiveness and hope, however misguided it might be thought now. I admire the selflessness and courage it took to travel into the unknown, to potentially hostile places, to risk their lives and preach the word of God and spread the values of the Christian religion. These self-sacrifices should not be dismissed or forgotten – or misunderstood.

On my way out of Paxton, walking south towards the Tweed, I came across another plaque, this one set up below a young copper beech tree by the side of the road.

Planted by Paxton Village Enhancement Group to commemorate the 2012 London Olympic/Paralympic Games and in honour of Eric Liddell, of Paxton descent, gold and bronze medallist [in the 200 metres] at the 1924 Paris Olympic Games.

It was good to see a good man not forgotten.

I had a problem. To make absolutely sure there was no way across the Union Bridge for a pedestrian (the alternative was to walk back to Berwick and cross the Tweed there – a long detour), I flagged down the postman. As he shook his head, good fortune drew up behind the Royal Mail van. It was John Home Robertson, the former Labour MP for Berwick and East Lothian, an MSP and a friend I hadn't seen for some time. 'I'll take you round to the English side of the Union Bridge,' he said. 'Save you a lot of time. But come and have a cup of coffee first.'

John's family had built Paxton House and some time ago he had handed it over to a trust, retaining the right to live in a small part of one of the wings. On our way there we drove past carnage, a trail of destruction that would constantly flank my journey up the Tweed. In late November 2021, Storm Arwen (a terrible, twee American habit of giving names and somehow anthropomorphising these disastrous events has stuck and is now universally used) raged across the north of Britain. Gusts of up to 98 miles an hour were measured in north Northumberland and they brought down mighty trees all over the countryside. On either side of the driveway up to the big house lay the massive trunks of the fallen. 'Keep Off. Rolling Logs Can Kill' notices stood near the piles of timber no one had ever imagined they would see lying horizontal. Over a welcome cup of coffee and excellent homemade shortbread, John and Catherine Home Robertson told me the estate had had to close because of storm damage and the path by the riverside was dangerous and in places impassable. Instead of feeling like a cheat on my intention to walk in step with the borderline, it seemed like good sense to accept the offer of a lift into England.

The approach to the Union Bridge remembers another, gentler, quieter age. At the foot of a steep incline on the English side, the road turns sharp left, a very awkward angle for cars but not the horses and carts the bridge was originally built to carry. Opened in 1820, it was then the longest suspension bridge in the world. Two hundred years later, having borne traffic a great deal heavier than ponies and traps, or even my dad's old Austin A40, it was in need of urgent repair. All I could see of the original bridge were the overhead cables that would carry the new bridge deck, one probably not made from railway sleepers. In an unusual and necessary cross-border collaboration, Northumberland County Council and Scottish Borders Council have raised most of the cash needed to make sure the Rumbling Bridge will rumble once more.

The massive stone pier on the English side was obscured by a lattice work of steel girders that hid a Latin motto whose words I had seen once before but couldn't remember. Even though there were no workers about on this side of the Tweed, I resisted the temptation to climb up the temporary structure. Much later I looked it up online. '*Vis unita fortior*' was carved below an entwined thistle and rose, and unusually it translates elegantly into English as 'United: Strength Is Yet Stronger'. In an age of division, disagreement and an emphasis on difference, I like that.

It is rare for music and politics to complement each other, particularly when lyrics and melody seem to crystallise mood and sentiment. John Home Robertson was first elected to Parliament in 1978 at a by-election caused by the death of John P. Mackintosh. A professor at Edinburgh University, he managed to combine academic work with his role as a constituency MP and in the House of Commons. He was also a forceful advocate for Scottish devolution. 'People in Scotland want a degree of government for themselves. It is not beyond the wit of man to devise the institutions to meet these demands,' he wrote. When the Labour government of James Callaghan enacted a bill to create a Scottish Assembly, a referendum was scheduled for the following year. John Mackintosh died before it could take place, but the chances of an Assembly being created were greatly reduced when a fellow Labour MP, George Cunningham, insisted that 40 per cent of the electorate had to vote in favour for it to come into being. That meant that all of those who did not vote in effect voted against a Scottish Assembly. This clause in the bill crippled the cause of devolution, and although a clear majority voted for it, the total number in favour did not reach the required 40 per cent and the legislation was shelved.

I believe that this was a crucial turning moment in Scotland and the United Kingdom's history and it would come to alter the relationship between Scotland and England. Mackintosh's enthusiasm for devolution was based not on nationalism, not on Scotland right or wrong, not on the glorification of the nation and the denigration of others, but on a democratic deficit. He believed in good government and giving power to the Scottish electorate. The failed vote clearly showed enthusiasm for an Assembly, one that might now have been more than forty years old, and forty years better, with most of the anomalies ironed out and the grit removed.

I campaigned in 1979 with John Home Robertson and a young Gordon Brown. Printed on my memory was the moment I arrived at a common room in Edinburgh University on the day after the vote. The count had taken a long time and it was early afternoon when I pushed open the door. Gordon was sitting in a window seat with a notepad on his lap. He looked up at me and shook his head.

A year later I heard the gravel-voiced singer Dick Gaughan perform a song he had adapted and set to music he had composed. Attributed to the great Borders poet and novelist James Hogg, the author of *The Private Memoirs and Confessions of a Justified Sinner*, the verses were originally published in 1819. The words refer to the corruption in the negotiations before the Act of Union in 1707, but are also conciliatory. Dick adapted them as a response to the failure of the vote for a Scottish Assembly and as I walked towards the Union Bridge the words echoed around my head:

What's the spring-breathing jasmine and rose,
What's the summer, with all its gay train,
Or the splendour of autumn, to those
Who've bartered their freedom for gain.

Let the love of our land's sacred rights,
To the love of our people succeed;
Let friendship and honour unite,
And flourish on both sides the Tweed.

No sweetness the senses can cheer,
Which corruption and bribery bind;
No brightness the sun can e'er clear,
For honour's the sum of the mind.

Let virtue distinguish the brave,
Place riches in lowest degree;
Think him poorest who can be a slave,
Him richest who dares to be free.

The second verse, the chorus, is repeated between all the verses and its sentiment perfectly caught the mood in 1979 and all its nuances. It still resonates.

Across the river I could see the walls enclosing the policies of Paxton House and as John Home Robertson waved me off and I began the long way round via Berwick back towards them, I walked a few yards towards a pretty little house along what looked like a private road. It was fringed with dense clumps of daffodils that had clearly multiplied over time. These golden stretches are now common on the verges of country roads and are a welcome harbinger of spring. There is no yellow more yellow and beautiful than daffodil yellow and as the buds open, the earth begins to come alive.

On the Scottish bank of the Tweed, close to the bridge

pier, I could see a salmon fishing shiel, a small, stone-built cottage with a long hut next to it. Both were boarded up with bright red shutters that would come off, not for the net fishing season, now consigned to history, but probably for holiday-makers. Close by was the door to an underground cold store dug into the riverbank, where fish could be kept fresh before being rowed down to Berwick for sale or processing. I wondered if structures like that had been an inspiration to J. R. R. Tolkien when he dreamed of the Shire and Bilbo and Frodo Baggins and their hobbit holes. It would have been no surprise to see a very small man with hairy feet open the white door in the little stone-faced façade, step out and light his pipe.

Stocks of Atlantic salmon are now so fragile that those fishing in Scottish rivers can catch them, but then they must immediately release the fish back into the river before they suffocate. The fact that the south bank of the Tweed is in England for about twelve miles does not introduce anomalies to this policy. Uniquely, the River Tweed Commission's powers cross the border and extend deep into Northumberland to include major tributaries like the Till and its catchment area. Dating from 1807, not long before the Union Bridge was built, the Commission has overseen fishing for two centuries and now protects the populations of Atlantic salmon in the river. It is an apposite example of the motto on the bridge in action.

I walked up the steep slope from the dismantled bridge past a honey farm before making my way to Horncliffe. Unlike Paxton, it is a destination, a dead-end, one road in and one road out. And it looks and feels immediately different. I sat down on a bench opposite a church and noticed a Union Jack flying on a tall flag-pole in the garden of a modern bungalow. Another unwelcome American import, the purpose of flying a Union Jack, a St George's cross, a saltire or a lion rampant in a garden or from a window baffles me. Perhaps those who do it want to advertise their patri-otism in an obvious and banal manner. It has nothing to do with geography: those who go to the trouble (where do you buy garden flagpoles? Can't be online – how would the white vans deliver them? Maybe they come in sections?) of running up these standards know where they live, as do those who look at them. This seems to me to be an unpleasant development, one with an all-too-audible military base note playing under it. Nuremberg rallies had thousands of flags flying as Leni Riefenstahl's floodlights played over all that orches-trated hysteria. Flags look right fluttering over Buckingham Palace, the Houses of Parliament or national sports stadia, but in gardens they seem sinister, even aggressive; planted on the border, they are unwel-come statements of the obvious.

Horncliffe is the most northerly village in England, but it could have been one of the most southerly, it seemed to me. Very different from Paxton, much older and more settled, with noticeably larger houses, it has a clear central square (rectangle, more like) and what looked like a manor house set in walled grounds. A sign on the gates called it 'The Garden House' and it appeared large and comfortable, with an expensive car parked outside. In the square stood 'The Old School', solidly built from very beautiful rose-coloured stone much spalled over the centuries. Workmen were unloading materials at a cottage nearby that was built in a similar style. I asked a young woman who was probably their client how I might manage to get down to the river and a path my Pathfinder had said would get me to Norham. Wearing outsize sunglasses and with two Jack Russell terriers on long leads, she was very polite and helpful. 'I'll show you,' she said, 'cos it can be confusing.' Perhaps I looked weary, probably confused, maybe even a little deranged. I was certainly forty years older than her. On our short walk, she told me that she had just moved to Horncliffe. 'Fed up with city life.' Although she didn't say which city.

Horncliffe sits high on a steep bank rather than a cliff and the views upriver from the top of the path are sweeping. Nothing gives a landscape a more classical perspective than a river winding into the distance. I felt I was looking at a Poussin or a Claude Lorrain. All that was missing were a few fluted columns of a ruined temple and a shepherdess or two. Clouds cleared as I made my way down the muddy path the young woman had shown me and the sun glinted off the great river. Rain over the previous few days had made the path slick and in places very slippy, but the heavily corrugated soles of my beige boots were equal to the task of keeping me upright and I reached the river without bouncing down the steps on my backside. A helpful wooden sign told me that Norham was three miles distant. A stroll in the water meadow, if not the park.

The surface of the Tweed was glassy, reflecting the high white clouds, as a pair of stately swans glided downstream with the current. The muddy path eventually led to a narrow wooden bridge across a ravine, with a stream gurgling at the bottom of it. I almost missed a message from Northumberland County Council: 'Footpath Closed Due To Landslip'. Next to it was a baffling map of what might have been the footpath, or might not. It had 'Road Traffic Regulation 1984' as a subtitle. What road? What traffic? Capital letters B, D, C and A were marked on points along a black line with a short sideways branch, but there was no key to say what they signified. I took this black line to be the path. To my left were wooden steps leading uphill, possibly to point D on the map. And that seemed to connect with a road, or perhaps a track. Was that where the landslip had occurred? Landslips need gravity and there seemed to be plenty up there.

All of this took some time to read since the map had been stapled to the side of the little wooden bridge at below knee height; bending is no longer something I do well or without the accompaniment of sub-vocal noises. Unable to make head or tail, I pulled Pathfinder 451, Norham, from my back pocket and all became quickly clearer. The path did indeed lead uphill to a track and not a road (these little maps offer that depth of detail) before proceeding towards Norham and then turning downhill to the riverbank about a quarter of a mile further on. No path beside the river was marked, even though I could clearly see one that looked well-worn winding through the long grass. Remembering that the Pathfinders are at least thirty years out of date, I decided to trust my instincts and stay on the low path. The worst thing that could happen was I'd be forced to turn back. But after the problems with the Union Bridge, I thought surely not twice in one day.

Ahead I could see the wide, flat river meadow marked on the map and also St Thomas's Island, where the Tweed divides into a narrow and a wide channel. All of it in England. The flat island looked like good grazing and I could see a small stone-built shiel used by the old salmon netsmen. The only place where the slippery path became a little tricky was at the foot of a river cliff, where it narrowed so much I had to be careful of my balance and go slowly.

When I at last reached the wide and sunny meadow, and flat, easy walking, I waved at a fisherman in full waders standing up to his backside in the river. Wearing dark glasses against the glare off the water, he was expertly using a twelve- or maybe fifteen-foot double-handed rod. His line was a luminous green and when he cast, it described beautiful, looping arcs as he landed his fly on a pool below the banks of St Thomas' Island. It was a place where the water was still and mirror-like behind a breakwater of big stones that snaked into the current. Many years ago, I had spoken to an old fisherman in Kelso who explained what these were. He called them yiddies, a Scots version of eddies. They are also known as croys and some are apparently very ancient, perhaps prehistoric in origin. The point of them, explained the old man, was to create pools of slack water where the salmon and other fish could feed without having to use their fins or their tails to keep steady in the current. And that was why the fisherman in the dark glasses had cast his fly expertly, elegantly, precisely behind the row of big stones. He was trying to tempt a feeding salmon.

Perhaps forty acres and broadly circular, the meadow behind me lay in a long, lazy loop of the river. Planted with what might have been winter wheat, it had attracted about sixty swans. They were probably grazing the green, young shoots. Down on the river two more took flight, their efforts to get into the air so laborious as to look almost impossible. Flapping their wings, they rose up a few inches out of the water and then seemed to run on the surface, their webbed feet frantically splashing, their short black bandy legs faintly comical. Once airborne, they wheeled around and flew directly over-head, no more than a few feet above me, their long necks outshot and their great wings fully extended and beating the air, awkwardness transformed into elegance. I felt their slipstream on my face.

Two more swans on the river had things other than the sweet young shoots of winter wheat on their minds. One was making a low clicking noise and the other sounded as though it might be snoring. There was a good deal of splashing and pecking as they circled around each other. Just as for the March hares up on the Berwick Bounds, it was springtime on the river.

As I walked around the long bend, enjoying the metro-nomic business of putting one foot in front of the other without having to watch where I was going on the good, flat path, I saw many other birds and started a large covey of partridges. After they exploded out of the long grass, I watched their whirring wings cross to the more peaceful Scottish bank. Two roe deer bounced through the willow scrub by the river and, walking through the sunlit late morning, the smell of wild garlic was everywhere.

On the crown of the bend stood another shiel. Like the one at the Union Bridge, it had well-shuttered doors and windows but I could see that it had been renovated. A shiny new metal chimney piece, complete with a cowl, suggested there might be a woodburning stove inside and the old stonework had been beautifully repointed, the mason mixing in some dark sand with his mortar to make it suit the russet colours of the sandstone, again deeply spalled by the winds and rains of many winters. So far as I could make out, he had patiently raked out all of the old white lime mortar and replaced it so that the new fitted seamlessly, as though it had always been there. And damp and draughts will have been reduced considerably, making a snug interior with the woodburner. A rough road with recent tyre marks suggested this might have been another holiday house in a lovely, isolated setting by the river.

It seemed a good place to pause, sit down on the dry step at the shaded side of the little cottage and take off my rucksack. At the beginning of each walking day I usually unclip my watch and put it in a pocket. Time can be distracting. I wanted to look around, not at my wrist, and think about what I saw, and enjoy it, make it timeless. I'd also not had the distraction of meeting anyone else on the path from Horncliffe, perhaps thanks to the message from Northumberland County Council. I had waved at the fisherman and that was all the human interaction I'd had. It was good to have the river and the border to myself. Once I remembered where I had put my watch, I was surprised to find that it was early afternoon. I was hungry. Unwrapping cheese sandwiches and twisting the top off a small bottle of fizzy water, I leaned back against the door of the shiel and realised that I was more than a little weary.

I shall be seventy-two later in the summer and of course my body doesn't work anything like as well as it used to. Aches and mysterious, random pains are so much part of life now that the brief intervals when nothing hurts come as a very welcome relief. So far, so unremarkable, and the same for most people my age, I expect. But last summer, for no reason I could work out, I woke early one morning in a rictus of back pain that was so severe it took ten agonising minutes to manage to sit on the edge of my bed. Walking was almost impossible until I'd taken some very strong pain-killers – paindullers, more like. Visits to chiropractors and doctors made little difference. I had an MRI scan that showed nothing. Only time and whisky seemed to help.

Now the pain is manageable, but more or less constant, especially in my legs while sitting typing. And if my back is not complaining loudly, the chorus is taken up by my shoulders, a legacy of playing rugby against men when I was still little more than a boy. But to my surprise I find that I can screen it out, even though it forces me to move more slowly and carefully. And on a sunlit afternoon by the Tweed, watching the swans, the scent of wild garlic feeling like a good accompaniment to a cheese sandwich, I realised how much I was enjoying myself.

A few hundred yards upstream, I passed another fishing shiel, this one a redbrick-built hut. Clumps of nodding daffodils welcomed me as I walked around it, noticing an incongruous hand sanitiser unit attached to a wall. On a paved area on the riverside, I imagined a barbecue and a few cold beers making a good end to a day's fishing.

When I rejoined the track, perspectives seemed suddenly to shift from the peaceful arcadias of Lorrain and Poussin, and looming up out of the mists of history was the great stone keep of Norham Castle. On the tree-lined horizon with the sun behind it, the dark fortress glowered over the river, altering the atmosphere. It exuded menace and blunt, brute strength, a memory of centuries of warfare. A breeze blew up the river, ruffling the water's surface, and I turned to watch some of the swans begin to lift off from the meadow behind me.

The path swung south, and ahead I could see dense stands of trees fringing the riverbank. Just before I left the open meadow, I saw that Northumberland County Council had left me another, much simpler message. 'Footpath Closed' was unambiguous. And this time there was no other footpath. Just the one. And it was closed.

So I walked on. There had been no problem after the first message and, anyway, how bad could this be? Norham Castle was close, maybe half a mile away, and the trusty Pathfinder showed another path on a slightly higher level, only a little way inland. I ignored the field name of Hangman's Land and a feature labelled Red Rock. What could possibly go wrong?

After about a hundred yards, almost everything. The path was slick with mud that looked like melted chocolate and behaved like it. Even on flat sections my boots slid just a little with every step. Perhaps if I went on a bit there would be a path up by a little stream marked on the Pathfinder that would link with the higher path? I hoped so because to my right was a near-sheer forty-foot drop into the dark waters of the river. Floating in the reeds was the white carcass of a dead swan. There was no path up to my left, just a cliff of weather-worn red sandstone, the very same Red Rock marked on the Pathfinder. The tree cover was so dense that the shadows made navigation more difficult. Shafts of a strange, ancient light penetrated the wood, grainy and dusty. I thought of fairy tales, of Hansel and Gretel, of Little Red Riding Hood, Tolkien's Tom Bombadil, of sinister wood sprites hiding behind tree trunks. On a short stretch of flat walking, I stopped to pull out my note-book. I quickly scribbled 'Scary path'. I should have added 'walked by an idiot'. On the steep bank below the red cliffs I noticed clumps of primroses and remembered reading of primrose paths in Shakespeare. This wasn't one of them.

Most difficult were places where the path climbed or descended, even for short stretches. I moved ever more slowly, taking baby steps, testing every one, grabbing a branch or a sapling where I could. A few inclines had sets of slippery wooden steps but most did not, and one or two controlled slides were needed before I found another way. I noticed that the exposed roots of some of the trees showed them also hanging on for dear life. Very gradually the path began to descend towards the river, and at a place where I could stand steady I worked out that, even though I couldn't see it because of the steep slope, Norham Castle was only about two hundred yards away. Looking out over the river from the shade of the dark and damp trees, I could see another island, Blount Island, green and glowing in the late afternoon sun. It looked like another world.

As I inched forward, streaks of light began to fall on the gentler slopes above me and when I turned downwards once more, I saw the ruined top of the castle keep. It was very close. Soon I found a better, flatter path and, crossing a ravine immediately below the rock the castle was built on, there was another narrow, wooden bridge. It seemed to lead straight into a rock face. To its right there had been a small landslip and the path had completely disappeared. Grabbing some exposed roots and a low branch of a tree on the riverbank, I scrambled up at the cost of only a couple of broken fingernails. Better than broken legs.

Then I entered another country. The path resumed and led me into bright sunshine and another flat meadow by the river, this one used as a football pitch by the village beyond it. Thank goodness.

I am growing a little too old for escapades, but I don't seem able to escape having them. The reason for that is obvious. A complete lack of common sense, a void where that should be, filled instead by idiotic foolhardiness and impatience. As I scolded myself, walking across the lovely, soft, flat, dry grass of the football pitch, I fought off the negatives with two arguments. First and most attractive was – what's the alternative? Sitting on the sofa working my way through the morning newspapers, maybe trying a crossword or two as mental exercise. Novels in the afternoon and television in the evening, all laced with undeserved meals and large gins and tonic. And naps. Every half hour. That way lies madness, to say nothing of pairs of jeans with waist sizes probably only available from a website that keeps emailing me with special offers. It's called Jolliman Quality Menswear. How do they know?

The second argument in favour of idiocy was less attractive. 'Not bad for seventy-two' is a phrase that might spin around my head, but it will never pass my lips. It's just an excuse for sub-standard work, lack of effort and frankly no use to anyone, me especially. Something is either good, or worth doing, regardless of the age of the person doing it. Or it's not.

I was looking for a viewpoint, a place where the story of modern painting changed. Beyond the far side of the football pitch, I could see that the path by the river extended a little way and it was by a garden wall that I stopped, turned and saw much of what J. M. W. Turner saw in the summer of 1797. The young painter toured Britain to sketch and observe, and after he arrived at Norham, Turner found himself captivated by the sight of the castle on its great rock. The large watercolour he painted was exhibited at the Royal Academy in 1798 and it made the young man's reputation. 'This is a work upon which we could rivet our eyes for hours and not experience satiety,' gushed the *Whitehall Evening Post*. After the show at the Academy the young Turner found his work was suddenly in great demand.

Light and its handling are what make this watercolour magnetic. The ruined castle keep is almost in the background, but it is made the focus not so much by the use of perspective but by the golden dawn sunlight rising behind it. Turner sat on the south bank of the Tweed close to where I was standing and he captured its reflections perfectly. A small fishing boat, its russet sail hoisted, drifts towards the darker waters below the castle, the site of the slippy path and the little landslide. On the north bank is a salmon shiel with another boat pulled up below it and three more fishermen working with nets. The rising sun catches them and the rocky riverbank above. Opposite the shiel some cows appear to be grazing while others stand in the water, probably drinking. I could see that Turner invented and rearranged the geography to suit the needs of his composition. Nowhere to be seen is the flat meadow below the castle; the Scottish bank seems to be far too steep, and goodness knows what the cows are doing on the equally rocky English bank, behaving more like mountain goats.

None of this matters. The watercolour is a stunning, atmospheric and revolutionary work of art. Turner knew that his painting of Norham Castle made his reputation and he came back at least twice to paint it again. Light obsessed him and his last painting of the same scene, begun in 1845, is almost completely abstract. The form of the castle keep is barely discernible, represented only by a fuzzy, glowering dark blue against the yellow light. A cow in the middle of the river is little more than a few dabs of brown paint, but the whole canvas glows with the atmosphere of the place, what I could see from where I stood. It would be difficult to read the late painting without having seen the watercolour of 1798. Turner can fairly be called the first impressionist painter and the famous French artists who followed him acknowledged his great influence. And that began at Norham.

The man who in turn influenced Turner was not a painter but someone born only a few miles from the village on the Tweed. In 1700 the parish minister of the village of Ednam and his wife saw the arrival of their first child. James Thomson was to become a poetic prodigy, his most famous work being *The Four Seasons*, a founding building block of what became known as the Romantic Movement. Almost unreadable now, it was immensely popular in the later eighteenth century and widely quoted. J. M. W. Turner was so impressed that he included these four lines in the 1798 Royal Academy catalogue, where his painting was so widely admired. It perhaps needs to be pointed out that they describe sunrise.

> But Yonder comes the powerful King of Day,
> Rejoicing in the East: the lessening cloud,
> The Kindling azure, and the mountain's brow,
> Illumin'd – his near approach betoken glad.

James Thomson's enduring monument is not his poetry (although he did write the words for 'Rule Britannia') but his influence on Turner and others. There is also an obelisk raised to his memory on a low hill near Ednam. When we cycled past it as boys, we had no idea who Thomson was, and few still do. But he was tremendously important in his time.

Directly below Norham Castle, and entirely absent from Turner's arranged compositions, is the reason for its existence. Blount Island is a grassy stepping-stone on a strategically vital ford over the Tweed. It had long been significant for armies moving north and south, and was originally known as Ubba's Ford, after one of the leaders of the Great Army of Danes who plundered England and the south of Scotland in the later ninth century. The castle was built much later, in the early twelfth century, by Ranulf Flambard, Bishop of Durham, to guard this gateway to England. He was an immensely powerful magnate. William I had made the bishopric into a county palatine, a semi-autonomous state that could act quickly if the Scots invaded and without reference to the king in the south. Ranulf Flambard behaved more like a prince than a bishop, and a monkish chronicler sniffed that he liked to have his meals served by ladies wearing tight bodices.

The magnificent Durham Cathedral was built on the fame and sanctity of St Cuthbert and its vast patrimony was based on the gifts of land to the old monastery on Lindisfarne, an island made holy by Cuthbert's time there as its bishop. After the Vikings sailed out of the sea-mists to attack Lindisfarne in the late eighth century, the first of many raids, the monks were eventually forced to abandon it. For almost a century, the Congregation of St Cuthbert wandered across the north, carrying his precious relics with them. It is likely that they first sought refuge, safely inland, at Norham. For many decades the church and the settlement around it were the *matrix ecclesia*, the Mother Church of Cuthbert's huge diocese.

The shadow of the saint is everywhere along the Tweed. A novice who first took holy orders at Old Melrose, he later sailed down the river and then made his way to Lindisfarne. Dozens of place names and dedications remember him.

The castle at Norham was understood as a northern bulwark, besieged thirteen times by Scottish armies and not often taken. The ruins of its massive keep and the curtain walls stand about four hundred yards from the village of Norham, leaving a clear field of fire around its landward bastions, emphasising a continuing military importance. Not until 1603 and the Union of the Crowns, when Robert Carey splashed across the fords with a message for James VI that told him he would become James I of England and Ireland, did Norham's walls begin to crumble.

I walked through the warmth of the early evening sun from Turner's viewpoint to the wide main street of the village and its well-set houses. Ahead I could see the village green surrounded by white bollards and fringed by daffodils. In need of a seat, I sank down on a bench close to an old stone column set on a tiered, wind-worn pedestal. At its top was a weather vane and, instead of a cockerel, a silver salmon swung with the changing winds. From my rucksack I pulled a bottle of fizzy water and a bar of Cadbury's Dairy Milk. I needed the energy for the last hour of a long day, an exploration of the little village. When I stood up, grunting with the effort, I noticed many brightly painted stones had been laid on the tiered pedestal. Perhaps they were some sort of secular offering.

Another cross stood in a small square near the gates to the churchyard. Dedicated to St Cuthbert, the village church lay to the west and it looked very substantial, as did its churchyard. Both seemed out of scale with the little village. I wondered if that was a legacy from the time of the wanderings of the Congregation of St Cuthbert. Was the wide perimeter the footprint of a monastic precinct? Around its walls were some large, grand houses, one of them the vicarage. A winding lane led off the square with the second cross and behind the houses that fronted on the village green. The lane led to the meadow where Turner had sat sketching. I half-expected to see Miss Marple in her coat and hat, carrying her wicker shopping basket, open the latch on a garden gate and nod to me as she passed by on her way to the butcher's shop. It took little effort or imagination to believe that I was ending my day in St Mary Mead on Tweed.

Paxton was only a very few miles distant but in fact a world away. It could never have been mistaken for an English village. Past that obvious observation, I wondered about the legacy of Northumbria and the cultural unity of the Tweed Valley that had existed between the seventh and eleventh centuries. Had it been completely submerged by medieval politics and the settlement of the border on the Tweed in the thirteenth century?

Day Three

The Haugh

On the morning of 12 June 1291, hundreds of servants and soldiers splashed across the fords below Norham Castle. Ox-carts carried all sorts of gear as they were goaded down the bank and into the river, and reluctant pack-horses were pulled into the current as grooms tugged on their halter ropes. Having waded or ridden the deeper channel, they skirted Blount Island and crossed a second branch of the Tweed to a place known as Holywell Haugh. Pavilions were erected and guyed and pennants planted in the tussocky grass of Scotland. Tallest was a red banner with three golden lions on it, their roaring jaws open and the claws on their forepaws clearly visible.

Five weeks before, England had come to Norham. Edward I had summoned his parliament to make the long journey north to help him settle what became known as the Great Cause, and thereby make the border politically meaningless.

At the end of the thirteenth century Scotland was a kingless country and drifting towards civil war. After the accidental death of Alexander III in 1286, the last attempt to find a successor from the line of macMalcolm kings had failed with the passing of Margaret, the little girl known as the Maid of Norway, in 1290. During the interregnum two bishops and four great magnates had been appointed as Guardians of the Realm. Nevertheless, unrest began to simmer as claimants armed themselves and an appeal was made to Edward I to mediate and facilitate the choice of a successor to the throne of Scotland.

Aggressive and expansionist, the English king immediately saw an opportunity. More than ten years before he came to Norham, Edward had humiliated Llywelyn, who had dared style himself Prince of Wales and had refused to do homage. In effect, he conquered much of the country, planting great castles around the coast at Conwy, Beaumaris, Caernarfon and elsewhere. Now the king looked north, and made his plans. Like his Plantagenet ancestors, Edward believed he had a legitimate claim to be overlord of Scotland and he sensed this might be the moment to enforce it. Alexander III had refused to comply, saying to Edward in public in 1278 that 'nobody but God has the right to homage for my kingdom, and I hold it of nobody but God Himself!'. Now that he had gone and no immediate heir could be found, this was the time to enforce the claim to overlordship and Edward gave instructions that documentary evidence to support it should be assembled.

Before the royal court made the long journey to Norham, a search of written records was begun and not only in the royal archives but also in the major monastic libraries across England. Despite a great deal of rummaging around, as chests were opened and dusty old scrolls unrolled, nothing much of substance turned up. But that did not sway Edward's resolve. When he called his parliament in the spring of 1291, the Guardians of the Realm and many other leading noblemen and burgesses were invited to assemble. They chose to stay north of the border, to meet in Berwick – then the richest, and probably the largest, town in Scotland. Robert Bruce (the grandfather of the victor of Bannockburn) and John Balliol had emerged as the leading claimants, or competitors, for the throne and the Scots expected that Edward I's arbitration would take place in Scotland. That was a miscalculation. Kings like Edward would not be summoned; they would do the summoning. And so after assurances of safe conduct and a renewal of the English promise in the Treaty of Birgham of 1290 that Scotland would remain 'free in itself, and without subjection from the kingdom of England', the Scottish delegation crossed the fords at Blount Island.

In the great hall of Norham Castle, in the presence of the king enthroned and surrounded by his great barons, Roger Brabazon, an English justice, told the Scots something they had not expected to hear. Edward I would not be a friendly arbiter but a supreme judge – as was his right, as the overlord of Scotland. And more than that, it seems that the king had encouraged many other competitors to present themselves for consideration. Instead of two, Bruce and Balliol, there would now be thirteen, almost all of them English noblemen descended from the illegitimate offspring of Scottish kings, of whom there appeared to be many. It was a genealogical maze, and probably a device to cloud the issue and make firm judgement all the more desirable.

Much winded by Edward's bullish and uncompromising approach, the Scots protested. One of the Guardians of the Realm, Robert Wishart, Bishop of Glasgow, seems to have been quick-thinking and eloquent, as well as courageous. The king had summoned many of his barons to the parliament at Norham and no doubt they rode north at the head of armed retinues. It was a show of England's great strength. Six hundred and fifty crossbowmen had also arrived to bolster the castle garrison, and anchored off Lindisfarne was an English warfleet. There was an unmistakable sense that if diplomacy failed, the English king would not hesitate to use force.

Nevertheless, Wishart spoke up and spoke well. Edward's demand to be recognised as overlord was something that could be conceded only by a king, and the Scots delegates were in no position to do that in the absence of a legitimate king. In addition, the bishop argued that it was not incumbent on the Scots to disprove the English king's claims but that he should prove them lawful. Edward was almost certainly not accustomed to being spoken to in such a frank and direct manner, nor to being contradicted so directly in public, and when Wishart made his final point, the king grew very angry. As Prince Edward, he had gone on crusade to the Holy Land, and as someone who had sworn the vows of a crusader, said the bold bishop, the king should not be threatening a defenceless people like the Scots with war. Edward exploded. He was indeed a crusader, the king roared, and he would lead a new crusade against the Scots.

Behind the formal scenes, like the meeting in the great hall of Norham, the chess pieces had been quietly moving. In a letter, Robert Bruce assured Edward I that were he to become king, then of course he would accept him as overlord of Scotland.

After the acrimonious conference, a three-week adjournment had been agreed and the Scots crossed the fords and returned to Berwick. But at the end of what might have been seen as a cooling-off period, the delegates refused to return to the castle and be surrounded once more by all that power and menace.

Edward and his counsellors were not dismayed. If what Robert Wishart had argued was legally correct, then all of the competitors for the throne should therefore be persuaded to acknowledge the king's overlordship before any judgement was made. Robert Bruce had already done so and the others should be encouraged to follow his lead, not something that would have presented much difficulty for the gaggle of English noblemen Edward's agents had persuaded to apply. What followed in the days of early June 1291 was a genuine turning point, a moment when Scotland's history abruptly moved first one way and then another.

I wanted to walk in the shadow of these men – of clever, stubborn Wishart; ruthlessly ambitious Bruce; John Balliol, the waverer; Edward I, a great and terrifying king – and to do that, I needed to find the precise place where history had played out, the meadow known as

Holywell Haugh. I believe in *genius loci*, that places have spirits and sometimes memory, and despite the intervening centuries I hoped to get some sense of atmosphere, if I could only find the place where they met.

Holywell Haugh appears on no map, not even the trusty Pathfinder. One very learned historian reckoned that the crucial meetings between the Scots and the English were held near the village of Upsettlington, but that seemed too far from the fords at Blount Island and the castle. I decided to walk the ground in search of the stage where those dramatic and momentous events had played out. I doubted I would hear any echoes, but perhaps I would see what the main actors saw and understand why they had agreed to meet at the haugh. Geography and borders lay at the heart of this story: a story that shaped Scotland, and England.

Walking west out of Norham village, I came across a road sign: Ladykirk 1 mile, Swinton 4 miles, and below it another that said, simply, Scotland. That way, it pointed. As the road swung north towards the river between high greening hedges and a handy footpath, I found myself blessed by another morning of brilliant sun. April temperatures meant a shirt, bodywarmer and a jumper, but the fresh brightness of the budding lime-green of the hawthorns showed me that it was growing warmer. Star-shaped violet flowers grew from a garden shrub of some sort that had seeded in the hedge and, beside them, behind a tangle of bare branches, was a clump of daffodils. It was a good day to go in search of history.

When I reached the elegant bridge over the Tweed, the views up and down the river were sublime, and on one side the morning shadows of recently planted poplars reached over the sparkling water to midstream. Upriver lay Canny Island and a long vista to the south. Built in the nineteenth century, the bridge is too narrow for two-way traffic and there is no pavement. About a third of the way across, I had a brush with death, as a very quiet hearse surprised me as it passed close. Heaped on the coffin were beautiful wreaths of yellow roses, but strangely there was no cavalcade of mourners' cars behind.

Once I had arrived safely in Scotland, a choice needed to be made. There was no road running parallel to the river and no sign of a track. But to find Holywell Haugh I needed to follow the Scottish bank closely until I was near the fords at Blount Island. Passing a lodge that might have been an old tollhouse at the end of the bridge, I noticed a wooden stile over a fence behind the house. Stiles usually mean paths and so I climbed it. And found a narrow, muddy path above a steep slope down to the river. My notebook entry made at that point was succinct: 'another crazy riverside path', followed by 'sheep are not so daft'. The latter referred to the safer option of climbing up the bank to a fence-line I could see on the horizon. Sheep had grazed it and I followed their zig-zags until I reached the top. From there, I found a sheepwalk along the ridge above the Tweed. The views east, south and west were breath-catching and the massive hump of distant Cheviot was clear of cloud. I was catching my breath after the steep climb, my woolly jumper stowed in my rucksack, and not long afterwards my bodywarmer would join it.

After a while, I climbed a short stretch of post-and-rail fencing into a large grass park where ewes and lambs skittered out of the way, even though I was keeping to the margins of the field. Deeply rutted by heavy tractors, a track led east, but it was difficult walking and I kept to the grassy crest as much as I could. To my left rose the magnificent outline of Ladykirk, a church built at the instigation of the pious James IV of Scotland in 1500. I planned to walk in a long loop that would later take me past it. Once I'd found Holywell Haugh. If I could find it. In front of me stretched broad fields of the green shoots of what I took to be young barley. Haughs are flat areas by rivers or streams and these fields high above the Tweed did not meet that definition.

What greatly helped my bearings was that the trees on the steep bank were mostly leafless and I never lost sight of the river. After about half a mile of stumbling along the rutted track, I expected to see the western tip of Blount Island. But I did not expect to see two cars parked on it. There were two fishermen in the channel beyond the island, but I could not see how they had managed to get their vehicles across the river.

After another few hundred yards I understood, because I suddenly came across exactly what I was looking for. Hidden by the trees on the steep bank, almost directly opposite Norham Castle, was a wide, flat meadow on the Scottish side of the Tweed. Holywell Haugh. Had to be. And leading into the haugh from the north was a well-made track used by fishermen which took me to a narrow and shallow ford.

I scrambled down the bank, past a modern fishermen's

hut with picnic tables on its deck, to reach the ford. I reckoned I could have made it across to Blount Island in my beige boots because the water was so low. The cars would have had no difficulty.

On 12 June 1291, it is probable that the Tweed was low enough for Edward I and his glittering retinue to ride across from Norham Castle to meet the Scottish delegation on the haugh, in Scotland. Show mattered in the Middle Ages and it is very likely that Edward was mounted on a destrier, a stallion trained as a war horse. Trumpets would have announced his arrival and he would have been preceded by bannerets, knights with their men marching behind their pennants. Skirted by a silk caparison bearing the royal arms, the destrier carried a great king in all his pomp. Surrounding him would have been a retinue of household officers and great magnates in all their war splendour. On that June morning, as the Scots watched and waited, colour and power came to Holywell Haugh.

A compromise had been reached. When the Guardians refused to return to Norham, the king agreed to meet in Scotland, just. The haughland was easily within bowshot of the castle walls, and the Scots would not have failed to notice that as men lined the walls to watch what happened on the flat meadow across the river. Both sides had also accepted something that would break the deadlock. Edward I had agreed that he himself would become a claimant to the vacant throne of Scotland.

It was a fudge, but one that the Scots could swallow. On behalf of all the other claimants and explicitly not as an overlord, Edward gained control of all the royal castles in Scotland for a limited period. In effect, until a new king had been chosen. It mattered very much that the Guardians of the Realm had granted control of the kingdom to Edward and that he had not taken it by force.

On Holywell Haugh, a ceremony took place. As I discovered when I finally found it, it was a perfect theatre. Almost completely flat, the haugh is overlooked not only by the glowering castle over the river but also by steep slopes on the Scottish side. Watched by the English earls, the royal retinue and household, as well as all the Scottish delegates, the Great Seal of Scotland was handed into Edward's keeping. It was the physical key to his temporary authority, for when it was pressed onto a blob of wax at the foot of a document, what was written above it became the law. In return, Edward made a solemn declaration. He promised to maintain the laws and customs of Scotland, and by implication agreed not to impose anything new or alien.

On the morning of 13 June, the parties assembled once again on Holywell Haugh and all the Scots present did homage to Edward, as the holder of the Great Seal and as 'chief lord and guardian of the kingdom, until a king is provided'. Probably hammered out in preliminary discussions leading up to the ceremonial business transacted by the river, it was also agreed that the momentous process of reaching a decision on who would succeed to the throne should begin in August, at Berwick and not Norham. As a claimant and temporary 'chief lord', Edward probably felt more comfortable in Scotland. There would be a huge jury empanelled to determine which man should be king. No fewer than one hundred and five would sit in judgement. Twenty-five 'auditors' would be appointed by Edward, including himself. Forty would be nominated by Robert Bruce and the same number by John Balliol. This last was undoubtedly a concession to the Scots delegates, a recognition that there were really only two credible candidates.

After much delay, most likely deliberate so that Edward's period of temporary control could be extended, the king arrived in Berwick on 1 June 1292. Arguments from other claimants were heard and dismissed, as Bruce and Balliol duly emerged as front-runners. But then another delay was agreed, as lawyers from the University of Paris were consulted on matters of inheritance and the definition of primogeniture. The auditors reconvened in October, and by that time even Edward's patience was running out. Bruce's arguments were finally dismissed. On 17 November John Balliol was awarded the crown of Scotland and the royal castles were placed under his control. Two weeks later, King John I sat on the Stone of Destiny on the top of the Moot Hill outside Scone Abbey, near Perth, and the crown was placed on his head. It was 30 November, the feast day of Scotland's patron saint, Andrew. But despite that happy coincidence, the auspices were not favourable.

Before the coronation at Scone, Edward I had insisted that Balliol accompany him from Berwick to Norham, into England, to swear fealty. There could be no ambiguity. Unlike Alexander III, the king-designate had consented to the English king's overlordship of Scotland and at Christmas, having been formally crowned, King

John I came to Newcastle to do homage for his kingdom as well as his lands in England. It was an arrangement that was doomed to fail, and quickly.

The new sovereign had to wait only ten months for his authority to begin to unravel. Macduff, the brother of the Earl of Fife, had been tried in a royal court and sent to prison. But Macduff appealed, not to King John but over his head to his overlord, Edward I. This in turn meant that John or a royal representative would have to plead in an English court to validate a judgement that had already been made in Scotland. It was unworkable, rendering the independence of the national crown as meaningless. When he refused to attend the English court or send a representative, Edward pronounced Balliol to be in contempt and demanded that he hand over several royal castles.

The English king then insisted that Scottish barons add their men to his army for an invasion of France. An uneasy year later, a parliament at Stirling removed Balliol's ability to govern and transferred power to a council of twelve barons and prelates. Politically neutered, King John I was now publicly humiliated. In a ritual usually inflicted on treasonous knights, he was physically stripped of all that made him a king. Edward I had Balliol dragged into the market place at Montrose and made to kneel. First, his knightly girdle was removed. Blazoned with the royal lion rampant of Scotland, his surcoat was ripped off and the royal signet ring pulled from his finger. Then the symbol of his authority, the Great Seal of Scotland, was smashed on the cobbles.

As his barons roared with laughter, Edward I was said

to have remarked, 'a man does good business when he rids himself of a turd'.

There followed perhaps the most famous sequence of events in Scotland's long history. The English king's attempts to convert the nation into a colony were met with sustained and ultimately successful resistance. William Wallace rose to prominence and won a signal victory at Stirling Bridge against a much larger army before suffering the horrific death of a convicted traitor after a show trial in London. When Robert Bruce continued to press his family's claims to the throne of Scotland and led renewed rebellion, his chances of success seemed at first slim. After his hurried coronation at Scone in March 1306, his wife, Elizabeth, was sceptical: 'I am afraid, my lord, that we have been made King and Queen as boys are made in summer games.'

After the death of Edward I a year later, as he prepared to invade Scotland, and the eventual triumph at Bannockburn in 1314, the hero-king appeared to have secured the independence of his realm. By that time Bruce was forty, growing old for the times, and his past began to prey on his mind. In 1306, he had been excommunicated, cast out of the communion of Holy Mother Church for the murder of his rival, John Comyn, in front of the high altar in Greyfriars Church, Dumfries. Condemned to die unshriven, the king asked his churchmen to write to Pope John XXII and beseech the Holy Father to rescind the sentence of the Church.

Three letters were sent to Rome, but only one survived and has become very famous, a canonical text in Scotland's story. Known as the Declaration of Arbroath (because it was probably the work of Bernard, Abbot of Arbroath), it puts forward a carefully argued and beautifully written case for independence under the rightful rule of King Robert. One passage is endlessly quoted as a caption under scenes of glory at Bannockburn, as the underdogs defeated the imperialist might of England.

> As long as a hundred of us remain alive, never will we on any conditions be subjected to the lordship of the English. It is in truth not for glory, nor riches, nor honours that we are fighting, but for freedom alone, which no honest man gives up but with life itself.

It is undoubtedly stirring stuff, but it diverts attention from the even more striking passage that comes immediately before it. Here it is:

> Yet if he [the king] should give up what he has begun, seeking to make us or our kingdom subject to the King of England or the English, we should exert ourselves at once to drive him out as our enemy and a subverter of his own right and ours, and make some other man who was well able to defend us as our King . . .

Although it is important not to overload the point, this was a clear statement of an embryonic political ideology that was some distance ahead of its time. It is also, I believe, a significant moment in Scotland's history, and the beginning of a halting, sporadic process of political change. Kingship was now conditional. There existed a contract between the community of the realm and the sovereign, which insisted on an absolute commitment to Scottish independence from England, and which obliged that community to remove a king who broke that commitment and replace him with 'some other man'.

But this passage is not, as has sometimes been claimed, an early form of democracy. The community of the realm most certainly did not include ordinary Scots, those who laboured in the fields, fished off the coasts or herded flocks in the summer hills. It comprised a very small group, the great magnates, the bishops and abbots and, to a limited extent, some burgesses, the men who conducted business in Scotland's few small towns.

Self-interest also helped create the intellectual basis for conditional kingship. The magnates did not want to fight in England's wars or be the servants of two masters, as had happened under King John I. But it was the Church in Scotland that had consistently and fearlessly opposed an English takeover. When he spoke up at Norham, the formidable Robert Wishart was by no means without support. His brother bishops also did not wish to come under the ecclesiastical control of York or Canterbury, and they insisted on a direct relationship with the Holy Father in Rome.

The longer-term significance of this key passage in the Declaration of Arbroath is, I think, harder to assess. North of the border there seems to have been less deference to medieval royalty, but the sources are very scant, although it was something that seemed to be picked up more strongly after the Reformation in 1560. Sometime after 1590 there was an encounter between the great churchman and academic Andrew Melville and King James VI at Falkland Palace. Here is a translation of Melville's Scots:

> I must tell you there are two kings and two kingdoms in Scotland. There is Christ Jesus the King, and his kingdom the Kirk, whose subject James VI is, and of whose kingdom he is not a king, nor a lord, nor a head but a member!

Melville concluded the lecture by reminding the king that he was only 'God's silly vassal' – although it must be pointed out that 'silly' in 1590 meant something like humble or lowly. James must have looked longingly to the south, where his mother's cousin, Queen Elizabeth I, was held in such reverence that no one would have dared speak to her in that tone. When the Stuarts did finally accede to the throne of England, it turned out to be a very different proposition. Heady stuff. Instead of hectoring ministers, they were surrounded by deference and very soon became believers in the divine right of kings – although that all eventually came to a sticky end.

Without over-egging the argument, I do think there is a real cultural difference here. By and large, Scots tend to be less deferential, but not in the threadbare phrase 'we're all Jock Tamson's bairns', meaning that there is somehow a natural egalitarianism north of the border. That seems rather too neat and smacks of self-congratulation. If there is less deference, I think it has more to do with scale. Compared to England, ten times its size, Scotland is a small country. Familiarity can breed contempt, of course, but it can also help soften differences in status. There is plenty of snobbery in Scotland, as well as racism and sexism and a shamingly large group of people whose poverty and deprivation close down their ability to engage in any creative or meaningful way. But despite those factors, Scotland's small scale and small population, concentrated in the Central Belt and the nodal cities of Glasgow and Edinburgh, means that the powerful and famous are often not remote figures but are more approachable than their English counterparts.

That sense of a wider community has been greatly helped by the reconvening of the Scottish Parliament, something that would have made Robert Wishart smile. Government is now closer and sometimes the better for that. But at the same time, and I'm certain many Scottish politicians would agree, there has been a huge increase in the ugly habit of what my mother used to call 'tall poppy syndrome'. Especially with the recent advent of social media, tall poppies, those active and prominent, are routinely and repeatedly scythed down, something that increasingly discourages young people from becoming involved in public life.

*   *   *

As I walked north from Holywell Haugh under a beating hot sun, I rummaged around in my rucksack until I found a hat. The back of my shirt was soaked with sweat, but in only a few moments it cooled enough to make me wince when I shouldered my pack again.

Even though they were stiffened somewhat by the history that had played out behind me on the haugh in the 1290s, these arguments felt soft, impressionistic. Was relative deference a real cultural difference between Scotland and England, or just a puff of wishful thinking? My instincts agree with it, but perhaps that is because I don't defer to status (respect is another matter entirely). Or I don't think I do. Everyone's experience is different.

As I crunched up it, the fishermen's track struck me as odd. Most of these metalled roads are formed from rammed aggregate and usually have a grassy crest in the middle. But this one was partly made from broken crockery, what looked to me like white china. I could see many recognisable fragments of saucers and plates – even the handle of a teacup, I was sure. All of which pushed matters of history and deference immediately to the back of my mind. Probably where they belong. What had happened here, on this track by the Tweed? Had there been some sort of almighty accident, resulting in tons of smashed china needing to be got rid of? Some sort of strange story had played out here. It was the nearest I'd ever come to actually walking on eggshells.

Idle, wandering curiosity (I can disappear down rabbit holes for hours, chasing intriguing stories) had taken me further along this road than I'd meant to walk. I pulled out the Pathfinder and saw that there was another track, one that led uphill towards a farm marked as New Ladykirk. On either side were wide fields, the green shoots of more barley. The track was dusty and the soil looked baked – in April. We'd had no rain for three weeks at our little place and clearly here, further down the valley, they'd had none either.

In 2022 we have experienced extraordinary, unprecedented cycles of weather, five periods of sustained drought when no rain fell for weeks, even during the winter. Not only does that dry up the ground – we have seen dust blown along our tracks in January – it also restricts the growth of new grass. We suffer a direct economic effect when it doesn't rain. My wife and I used to breed horses, and although we will have no more foals (backs and shoulders are beginning to creak too loudly), we do have a duty of care to our retired brood mares and other older horses. They are not clapped-out machines to be parked somewhere round the back and forgotten about. Our horses are living creatures, each with their own character and foibles, and we love them. And so when there is very little spring grass, we have to keep feeding them expensive hay and haylage. They live outside, well rugged against the cold, but when the old ones get to the end of a winter and all its privations they need a bite of sweet grass and all its esters.

Much more problematic is our water supply. For twenty-five years we have drawn our water from an ancient well up near the top of our hill. Dedicated to St Mungo, it supplied the town of Selkirk until the nineteenth century. But in the last year, and occasionally before that, the flow has been very low, almost a trickle, too low to provide for us and our neighbours. We have endured long periods with no water at all at the farm. Mercifully, a stream runs through our meadow where the old horses live out and the troughs above our holding tank have never run dry. But around the farmhouse, the barns and outbuildings, and the stables, sometimes nothing comes out of the taps, scarcely even a drip.

A complete loss of water for weeks is more than an inconvenience. It not only means none to drink or cook with but also no toilet flush, no shower, no washing machine, no dishwasher and, most important, nothing for the water buckets of the three horses who come into the stables overnight. Compensating for the loss of all these facilities takes up a tremendous amount of time and effort, hours of ferrying containers back and forth every day.

Our son lives on the farm with his family and without his help we could not cope. Each morning he drives to the local garage, who kindly allow him to fill up a dozen thirty-litre containers. They are very heavy and I can't carry one very far. My job is to go to the local super-market to buy ten-litre boxes of drinking water; demand has been such, that over the last year a quota was imposed at one point. There are many farms in the Tweed Valley, and especially in the western hills, on private supplies. Kettles are boiled for washing and we bought a camping shower that works from a bucket of warm water with a battery-powered pump. And we cook as much as possible in the oven and the microwave to avoid having to wash up pans.

The cause of these droughts? Anyone who thinks the climate isn't changing isn't paying attention. Those of us who work on the land every day have seen mounting, clear and unambiguous evidence of extreme weather, such as droughts and the increasingly regular and violent storms that have blown down so many trees that the look of the landscape is changing. Gaps have appeared in familiar horizons, and fields once well-sheltered are now open to the winds. Governments are not acting fast enough and they won't react until it's too late. All we can do is change what we do. That means consuming less and conserving more. Not a message many people want to hear. And for our immediate difficulties, I shall need to find a great lump of cash to get us connected to the mains water supply. Sooner rather than later.

Our present troubles sometimes interfere with my enjoyment of beautiful, dry sunny days. There have just been too many of them. But not on the morning I walked over the broken crockery to New Ladykirk Farm. A well-set, tidy steading reminded me of the past, of farming even sixty years ago. There were several empty cottages no longer inhabited by farm workers – the men, women and children needed in the labour-intensive centuries before mechanisation emptied them. I guessed that after the Second World War perhaps forty or fifty people may have lived at New Ladykirk Farm. When I walked past the barns and old cart sheds to the tarmac road, I met no one. But an atmosphere was still in the air, a scent I remembered from childhood. At the gable end of a barn stood a stack of last year's silage bales and their sweet aroma filled the sunlit morning, a memory of good summer grass.

A long, straight road stretched out in front of me, and on the horizon I could see the outline of the Ladykirk, the church built for James IV in 1500–01. Young trees not yet in leaf lined the route and I paced out the distances between them. It was either sixty yards or thirty, a memory of a decision on a winter's day, of the men who planted the young, dormant sticks perhaps twenty years ago and their wish for some order.

Where the road dipped, turned and crossed a burn was another farm steading, Old Ladykirk. Its substantial cottages still had their old pigsties behind them, one set having been converted into what looked like a conservatory, or perhaps a greenhouse. Hearing the purr of a quad bike, I looked around to see the farmer pulling a small trailer. As most people in the countryside do, he raised a hand in greeting as we passed each other. On the far side of the brae, I came upon early summer, a row of chestnut trees that had flushed into lush, green leaf and I imagined their ancient taproots drinking deep from the burn trickling below them while their canopy unfurled to be warmed in the long hours of April sun.

The Ladykirk loomed up on the right, its chunky solidity sitting on the crown of the hill. I saw that it was roofed not by slates but by stone flags. The patron, James IV, had a reputation for piety, perhaps a piety fuelled by guilt. His father, James III, had adopted a deeply unpopular, pro-English foreign policy and had contracted to marry his heir to Cecily of York, the daughter of Edward IV. His turbulent reign was an example of the Declaration of Arbroath in action. The great magnates and prelates feared for Scotland's independence and there were two rebellions that attempted to remove the king and replace him. Frustration boiled over in 1488 when James III fought a rebel army at Sauchieburn, near Stirling. In the ruck of battle, the king was killed and James IV quickly crowned in his place.

All his life the new king bore an intense sense of guilt for his father's death and he often did penance. Pilgrimages to the shrine of St Ninian at Whithorn and to St Duthac in Tain, churches that lay at each end of his kingdom, were undertaken almost annually. The length and difficulty of the journey mattered; it was part of the act of penance. During Lent, James wore a *cilice*, an iron belt, next to his skin, adding an ounce to it with each year that passed since the events at Sauchieburn.

In the summer of 1497 James IV led an army to lay siege to Norham Castle. Some of his forces crossed the ford at Blount Island so that they could attack from the west and the south. After the king mounted his horse to splash back to Scotland, a flash flood suddenly swept him downstream and into a deep pool behind a yiddie, a Scots version of an eddy. Also known as steills, these were places where salmon could be caught by netting. Hauled out before he drowned, the pious James believed that the intercession of the Virgin Mary had saved him and he determined to do her honour. The full name of the church he had built in gratitude is Our Lady Kirk of Steill.

The door was unlocked, a welcoming and ancient cultural habit of trust that assumed no one would damage or desecrate a church, and one that encouraged those who might wish to spend a few moments in prayer or contemplation or to simply seek some peace. I doubt if many churches are unlocked in towns or cities nowadays. Inside was the familiar chill and quiet of an old place lit by shafts of vivid colour as the sun streamed through the stained glass.

In a side chapel was something I hadn't seen before, a series of framed lists headed Cradle Roll. It recorded baptisms, an old tradition enlivened by fashionable twenty-first-century Christian names: Kia, Leoni, Brodye, A-Jay and Nathan, the latter an appropriate biblical revival. Top of the list was one that stirred a memory, a continuity, community of a kind. I guessed that Charlie George Mole was the grandson of someone I once played rugby with. At Kelso we had a pack of giant forwards (at 13 stone, I was the lightest) but too little talent in the backs, except for Drew Mole. A skilled, tidy player, he had been a farmer in Berwickshire and here, I think, fifty years after we'd played in the same teams, was an important event in his life remembered in a kirk that was five hundred years old, no doubt the repository of many thousands of such connections.

Ladykirk is a tiny hamlet. No more than half a dozen houses surrounded the old kirk. Beyond them, stretching almost to the horizons on every side, were the fertile fields of the area known as the Merse. The name is cognate to Mercia, the old Anglo-Saxon kingdom in the midlands of England, and it means the marches, the borders. And it was on the southern borders of Northumbria, for a time the most powerful of all the kingdoms. The Merse is some of the best farmland in the north, and my ancestors helped plough and reap its fields for generations as they moved from farm to farm in the eighteenth and nineteenth centuries. I like fields – a tidy, working landscape. The countryside isn't only a place of peace and quiet beauty, somewhere to be idealised and admired. Nevertheless, this is overwhelmingly how it is seen by the vast majority of town and city dwellers. It's good that the land is loved, but a shame it is not better understood. Here is Enid Blyton, rhapsodising in 1930. She was on a trip to Portugal, but her heart clearly wasn't in it: 'But I thought I hadn't seen any countryside anywhere that I thought was lovelier than England's. I had seen no animals nicer than ours, and no children that I liked better than English children . . . and I know that, no matter where I go or what I see in other countries, I shall always love England best.'

There's nothing wrong with that sort of sentiment, except that it has been so pervasive, as well as being bland and uninformed. Enid was a cultural phenomenon who wrote a mind-bending seven hundred and fifty books and sold an astonishing six hundred million copies of them. This simple piety of 'there's no place like home' was obviously enormously influential, but for me it's only part of the story. Picturesque is by no means enough. Perhaps this comes from the old ploughmen and carters, the generations of Moffats who worked the rich Berwickshire soil, but what I find attractive is how productive the land can be. Of course, farming methods can and have been brutal. One only has to remember Rachel Carson's powerful polemic *Silent Spring* in the early 1960s, which worried about the effect of pesticides in America. But done sympathetically, as well as unsentimentally, farming can be immensely satisfying. Horse-breeding isn't even recognised by the government as an agricultural activity, a notion unimaginable in a world before the coming of cars and lorries, but it is about growth and using the land. Our little farm is a working landscape that has produced beautiful horses that have given immense pleasure, as well as generating economic benefit because of that. One of our mares is a British dressage champion with a social media following, and others have done well for their riders and owners.

The road out of Ladykirk led to a crossroads and on my left a steep incline down towards Norham Bridge, the place where I had started early that morning. My plan was to begin to walk along the Scottish bank of the Tweed, but first I needed to find a bench, sit down and have some lunch. And only fifty yards along the path there was one. Hallelujah! It was dedicated to Bert Foreman, 1933 to 1999. Many thanks, Bert. One end was shaded by the trunk of a tall ash and I gratefully unshouldered my rucksack, sat down and stretched out my weary legs. The Pathfinder maps' scale is in imperial – miles, yards and inches, two and a half of the latter to the mile – and I reckoned I'd done about four and a half, maybe five miles, with all the messing about looking for Holywell Haugh.

Before I started out in Norham, I'd bought myself two treats from the excellent butcher's shop, rolls filled with bacon, brie and cranberry, and I had two small bottles of fizzy water. Joy! It was good to be hungry and not just because it was lunchtime. While I watched two fishermen casting below the bridge, I feasted and drank deep.

But not for too long. At my age, stiffness soon sets in. The riverside path led south to Ladykirk estate and home farm. The Pathfinder used the older name of Upsettlington to describe the whole area, what was almost a river peninsula as the Tweed turned south-east and then south-west. I wanted to spend some time there because it was the birthplace of a hero. In the distance, on the English bank of the river, I had seen what looked like two towers. They glowered over the river like the grim keep of Norham Castle. I looked in vain on the map for what they might be, but as I walked closer I could see that they were tall grain bins, a fitting memorial to the man I admired so much.

James Small changed the landscape. And the world. Born sometime around 1740, the son of a farmer at Upsettlington, he was apprenticed to a carpenter and ploughwright at the village of Hutton, not far from Paxton. Small was kept busy repairing the old Scots plough. Forever breaking down, the design of these had varied little for centuries. Essentially a large, flat-sided wooden wedge tipped with iron, it was dragged through the ground by a team of oxen. Ploughing was a highly labour-intensive, slow and halting business. The plodding oxen were led and prodded on by a goadman, the plough itself guided by another who held the stilts steady and a third man who often had to sit on the beam, his weight needed to keep the wooden mouldboard from jumping out of the ground when it hit compacted earth or big stones. Furrows were shallow and the plough was often damaged. Because it was flat-sided, the mouldboard did not turn over the furrow-slice completely. That meant several plough-followers were needed, usually women and children, to pull out the weeds and bash down the big clods with a mel.

As broken ploughs came into the workshop at Hutton,

James Small began to think about change, about how a better plough could be made. In 1758 he travelled to Doncaster, where he found work as 'an operative mechanic'. Perhaps Small had heard of the Rotherham plough. Designed by Joseph Foljambe sometime after 1730, its mouldboard had a slightly different shape and, crucially, it was plated with iron. Not only could it cut through the ground with less resistance, it also broke down much less frequently.

Six years later, when he might have been twenty-four, James Small came back home. While he'd worked in Yorkshire, a radical idea had been forming and it seems that he wanted to develop it himself with the help of his own people.

Much intrigued and moved by the story of this man, one of the very few from what might be called the working classes to make a positive mark before the nineteenth or twentieth centuries, I drove to Berwickshire one summer in search of him. In 1764 he had been set up in business by John Renton, a wealthy farmer, at Blackadder Mount Farm near Duns. What I found was a near-complete loss of historical memory, a world-changing invention unremarked, not memorialised or celebrated in any way. On the road to the farm, I stopped at two sets of buildings hidden behind a high beech hedge. I only found them because I had done some research beforehand, and even though they had been listed on the Canmore site, the national record of the historic environment in Scotland, there was no information about James Small, or indeed anything else.

Cottages had been made out of the west end of each

of the ranges by the roadside, but the rest of the buildings were empty, semi-derelict and overgrown with
willowherb, rowan and a tangle of scrub. The architecture was formal, though, and not like the usual style on
farms. There were severely pitched gables topped with
decorative finials, regular fenestration and a very pleasing
symmetry in what I could see of the overall design. These
were not tumbledown ruins but the abandoned remains
of serious business. In the southern range of one set,
which formed a courtyard with the U-shaped northern
buildings, there was a high double doorway in the gable
end. Beyond it sat the reason for the existence of this
little complex of buildings. Just discernible in the gloom
of a summer interior was the massive chimney of a
blacksmith's forge. A huge yellow sandstone mantel,
beautifully chiselled and squared, projected from red
sandstone mountings with flues cut into them. Below
the lum was a half-broken fireplace that once rose to
waist-height. The forge was clearly large enough to heat
substantial items of metalwork.

It was here, at Blackadder Mount, that James Small
began to work on prototypes for his new design. Having
seen the Rotherham plough, he had the breakthrough
notion of not plating the wooden mouldboard but of
discarding wood entirely and casting the whole thing in
iron. But the shape of the mouldboard had to be precisely
right. So single-minded that he made scores of prototypes, using his carpentry skills to carve slightly different
shapes, Small experimented again and again. He had the
wooden prototypes pulled through the ground so that
he could trace accurately the points of hardest wear and

greatest stress. Many were discarded and sometimes even smashed to smithereens by Small as his frustrations boiled over. But finally, he found the right design and sent it to the Carron Ironworks in Falkirk to be cast in iron.

The result was revolutionary. All of his experiments had convinced Small that the shape of the mouldboard had to change, had to be not flat-sided but slightly screwed, much like the modern plough. This not only allowed it to delve deeper but also turned the furrow-slice completely, so that it covered the weeds and made them into a mulch and extra fertiliser. And because it could delve deeper, the new plough helped enormously to improve drainage.

As I walked uphill from the riverbank, past more mighty trees felled by the fury of Storm Arwen, I looked out over the fields around Ladykirk Home Farm. It is easy to forget that two hundred years ago they looked very different. The old runrig system was still in use. Long, narrow strips were ploughed by ox-teams and between them ran drainage ditches for the excess rainwater that ran off the rigs. It was a very inefficient way of farming and Small's plough changed it radically. Wide fields were enclosed, underground drainage painstakingly dug and laid, and, as a result, much more and much better land came into cultivation. Farms also looked different, as the homely geometry of fenced and hedged fields was laid out and the open rigs disappeared. Only one man was needed to guide the new plough, as he wrapped the long reins of two strong horses around his hands, gripped the stilt handles and clicked his tongue to get the animals moving. That released others for the work of improving the land and bringing many more acres under the plough. It was an agricultural revolution that spread all over Britain and to North America, where the prairies became one of the bread baskets of the world.

For reasons that remain unclear, James Small never patented his design, made no money from it and, in fact, died in poverty in 1793, worn out by all that he had done. I've no doubt he was more than a genius. He was a great and good man, and he should be better remembered.

By the time I'd walked back down to the Tweed, it was early evening and the westering sun threw long shadows through the trees on the far riverbank and over the slow-flowing water. Motes danced in the air above the surface and there seemed to be no breeze, only a great stillness settling over the land. On the high grass banks to my right, the ewes had scarted out shelters from the east wind that blew in off the North Sea on winter days. The strips of baked earth were ochre-coloured against the green of the grass. To catch the last warming rays of the sun before the chill of the night, lambs were basking in the sheep-scrapes, their forelegs tucked under their chests, their ears flicking at the insects. Perhaps siblings – now that all ewes appear to have twins these days – some were lying very close to each other, borrowing body warmth. With such an open evening sky, I thought it would be a cold night, perhaps even frosty, but the forecast was for another sunny, rainless day.

Day Four

War Border

Woken by the welcome drumming of steady rain on the slates, I didn't curse a wrong forecast but instead blessed the occasional waywardness of the Met Office. The unexpected rain would do nothing for our failing water supply. That would need a real downpour, and days of it. But grass has shallow roots and even a couple of hours' steady rain encourages noticeable growth if it's followed by warmth. And it was.

By the time I walked down to the track by the Tweed below Upsettlington, the sun was climbing behind me, throwing a long shadow. The English bank was still in shade but the butter-coloured light had unfurled across the haugh in front of me.

On the track the dust of the day before had become a thin slick of mud and I noticed it had been decorated by a delicate tracery of many lines. They seemed to lead nowhere, looping in circles around each other, crisscrossing and disappearing at the edge of the grass. The creatures who had etched these random trails had disappeared back down their burrows having, like me, blessed the rain.

I was looking at worm trails. I'd seen them before, almost always after long periods of sunny weather. Down in their underground world, it had become too dry for worms. They breathe through their skin and it needs to be moist, with a mucus-like sheen. And so when the worms felt the night rain begin, hundreds, perhaps thousands, had come to the surface at a time when predatory birds could not easily see them and they slithered around on the muddy track by the river. That was why the trails seemed aimless, describing random journeys. The worms weren't going anywhere.

On both sides of the track were high stacks of cut logs, each one about twelve feet, the preferred length for sawmills. It was more of the sad bounty of Storm Arwen; the wrecked wood behind looked as though it had been shelled by artillery. A forester told me recently that it had been no storm, that in America they would have called it a hurricane. 'Like standing in the way of a jet engine,' he said. 'Not a gusting storm, but a constant blast of ninety-mile-an-hour wind.' He said it had been worst in a twenty-mile corridor down the eastern coastlands of Berwickshire and Northumberland. 'From about Cockburnspath to Alnwick, hundreds of thousands of trees went down.'

Much of what the foresters had cut was Scots pine, a beautiful orange-coloured wood with deeply corrugated dark bark. When I passed the stacks, I caught the sharp and clean scent of pine, something elemental that would live on after the death of the trees. Beyond, where the remains of the woodland ended, was a solitary hardwood tree, its smooth bark saying it was probably a beech. Almost all of its main trunk had been amputated by chainsaw. But growing vertically out of it was a single, long, skeletal branch, reaching for the sky, and at its top were the tiny, perfect, unfurling leaves of survival.

Across the river the sun lit a series of large houses that looked north to Scotland. Each seemed well-set in large gardens. One had a long and rather grand pillared verandah. It would not have looked out of place in colonial South Africa or Zimbabwe, while another had been painted a light cream, a perfect match with the ochre of the pantiled roofs and the green of the trees on the bank behind it. As ever, England looked more prosperous.

When the track by the river had skirted the wide haugh below the walls of Ladykirk Estate, I came upon welcome new information. Thirty years old at least, the Norham Pathfinder sheet couldn't tell me if the path continued through the stands of riverside trees I could see ahead of me. But a fencepost could. With the town's crest in the middle, a small disc informed me that I was on one of the Coldstream Paths and a helpful arrow pointed straight at the woods. Very different from the prohibitions and confusions of Northumberland County Council.

It was a still, warming morning, and when I stopped to peel off my jumper I sensed rather than saw some movement on the far bank of the river. Just a flicker in the corner of my eye. When I'd shouldered my rucksack, I pulled the Pathfinder out of my back pocket and noted that the oddly named Bendibus Island was on the opposite side. As I looked up, a black bullock suddenly thrashed through the bushes and seemed surprised to find itself on a shoal of bleached stones by the river's edge. We looked at each other, this English cow and I, both of us more than surprised. Moments later, four more bullocks followed and they stood in a line, staring at Scotland. I guessed that the narrow channel behind the island must have been very low, and the grass is always greener, especially in spring after six winter months in the byre eating nothing but silage. I looked up at the grain bins, the tall green towers I'd seen from a distance, and smiled at the thought of the farmer trying to retrieve his stock as they considered becoming immigrants.

As I walked on, the path flat and easy, wondering if J.M.W. Turner would have liked to have painted those wandering cows, I fell into the metronomic trance of putting one foot in front of the other.

The image of the tall bins, the towers sparked a very distant memory of a young man and his first real job fifty and more years ago.

'Mind, son, we work on grip. On bonus. Nae time and line'. Louis Poloczek had fought with the Free Polish forces in the Second World War and been posted to the Scottish Borders. When it became clear that the Soviet Union was going to exert great influence over his homeland, he decided like many of his compatriots to stay where he found himself when the Germans at last surrendered. Having fought against one tyranny, Louis didn't want to find himself living under another, and there had been dark rumours about what might happen to returning soldiers who had campaigned with the allies. In 1947 the new Labour government used its huge majority to push through the Polish Resettlement Act, the most wide-ranging and inclusive legislation ever passed into law on immigration in Britain. It made 250,000 Polish soldiers British citizens overnight. It was an act of compassion – and gratitude for their bravery and sacrifice – whose scale shames contemporary governments and their callous, cruel attitudes to relatively tiny numbers of refugees and immigrants.

Louis was the ganger, the leader of a crew of four who built grain bins like those I could see rising above the trees on the opposite bank of the river. 'The towers hard work. No' bugger about now,' said Louis, looking at me very directly, his face not far from mine. I'd heard he'd been an army boxing champion. 'You bugger about, everybody lose. Understand.' It wasn't a question.

I did understand, and needed no second telling. It was the summer of 1969, the long vacation between my first and second years at university, and I needed to earn money to pay off my overdraft. The agricultural engineers who had taken me on were very busy and short-handed. That was the only reason Louis agreed to take me, an inexperienced late teenager, into his squad. There wasn't anybody else available.

'Start six o'clock. No' be late,' said Louis. 'And bring big piece. We stop only when too dark to see.' Right. OK. My dad was an electrician and the night before I started on the towers, my mum took a whole Scottish plain loaf out of its waxy tartan wrapping paper, divided it and made two tottering piles of sandwiches, including the heels, for our pieces. She used the wrapper to keep mine as fresh as possible and put them in an old duffel bag with an apple and four Penguin biscuits. 'You'll need all that,' she said, 'and I'll make up a flask of tea in the morning.'

At 6 a.m. sharp on a bright July morning we piled into the Commer van and drove from the works down to the newsagents in Kelso Square. Louis, Sandy and Jock the Weasel (I can't remember his surname) all bought a paper, cigarettes, chocolate and a big bottle of Middlemas's sweet lemonade. 'Aye, the Student Prince,' said Sandy when I bought *The Scotsman* and not the *Daily Record*, 'you'll no' have time to read all that.' It was a routine repeated every morning all that hard-working summer. When we left the shop, Mick Bennett was waiting outside with his Jack Russell terrier. He had the same reply for all of us as we passed through the shop door and said, 'Morning, Mick'. It was an emphatic 'Fuck off'. A man with Down's syndrome, he was always up early to say his version of good morning to the men who came to the paper shop. When we waved at him as Louis drove away in the van, Mick gave us an unmistakable V-sign.

When we arrived at Barmoor Mains Farm in North Northumberland, only four or five miles from where I was walking, Louis, Sandy and Jock the Weasel went over to check the prefabricated piles of green metal sheets and fittings for the tower while I was told, 'Get the black shite out of the van.' As I would shortly discover, drums of this sealant were needed to plaster the edges of each sheet as it was fitted. It would be my job, that and holding the nuts with a spanner as bolts were tightened with what we called the burp gun.

The towers were simple buildings but to store a farm's grain safely, keep it dry and keep out vermin, they needed to be completely sealed, no missed bits, no gaps. Black shite mattered. The process of construction depended on a system of jacks. On a concrete base we built the roof first, then jacked it up before attaching the first ring of curved metal panels. Once the edges had been smeared with black shite, the panels were bolted on. With Jock the Weasel and Louis on the outside heaving the panels into place, Sandy tightened the bolts with the burp gun while I was on the inside with a spanner, trying to ignore the constant vibration in my hands. There was a lot of shouting as the prefabricated panels, not so much heavy as big and awkward, were manouevred into position. 'A ba' hair,' was a smaller, more precise measurement than 'a wee shadie.'

'Aalreet?' An old man had come around to the steading to watch us work. Wearing a bunnet well scrugged down over his forehead, he sat on a stone mounting block. As he eased himself down, using his horn-handled crook as a third leg, there were grunts of effort as old bones creaked. When he let out a high-pitched whistle, an arthritic black and white collie trotted out of the farm-house kitchen door to sit at his feet. Grey around the muzzle, the dog sized us up with the collie's keen eye. We all nodded at them both and I noticed that the old man had long side-whiskers. They had been long, long before the teddy boys grew them long.

After watching us work for a while, the patriarch seemed to become amused at how awkward it could be to get the bin's panels to fit. Sandy was having trouble getting the holes forent with a podger, handy Scots words meaning aligned and a short, tapered steel rod that could be pushed through the bolt-holes to force the panel into alignment. It was then I heard a sentence in another language.

'Wey,' said the old man, 'it's a boogah when a mun cannot get his buowlt in the hail.' Sandy, Louis and Jock all turned and laughed but I was confused for a moment. The vowel sounds, and I can hear them clearly in my mind's ear now, were completely different from the Scots we spoke.

While bugger was pronounced boogah and its 'u' sound and in other words was spoken as a double 'o', other vowels simply had no equivalent. Buowlt is as close as I can spell North Northumbrian for bolt but it does the richness of the sound no justice. Later in my life as a student prince I learned some German and the old man might have been pronouncing a Northern European umlaut 'o' with two dots above it. It also exists in Scandinavian languages. I looked it up and the advice was to make the an 'e' sound and purse your lips into an 'o' shape. Didn't work. As for hail for hole, it might be a non-close front rounded vowel. Apparently.

Whatever, the old man could never have been mistaken for a Scottish Borderer, but he was a borderer nonetheless. He and I lived only a few miles apart and yet his accent was so different that I had to listen carefully to understand what he said.

No doubt the internet, TV and the general Americanisation of English amongst younger people has flattened out some of those pleasing linguistic bumps in the roads across the border. The old man was talking to us more than fifty years ago and will be long dead now. Perhaps very few in North Northumberland talk now of buowlts and hails.

It was hard work on the towers and on the first day I was knackered by midday piece-time and famished. That was when I made the great mistake of eating most of the sandwiches my mum had made for me the night before, not leaving much for a second break at about 5 p.m. I knew that the other three were watching, judging, making sure I didn't slack. And I didn't. Instead I nearly collapsed. Around 6 p.m., when the sun was dipping behind the western hills but we could still see to work, I began shaking. Couldn't control it. 'You knackered, son,' said Louis. He gave me a bar of chocolate and his half-empty lemonade bottle. 'Eat this now. Eat lot. Drink quick.' When I'd washed the Cadbury's Dairy Milk down with a good swig of lemonade, the effect was almost instant. I felt much better and stopped shaking. What we'd now call a sugar rush had come to my rescue.

I made a lot of money on the towers and we had a lot of laughs, often at my expense. At another farm in Northumberland we had to build a grain bin in a very awkward place in a corner of the steading. It was difficult to get around the back to use the burp gun without scuffing an elbow on the wall of a barn. By the time we had built the roof and attached two or three rings of sheets, Louis called a smoke break to see if we could work out how to make things easier and, crucially, faster. That mattered because we were working on bonus and the next job was waiting. Sandy couldn't find his lighter. 'It's on the bloody roof, I think,' he said. Each bin had a ladder on the outside but we had never had occasion to use it. It had a tube-shaped latticework of metal, a safety structure to prevent falls and Sandy was a big fella. 'I'll get it,' I said.

On the roof, I made the mistake of showing off. Instead of crawling up, using the slightly proud bolts for purchase on the otherwise smooth, slippery surface, I stood up. Spotting Sandy's lighter, I reached for it, lost my balance and began to slide slowly off the roof, wind-milling my arms wildly, unable to stop as gravity tugged at me. We had got the tower about twenty feet high and I fell feet first, tried to land on the top of a breeze-block wall, fell forward and found a very soft landing. Face first in a silage pit.

When Louis, Sandy and Jock ran round, they gasped and started to laugh so hard that they wept. Losing their breath, they leaned against the tower, Sandy banging the sheets. Out of the black, treacle-like morass of rotting grass walked the Creature from the Black Lagoon.

'No' funny, no really' said Louis, still snorting with laughter. 'That stuff no' good on skin.' He ran over to an outside tap in the steading and quickly unwound a hose. For some reason, as I wiped the gloop off my cheeks, I remember the hose was yellow. Using his fingers to create a strong jet, Louis played it up and down, soaking me in freezing water but getting most of the sticky, sweet silage off.

The prolonged laughter and the commotion had brought the farmer's wife out of her kitchen. 'Here,' she said, 'give me those jeans and that shirt. I'll get them in the wash now. If we leave them, you'll never wear them again.' An older lady, wearing a wrap-around floral-print apron and her hair scraped back in a bun, she didn't wait for an objection. Sandy and Jock were still laughing at this sodden item standing in his underpants and socks. 'Aye, these too,' she said, pointing to my pants. 'It's no' as if it's something I have not seen before.' I thought Sandy would have a hernia. I hoped he would have a hernia. Bastard. Louis threw me a filthy, oil-stained towel from the van, which I wrapped around my waist instead of drying myself. 'Ye'll get your clothes in the morning,' said the farmer's wife, handing me a set of old overalls. Good job it was July. I looked like one of the Waltons.

Hoofbeats jolted me out of my reverie. I heard them behind me before I saw a rider come out of the wrecked wood and move from a canter into a gallop across the open haugh. Perhaps it was someone from the stables at Ladykirk. She was certainly a confident rider, steady and her backside was well up out of the saddle as the big grey horse sped across the grass in a wide arc before wheeling back to the trees.

Ahead I could see the dense wood by the river and, beyond that, on the high ground, a field of rapeseed – so bright, vivid and yellow that it looked as though the sun was shining only on that field and all around paled by comparison. In front of me a newly mown and very tidy path lay on the other side of a five-bar gate and a cheering surprise. On the gatepost, under the Coldstream Paths sign, was another. Headed Border Brains Walks there was in the centre of a disc a drawing I recognised instantly. It was a swing plough and below it was 'James Small Walk'. Hooray! Recognition at last, no matter that it was only local. Quite where the walk would lead I wasn't sure. Blackadder Mount is some distance to the north, but that didn't matter.

The mown path led me past a long run of beautifully weather-worn sandstone walls. They were not drystane dykes but walls built with squared, well-worked stone and set in old-fashioned lime mortar. A mason who knew his business had recently repointed all the coping stones along the wall-head and the top two or three courses with modern cement. That would keep rain-water and the drip off the trees in the wood behind from getting down into the walls and dissolving the old lime. After a very easy and pleasant walk past all that skill, I came on a deeply eroded sandstone cliff that was overhung by big bushes and trees. Set in what was almost a cave was a bench, a real temptation. I resisted, knowing that I had miles to go and stiffness would be kept at bay by keeping going. But I did plonk my rucksack on the bench and drink some orange Lucozade. The back of my shirt was damp with sweat and, even in the moments it took to drink, it became so cold that once again there was a shiver when I re-shouldered my pack. But at least it was a few ounces lighter.

Beyond the cliffs lay more lush haughland and a reminder of how we used to pollute the beautiful river. Snaking into midstream was what might have once been a sewage pipe, no doubt long since redundant. When I was growing up in Kelso, the town's sewage was piped straight into the Tweed, untreated. And we swam in it. Sometimes in hot weather children came out with what we called water-blobs, large blister-like swellings. Amazing.

The Coldstream Paths sign (James Small made only intermittent appearances) led me into a completely unexpected Garden of Eden. First I crossed a wild garlic wooden bridge, the white flowers and their savoury scent surrounding it, blanketing both banks of a trickle of a burn. Down some well-engineered steps with hand-rails, a technology clearly unknown to Northumberland County Council, I came across another riot of white. Thousands of sweetly scented flowers grew along the steep banks above me. Like miniature chrysanthemums, they carried the faint perfume of the summer to come.

All this wildwood glory had a soundtrack. On an otherwise silent and still morning, the river began to chatter, its stately flow suddenly speeded by what looked like a man-made weir strung out in a long, looping curve from Scotland to England. The white water of these brief rapids seemed to chime with the white all around me.

The path wound its way around the boles of mighty trees before it arrived at a doorway. Set into a wall built from strangely ordered courses of stone that might once have served other purposes, it led to the edges of the policies of a grand house. Signs marked 'PRIVATE' blocked paths up the bank, and above me I could make out the upper storeys of what I took to be Milne Graden House. Dominating the woodland by the river was an immensely tall Wellingtonia, a tree whose tight grip on the ground had helped it survive the great hurricane.

Beyond it the path climbed once more and the scents of flowers filled the still air. On each side were dozens of yellow buddleias, probably self-seeded from the gardens around the grand house. Under them were clumps of purple campions just coming into flower and delicate blue forget-me-nots. It was magical, lingering amongst all that new blossom and beauty, high above the sunlit glint of the river, listening to the carrying voices of two fishermen about four hundred yards away. They stood near the English bank in their waders, casting flies into Scottish water.

Abruptly, the path led up to a road and out of the magic wood. After checking the Pathfinder, and another shiver on my damp back as I shouldered my pack, I saw that I had about three miles to go before I reached Coldstream. Walking was easy on the tarmac, and more flowers grew in the lush verges.

During the winter, farmers had trimmed the hedges that lined the road into a good, compact, bushy shape that would become a well-camouflaged home for many nesting birds. Through a gap I saw a small herd of black cows and their calves lying or standing close to each other, gormless, motionless except for tails and ears flicking at the insects. The scent of buddleia was replaced by milky cowshit.

On the heights above the Tweed a breeze began, and when the road became an avenue of cherry trees, blossom snow fell. Spinning and floating, the tiny white petals seemed all to fall at once. Further up the road, the blossom was pink and it drifted against the grass of the verge like candy floss.

Ahead I could see the outline of Lennel Kirk and the walls of its graveyard. Next to it I found Scottish Water's sewage works and a very different aroma filled the air. While the church had long since become ruinous, the graveyard was still in use, some of the headstones commemorating very recent interments. It was such a shame, as well as more than insensitive, that the burial of loved ones should have to take place next to a sewage treatment plant.

Lennel Kirk is ancient, more than a thousand years old, founded by King Edgar of Scotland sometime between 1074 and 1107. Roofless now and with only one gable still standing, it lost its role as a parish church in 1705 when Coldstream began to grow. Once I had walked through the little village downhill towards the town, I came across a melancholy roadside sign. Coldstream Business Park, it proclaimed proudly, was underwritten by the European Regional Development Fund, and side by side with a saltire was the blue EU flag and its circle of stars. And behind the sign was an empty field. The result of the Brexit referendum was not the first time that international and national politics had directly affected Coldstream.

★   ★   ★

When the prioress saw puffs of smoke rise, she knew
that a moment later she would hear the distant thunder
of the cannon. It was the afternoon of 9 September
1513. The blustery morning rain had cleared and a pale,
watery sun lit the beginning of the bloodiest battle ever
fought in Britain. Standing on the walls of her convent
of Cistercian nuns, Prioress Isabella Hoppringle gazed
to the south-east and listened to the great guns roar and
watched the grey smoke billowing. Hidden by the gently
undulating ridges beyond the Tweed, James IV was
about to charge at the head of the greatest army ever
raised in Scotland and clash with a smaller English force
commanded by Thomas Howard, Earl of Surrey. The
Battle of Flodden was beginning.

Almost two weeks before she climbed up to the wall-
walk, Prioress Hoppringle had bowed her head as her
king led his vast army across the fords at Coldstream.
Immediately below the walls of the nunnery, where the
little Leet Water joins the Tweed, more than forty thousand soldiers and many camp followers waded into the
shallows of the broad river to invade England.

Under the royal lion standard, the king was followed
by the knights and servants of his household. Ox-teams
pulling five great siege guns were encouraged into the
water and palfreys hauled ten lighter pieces behind them,
keeping them as dry as possible. All Scotland, it seemed,
followed their king. Lord Home rode at the head of
three thousand Border horsemen and the Earl of Huntly
led the men of Aberdeenshire and the Moray coast.
Thousands of soldiers, rank upon rank, shouldered a
forest of eighteen-foot steel-tipped pikes, which they

would lower and level at the lines of their enemies. The Earls of Errol, Crawford and Montrose had come south with the levies of Perthshire, Angus, Forfar and Fife. Prioress Hoppringle may have raised an eyebrow and looked sternly around at the nuns beside her when she saw the Earls of Argyll and Lennox with their plaided Highlanders. Men from clans MacKenzie, Grant, MacDonald, MacLean and Campbell lifted up their linen sarks to wade the Tweed bare-arsed. Town levies from Edinburgh, Glasgow, Ayr, Haddington, Selkirk, Hawick and Galashiels were commanded by the Earls of Cassillis, Morton and Rothes, and they were accompanied by archers from the Ettrick Forest and Lowland conscripts from the Lothians. Men from every corner of Scotland had come to the muster on the Burgh Muir in Edinburgh, and those from the Borders and Galloway had joined them at Ellemford in the Lammermuirs. The prioress and her nuns had seen nothing like it. No one had.

When I walked down the hill at Lennel and into Coldstream, I wanted to see if I could find any remnant of the priory, or at least work out exactly where it might have been. Having been born and raised ten miles away in Kelso, I knew the little town but had mostly driven through on the main road to the Tweed Bridge and onwards into England. To my shame, I'd never stopped to walk around and look. To the south of the High Street, the Market Square is pretty if a little run-down but only its name remembers its function. The sole shop, an upholstery business, had long since closed down. But the town's museum was open, welcoming, well laid out and disappointing.

Its major focus was the history of the Coldstream Guards. Raised in 1650, it is the oldest and one of the most distinguished regiments in the British Army. It played a crucial role at Waterloo, holding the chateau at Hougoumont on Wellington's right flank. Napoleon threw wave after wave of attacks at the walls but the massively outnumbered Coldstream Guards held them off and thereby prevented the French from directly attacking British lines or outflanking them. There was a beautifully made model of the engagement, with hundreds of tiny, very detailed figures of soldiers. But it wasn't that story, or that battle, I wanted to find out about.

The gentleman at reception was the first person I had met or spoken to on that crystal morning. He was very kind and helpful, but didn't know where the priory had been and, apart from one or two fragments of masonry and what might have been two fonts or stoups that held holy water, there was nothing much to be seen of the old church in the museum. Yet more forgotten history, even though the nuns had been witness to momentous events.

Street names offered some clues. Abbey Road led off the Market Square towards the Tweed and the house name of Whithou might have been an echo, if it was a version of White House (Cistercian nuns wore mainly white habits belted at the waist). There was also a sign pointing to an 'Abbey Cottage East'. Behind the frontages on the south side of the square was a scatter of much older buildings and it looked as though others had been demolished. In the museum one of the fragments of masonry, a beautifully carved capital, had apparently been dug up in the garden of the Crown Hotel, which was said to be in the square. Another three had been found nearby. The whereabouts of these was not made clear, and the hotel had disappeared.

But it turned out there was continuity of sorts, as often with sacred sites. On a steel plaque fixed high up on the gable of a block of new flats was this:

ADAM THOMSON COURT
In honour of the Rev. Adam Thomson D.D. (1779–1861) who was born in Coldstream and was minister of the Secession Church here for 55 years. By his labours and the establishment of the Bible Free Press on this site the Bible printing monopoly was broken. The price of Bibles was reduced by half, making them available to all at a price they could afford.

"Freely you have received, freely give." Matthew 10:8 unveiled by

The Moderator of the General Assembly of the Church of Scotland

THE RIGHT REV. JOHN M.K. PATERSON
April 17, 1985.

The deeply contentious issue of patronage split the Church of Scotland again and again. Should the lairds, as in England, decide the appointment of a new minister, or should it be the kirk session, essentially the elders, who controlled the process? By the early eighteenth century, the Secession Kirk had broken away and was particularly popular in the Tweed Valley. Thirty congregations were quickly formed, one of them in Coldstream. But that was by no means the end of it.

In 1744, the Secession Kirk split over the issue of the Burgess Oath, which prominent members were required to swear to a secular authority (as rebellion was brewing in the Highlands) and which, some argued, bolstered the legitimacy of the Church of Scotland, which they believed to be illegitimate. Therefore the Burgher Secession Kirk was set up alongside the Anti-Burghers. Further disagreement led to yet another split over the state's support of the Church of Scotland, and the Auld Licht Burghers and the Auld Licht Anti-Burghers and the New Licht Burghers and the New Licht Anti-Burghers formed separate congregations. Ultimately both sects of the New Lichts decided to forget the origin of the second disagreement and they merged with the United Secession Church (New Licht). The merry-go-round finally stopped when in 1900 and 1923 most of these sects reunified. The die-hard Auld Lichts of the Secession Kirk held out until 1956.

Despite the bewildering choices facing the godly, and what seem now like petty disputes, these sects showed not only a genuine piety but also a pleasing disregard for established authority. I can't help thinking the contrast with the relative stability of the Church of England was stark. Of course there were breakaways in the south, like John Wesley's Methodists, as well as Baptists, Quakers and others, but what strikes me is how deeply political religion was in Scotland. The issue of patronage was an affront to the essential democracy of the priesthood of all believers, a doctrine that had never had much traction in England. South of the border, stability and tradition seemed more important than principle. Old maids cycling to communion in the morning mist.

Emblematic of that cultural difference was the Bible printing monopoly. Far from being able to read the word of God for themselves, most Christians could not even afford to own a Bible. Since the reign of Elizabeth I only the royal press and the presses of the universities of Oxford and Cambridge were permitted to print Bibles, and they were expensive. In Scotland, there was a similar restriction. By some circuitous route that I have not been able to trace, the monopoly had been acquired in the nineteenth century by Sir David Hunter Blair and a Mrs B. Bruce. They made the huge annual profit of £6,000 between them.

A child of the Secession Kirk and its endless disputes, the Revd Adam Thomson changed all of that. He thundered from the pulpit and elsewhere that 'all monopolies are bad, but of all monopolies a religious monopoly is the worst and a monopoly of the word of God is the most outrageous!' Thomson lobbied MPs, arguing that the renewal of these copyrights should not be waved through and in 1837 a parliamentary committee took evidence from Scottish members. A decision was taken that there should be no sole right to print Bibles. It was a triumph, but not yet complete. Thomson travelled to London to meet the prime minister, Lord Melbourne, and a Bible Board was set up. Prices immediately fell, as the existing publishers cut them by 20 per cent to 40 per cent, but in Scotland there was resistance from the trade, from printers, binders and booksellers. And so the Revd Thomson went into business.

Next to the steel plaque on the gable end of the new flats was another street name with a story behind it.

Bookie Lane led to an open space and on one side there was a range of buildings that looked neither domestic nor part of a farm steading. A man who was unloading scrap metal from a skip told me they were part of a printing press but most of it had been demolished – as late as 1983. 'Before then this part became a brewery,' he said, smiling, pointing at the derelict building. 'Bibles then beer.'

In its heyday, the Coldstream Free Bible Press was big business. Three hundred people were employed and in one year, 1845, a staggering 178,200 Bibles were printed and bound. But there was a looming problem. The English monopoly remained in the hands of Oxford and Cambridge university presses and a company called Spottiswoode & Co. They began to dramatically undercut the prices of Coldstream Bibles to tenpence, and even sixpence per copy. Soon Thomson's press was forced to sell below the cost of production and it drove the minister and his family into poverty. He was seventy-three by this time. Thomson's congregation and others came to the rescue, but by 1850 the business was closed. It was a noble enterprise and a great personal sacrifice that deserves to be better remembered.

I walked down Abbey Road and found myself beside more wild garlic, this time on the banks of the Leet Water. The afternoon sun dappled through trees just coming into leaf and I discovered a very pretty stretch of haughland where several dogs were being walked by the Tweed. After three weeks with little or no rain the river was very low, with wide shoals of bleached stones showing on either bank. It was easy to see where the ford was, but I could find no sign of a track leading to or from the crossing.

I made my way back up to the higher ground above the haugh and came across some remnants and memorials. Under a flagpole flying the saltire was a boat-shaped plinth with a long iron broadsword mounted lengthways on it. The sword pointed south-east, in the direction of Flodden, the direction Prioress Hoppringle had been looking on the afternoon of 9 September 1513. Behind were two large upright plaques. On one was inscribed, 'Near to this spot stood Coldstream Priory'. Below it was a stone capital like the one in the museum, and to the right was a tiny, high-walled graveyard behind a locked, cast-iron gate. Set in the far wall were two headstones for the Marjoribanks family, one as recent as 2013, and between them a Celtic cross marked another grave. Nearest to the locked gate was what seemed to be the oldest relic of sanctity, a stone-bordered grave with a lattice of thick iron bars over it. I could not get close enough to see if there were any inscriptions and the grave lay at an awkward angle to its surroundings, a hint that it had once been in another setting.

This was holy ground, a place sanctified by prayer and the tread of generations of nuns, women who had given their lives to God. And clearly people still wished to be buried here, in this little scrap of half-forgotten history, the site of St Mary's Priory.

And yet from the bits and pieces I could discover, it was a very important meeting place. Within the width of a haugh and the fords over the Tweed, the convent sat in a pivotal position as the winds of history swirled around it. I'd been surprised to read passing references to Prioress Hoppringle that insisted she was an English spy. Isabella was a confidante of James IV's queen, Margaret Tudor, sister of Henry VIII. Thomas Grey, Marquis of Dorset, recorded the queen's comments: 'Her Grace reported that the prioress had been very good and kind to her . . . another cause which moved us to assure the said house was because the prioress there is one of the best and assured spies that we have in Scotland.'

Ten years after the disaster at Flodden, Isabella's view of the Queen Dowager Regent wondered about her credibility and consistency: 'She is very fickle, therefore counsel the man you know not to take on hand overmuch of her credence.' Which means, I think, that she was economical with the truth and changed her mind – too often.

Other evidence suggests that the prioress was less of a spy and more of a diplomat, working to secure peace and to protect her convent in its vulnerable position on the border. In 1509 James IV granted an unusual dispensation. Isabella was permitted to entertain up to twelve English people at any one time, and she could also communicate with her guests at any time, whether or not England and Scotland were at war. Probably especially then. It seems that diplomacy and the gathering of information rather than espionage was Isabella's role. In the early sixteenth century spying probably meant something slightly different. The priory stood precisely on a key crossing point on an international frontier and English envoys often splashed across the ford. Even after

Flodden, these arrangements continued. When King Henry VIII sent large raiding parties into the Tweed Valley in 1515 and 1523, he placed Isabella's community under his protection. By contrast, other churches in the Borders, especially the great abbeys at Kelso, Melrose, Jedburgh and Dryburgh, suffered terrible damage at that time.

After the exchange of cannon fire had stilled and the grey smoke had blown away on the afternoon of 9 September 1513, Isabella will have heard the din and clash of a distant battle rise to crescendos and fall into lulls. Almost seventy thousand men fought to the death only three miles away at Flodden and their war cries, shouts and screams rolled over the ridges above the Tweed like a tide of fury.

As his army charged downhill to engage the English, James IV was on foot, in the van of the largest battalion. But after their ranks had been badly thinned by cannon fire, the Scots found themselves quickly floundering. At the bottom of Branxton Hill there was boggy ground made much wetter by the morning's rain. In the churned mud, the Scots pikemen could not maintain formation. Many quickly took off their boots or shoes to get a better grip of the ground. Some men sank to their knees in the morass. With shorter pikes, known as bills, designed to act like spears and axes, the English infantry coped better and began to advance slowly, with murderous effect. If a man lost his footing and went down in the ruck of the fighting, he was as good as dead. As those behind the front rank moved forward, they hacked, stabbed, kicked and slashed at him. Most men who died quickly suffered terrible head wounds.

After furious fighting in the quagmire on either side of the stream at the bottom of the hill, the huge Scottish army wavered and suddenly began to disintegrate as panic crackled like wildfire. In the rear of the vast battalions, the less well-armed, less disciplined and much less motivated ordinary soldiers could see the long Scottish pikes falling in front of them, and their lords and captains going down with them. Perhaps some saw the royal standard disappear into the melee. Perhaps there were shouts that the king had been killed. A few turned away and fled as a trickle quickly grew into a flood. When it was clear that all was lost, Lord Home and his Borders horsemen and the Earl of Huntly led their men off the field in good order. But for others, particularly the thousands of camp followers, many of them women, terror drove them north as they ran towards Scotland, towards what they hoped was safety.

As the sun set behind her in the late evening of that terrible day, Isabella Hoppringle watched thousands of fleeing refugees wade across the fords of the Tweed at twilight and stream past the walls of the convent. It was clear that the battle had gone badly wrong and some may have shouted to the sisters that the king was dead and Flodden a field of carnage. It was too late and too dark to do anything but the prioress would exercise her diplomatic immunities in the morning and she no doubt issued instructions before a sleepless night.

When dawn broke at Flodden, sometime around 6 a.m., a pale, grey light revealed the horror of the battlefield, the slaughter and the agony of the mortally wounded who had somehow survived the night. Almost ten thousand men, most of them Scots, had been killed or would die of terrible injuries. Flodden was fought not with bullets but with bladed weapons and many of those bludgeoned into the mud will not have died quickly. During the night, holding torches high, parties of scavenging camp followers and soldiers anxious for loot stripped the dead of their clothes, weapons and anything else they could find in the blood-soaked morass. As they pulled at limbs and rolled over bodies, any that were not dead had their throats cut. In unspeakable agony, others will have moaned pitifully, passing in and out of consciousness. Some found themselves trapped under mounds of the dead in fields that had become a charnel house. Everywhere there was the stink of death, of blood, of entrails slithering out of slashed bellies, of shit from voided bowels.

When Prioress Hoppringle, her nuns and their servants came to Flodden in the morning with their carts, hoping that their white habits and God's grace would protect them, the shock of what they saw must have been profound. No doubt some of the women vomited. Most corpses had been stripped and many had suffered terrible wounds to their faces and heads, but as Isabella walked through the carnage, perhaps lifting the skirts of her habit out of the mud, she looked for those lords she knew and could recognise.

When their carts could carry no more, the convent's servants led the horses up over Barelees Rig and down to the Coldstream fords. It is likely that there were so many dead that Isabella was forced to have communal graves dug. But at least she could do these lords the service of a mass and burial in sanctified ground. This mattered very much because it was widely believed that holy soil would physically cleanse corpses of mortal sin as they rotted to bones in the ground. That is why in old churches many are buried under the nave or in side chapels. The closer to the high altar, where the host descends, the better. Time in purgatory could be much reduced by burial in places blessed by prayer and praise, and made holy by the tread of monks and nuns.

The location of the mass graves is long lost under the houses and buildings of Coldstream. Beside the memorial to the battle, there were two houses whose windows looked over the Tweed, and they had back gardens. But when I rang doorbells there was no one at home to ask if they had ever dug up anything that might have come from the priory. Along a lane that led back to the Market Square there was an old and very substantial wall that certainly predated all the buildings around it, but I doubted if it was a remnant of St Mary's. It looked to me more like something built from stone robbed out of the ruins of the old convent. It was clear that it had disappeared entirely, the chapel and the buildings around it razed and its foundations forever buried under the modern town. Perhaps I should go and look in the obvious place for relics of that disastrous September day in 1513.

Battlefields are often mute. Either modern development has obliterated them or the horrors that took place have sunk into the grass and passed out of memory to become little more than statistics. Flodden seemed to me like a blank. Where the Scots advanced downhill was planted with barley, its straight rows still visible against the parched soil. Modern drainage has removed the fatal morass and only the memorial on Branxton Hill remembers what happened and makes the site different from the rolling farmland around it. When I reached it and turned north-west, I could clearly see Coldstream and the row of houses where the convent had been. Even though Isabella Hoppringle did not have binoculars, I'm certain she will have seen the silhouette of the melee against the horizon, the pennants in the breeze, heard the trumpeters sending signals, watched movement of the heaving ruck as thousands of soldiers advanced down the hill.

But I could visualise very little. Flodden is wide and empty, and a little desolate. I walked down the hill and into the little village of Branxton. Opposite a large house with another flagpole flying the cross of St George, and next to a board commemorating men who fought in the Great War, was the Flodden Visitor Centre. It was an old red phone box. A map of the battlefield had been fixed to the back, where the coin-operated telephone had once been, and some leaflets placed on the shelf that used to hold directories.

It seemed to me both insulting and emblematic, a jaunty little joke that misfires badly. Disrespectful doesn't even get close. In Scotland, Flodden is seen as a national tragedy that affected the whole nation, from the Hebrides to the Borders. Ten thousand died. Not only did we lose, but for once we should have won. James IV's army greatly outnumbered the English. Scotland's noble families were decimated, something that would not happen again on that scale until the First World War. In England, Flodden is barely remembered and the phone box seemed not only to verge on the obscene, making light of all that suffering, it also put the Scots in their place – marginal in all senses, in a box.

But Isabella Hoppringle never forgot what she and her nuns saw. Here is a dispatch from her in 1523, complaining about the widespread lawlessness that followed the battle, about Border Reivers and their raiding:

> Lately heard from her that the queen is gone to Stirling, and has taken with her all the Frenchmen that were about her son. Monday after Palm Sunday the Lord Lieutenant was with Dacre at Morpeth. The latter has undertaken that the Redesdale men shall make redress for all the robberies committed by them since Lord Ross's departure, by the 1st of May. Ralph Fenwick has done the same for the Tynedale men, and brought in half a score of them as sureties. My Lord Lieutenant and himself have made proclamations for injured persons to bring in their bills to them. Since his coming hither, strange to say, there have been no offences on either side. Seldom has there been peace so long.

When I left Branxton, the sun had gone and a west wind was blowing heavy, steel-grey clouds over the western hills. At last some rain to help the grass and the barley.

Day Five

To the High Country

'With the greatest respect to his family,' thundered Major-General Sir John Swinton, Lord Lieutenant of Berwickshire in 1998, 'who the hell was he?'

This outburst attracted the attention of the *Sunday Times* and the journalist John Linklater. The headline was 'No Takers for a Seventy Foot Statue of a Nobody'. The article continued: '[It has a prominence] out of all proportion to the obscurity of the forgotten man it was supposed to commemorate. The truth is that Charles Marjoribanks was a political nobody whose career ended almost the moment it began.'

It is certainly prominent, the statue of the MP for Berwickshire between 1832 and his death in 1833. I was standing under it, about to walk from Coldstream across the Tweed Bridge and into England, and like Sir John and the *Sunday Times*, wondering why it was erected and why it dominates the town. The inscription did not add much, except that Marjoribanks was amiable and had many friends, some of whom clubbed together to have this overblown tribute erected. In 1998 the column was crumbling, would need money spent to restore it, and Sir John and the *Sunday Times* wondered if that was a good use of resources. When I shaded my eyes to look up at this man, I noticed that he had one foot slightly over the edge of the plinth as he gazed north over Berwickshire.

The Marjoribanks family were once important around Coldstream and were related to the Pringles, descendants of Prioress Isabella. Charles is buried in the little walled graveyard I had seen while looking for any remains of the convent. What intrigued me was not that fame and renown are transient. There are plenty of statues to forgotten people in our towns and cities. It was the scale: a Borders version of Nelson's Column. What did this man have that motivated his friends to think so big?

When I reached the midpoint of the Tweed Bridge and looked down to the river, I noticed a heron standing very still in the shadows of the trees by the Scottish bank. Black and grey, and very elegant, it seemed to me like a Presbyterian version of a flamingo. A cold wind was blowing up from the east and I hurried past the England and Northumberland signs towards Cornhill.

It was early morning, blustery with smirrs of rain blowing up the river, and I was thinking about lunch already. Instead of making the usual cheese sandwiches, I was heading for the good food emporium that is the Cornhill Village Shop. Its delights are legion, but I rarely get further than the filled roll and pie counter near the entrance. Rolls, also known as baps, buns and sometimes butties, are usually either white or brown, well-fired, even slightly blackened or soft, or, for some misguided reason, sometimes wholemeal. At the Cornhill Village Shop, the selection is encyclopaedic, causing endless chin-stroking and umming and ahhhing. There are rolls crusted with sesame seeds; cheese and onion baps; oblong white sandwich rolls; one sort with what look like nuts baked into them. The list is long. And the fillings! Oh, the fillings!

Next to the rolls are the pies, and they are to die for, or perhaps of. There are quiches and pies in foil to be heated in the oven, but the takeaway section is the principal glory. Scotch and pork pies of course, but many variations on those themes, and also stovie pies, haggis, neeps and tattie pies, curry, steak and too many others, including a Balmoral pie topped by a tomato. My problem is not so much swithering over choice but quantity. One pie is often not quite enough and two is always too many. So I bought two, a spicy pie, and a chicken and mushroom pie. I'd think about fruit, vegetables and my arteries later.

The place name of Cornhill has nothing to do with corn or hills. The second element derives from the Old English *halh*, a corner of land and a likely reference to the great, looping bend of the Tweed after Coldstream. *Cron* or *cran* meant a crane or a heron, a name conferred long before Presbyterianism was ever thought of. Heron Bend is a small village, and certainly no picturesque St Mary Mead, with a population little more than three hundred. But it is alive, warm, vibrant and its beating heart is the village shop. A high volume of passing trade that parks right outside makes it viable, but its roots in the community are deep.

When I joined the queue for my pies, trying to look over shoulders at the day's selection, I listened to local people who had come in for the morning papers (and, it turns out, two unplanned slices of a very cheesy quiche just out of the oven) and there was no rush, as banter, questions and pleasantries were exchanged. Others passed us on their way to the excellent coffee shop at the back. During the Covid pandemic the shop began to run a delivery service in Cornhill and the surrounding villages, a lifeline, especially for elderly people on their own. Later, I found a photograph of an improvised poster in a Cornhill house window: 'To our village shop and staff for serving our community in these uncertain times and being so cheerful at all times. We salute you! THANK YOU!'

The shop has won many awards for its food and its exemplary service. But the way the staff and owners coped with the pandemic was not unique. Over the years, it has raised more than £100,000 for Macmillan Cancer Support and done much for other causes. Posters advertising bingo in the church hall (eyes down at 7 p.m.) and a myriad of other local activities are put up and taken down every week, it seems. The shop is a hub and adds colour, quality and meaning to the life of Cornhill and those like me who pass through. In an online and helpline world of increasing numbers of faceless, keyboard or telephone transactions (where have all the branches of banks suddenly gone?), the staff instinctively understand what community means and what it needs to sustain it. Cornhill doesn't need an overblown monument to a forgotten politician to announce itself. It already has something monumental to be celebrated, something much more valuable.

With my pies safely stowed in my rucksack, I walked downhill to where a little bridge crosses the Duddo Burn and found myself on the English side of the Tweed. The border follows the midstream line of the river, but just beyond the junction with the road up to West Learmouth Farm it abruptly shifts. Climbing up out of the southern riverbank, it follows the line of the road for about a hundred yards and then marches north-west across a flat field before resuming the midstream of the Tweed. It is an odd kink, one with no geographical logic. However, there is an emblematic story of the border behind it and a blatant episode of cultural appropriation.

From a distance, the flat field carved out of England looks indistinguishable from its neighbours on either side of the road. After consulting the Pathfinder and lining up my location with such landmarks as made sense, including a classical folly on the Scottish bank, I came to a gap in the hedge, one that seemed always to have been there. Beyond it stretched a faint shadow of the old borderline. On its eastern side about two acres of barley had been planted, while on the west was pasture. Between them I could see an arrow-straight line of slightly raised, tussocky ground, about the width of the tarmac road. It led to the riverbank before turning a dog-leg left and finally disappearing into the water just upstream from a weir. Along the length of this boundary was a row of rotted stumps of ancient fence posts. Once upon a time they, the hedge by the road and the river had delineated a huge rugby pitch, as well as an international frontier.

Locally known as the Ba' Green, it was the venue for annual matches between the Englishmen of the nearby village of Wark and the Scotsmen of Coldstream. An early version of rugby, the ba' was once played all over Britain by teams that sometimes numbered in hundreds. The object was to score hails or goals by carrying the ba', made of leather and slightly smaller than a football, over a line. This could be marked by flags, a fence, a wall or even a stream. Players could run with the ba', be tackled and often huge scrummages piled up. These have the wonderfully suggestive name of 'strows'. Sometimes no one was sure where the ba' had gone, for one player would shove it up his shirt while half a dozen of his teammates would run in different directions. Games went on for a long time and results were often disputed. The ba' is still played in the Borders, notably in Jedburgh and the villages of Hobkirk, Denholm and Ancrum. There are also annual games as far north as Kirkwall on Orkney and as far south as St Ives in Cornwall.

The ba' games are clearly the forerunners of the modern game of rugby. Nevertheless, in 1876 a big lie was told. Matthew Bloxam, a former pupil of Rugby School, claimed that the game had been invented, spontaneously, fifty years before by a schoolboy. During a football match, William Webb Ellis caught the ball and 'rushed forwards with the ball in his hands towards the opposite goal'. And that was it. Rugby was invented. Ever since then this evident tosh has been endlessly peddled, repeated and widely accepted. Winners of the Rugby World Cup are handed the William

Webb Ellis trophy and since the game was clearly English, invented in the Midlands of England, the national association for its administration and promotion is called *The Rugby Football Union*, and not, as it should be, The English Rugby Football Union. Their stadium at Twickenham is commonly called 'HQ'.

All of that really annoys me. The game was played and its rules evolved all over Britain and yet England appropriated it. On the basis of a myth, a laughable, completely incredible story, the so-called Rugby Football Union has gone on to have a baleful effect on the best game in the world. And that really, really annoys me.

Having been invented at a private public school (how does that particular paradox persist?), rugby quickly became posh, the preserve of the middle classes, run by former public schoolboys and fuelled and fouled by undisguised snobbery. Except in two places in Britain.

South Wales and its mining communities adopted the game early from public schoolboys who strayed too far west and it quickly became very popular. By the end of the nineteenth century and the introduction of the five and a half day working week, Saturday afternoon club games regularly saw crowds of thirty or forty thousand. Teams were made up from working-class young men who had never seen the inside of a private public school. The national team became very successful and Wales was unbeaten against England for ten years at the beginning of the twentieth century, as well as beating Scotland and Ireland too often and even defeating New Zealand in 1905. Rugby quickly came to be seen as a key component of Welsh identity and it was at the international match of that year in Cardiff that national anthems were first sung as a prelude to the match. The idea was to match the intensity of the haka, the Maori war dance performed by the New Zealand team before the kick-off. And it is surely significant that instead of singing about the queen or other monarchs and old battles, '*Hen Wlad Fy Nhadau*' ('Land of My Fathers') hymns the people of Wales, their language, their land – and it does that in Welsh. The song is without doubt the most stirring of all the anthems sung at the annual Six Nations rugby tournament. It comes from the heart and not a cold collation of traditions, most of them invented.

The only other place in Britain where rugby is played by ordinary people is the Scottish Borders, and it's my firm contention that the game's popularity descends directly from the ba' and how it involved entire communities – of men. The clubs are based in the towns of Kelso, Hawick, Melrose, Galashiels, Selkirk, Langholm and Peebles, and in 1901 five of them formed the earliest rugby league in the world. Ned Haig of Melrose invented rugby sevens, now an Olympic sport and played all over the world.

And yet, just as in England, for most of the twentieth century, the game was controlled by the former pupils of the fee-paying schools of Glasgow and Edinburgh. They thoroughly disapproved of the Border League because they thought it might lead to professionalism, the game being played in the Tweed Valley by working-class men who might need the money. There was a lot of lofty talk about the amateur ethos, the Corinthian spirit, from people who had plenty of cash.

In the north of England, several clubs wanted to form a league and also compensate their players for the loss of wages when they played. The Rugby Football Union looked down its upper-class nose at that, and what became known as the Rugby League broke away and became professional. Occasionally a very good Borders player would turn professional and sign for a rugby league club, the likes of Huddersfield, Workington, Leeds or Hull Kingston Rovers. The Scottish Rugby Union would then ban that player for life from entering the grounds of any of the clubs in Scotland, including that of his old club, even though he had been a notable player as an amateur. It was a shameful, disgraceful exhibition of pure snobbery and the attitudes of the former pupils on both sides of the border not only split the game into two codes, thereby weakening British teams and ensuring regular defeat by New Zealand, South Africa and Australia, they also inhibited the development and modernisation of the game. For example, there are far too many players, thirty of them, milling around on the pitch in rugby union, and league cut the number to twenty-six, very sensibly, opening up the game, creating more space. Of course the Corinthian former pupils could never imitate the professionals, but it is a great irony that as it was finally forced to professionalise, rugby union has come to resemble rugby league very closely.

I know this is fast turning into a rant, but I have skin in this game. It was often said that a Borders player had to be twice as good as a former pupil from Edinburgh or Glasgow to get into the Scotland team – any Scotland team. And it was true.

At the end of March 1968, when I was seventeen, I first played for my home town of Kelso. Pulling on the black and white jersey as a schoolboy alongside men who had been my heroes is graphically printed on my memory. Our opponents were Edinburgh Wanderers, at that time one of the strongest sides in Scotland, and we played them on the international pitch at Murrayfield in front of a crowd dwarfed by the huge stadium. All our captain had to say in the dressing room under the west stand was, 'Right, lads. Remember, this is a city team. Just a lot of solicitors, accountants and teachers.' It was enough. The forwards growled. We lost, but the *Scotsman* newspaper wrote that I was the pick of the Kelso forwards. I have the faded, yellowing cutting still.

I'd also played for the South of Scotland Schools against Edinburgh, Glasgow and the North Midlands Schools, only losing narrowly to Glasgow. The Scottish Schools team was picked a couple of weeks after I'd first played for Kelso and I was more than dismayed to discover that in my position of loosehead prop, a boy from Loretto, a private school we didn't play against and which didn't allow its pupils to play for Edinburgh Schools, had been preferred. In fact, the dominant South had only one player in the team. It was an absolute travesty and I remember our PE teacher being upset when he told me I'd been missed out. It was something born out of pure prejudice. Fifty-five years later, it still makes me angry.

Personal issues aside, the influence of the former pupils of private schools in England has been baleful. Rugby could have been Britain's national game and we could have led the world but blinkered thinking and blind snobbery choked off that possibility. And now we are saddled with football, which the English also appropriated, a tedious game played by wildly overpaid prima donnas.

But the tale of the Ba' Green did snap me out of bitter old memories. The story goes that as Coldstream grew larger than Wark, reversing the age-old advantage England has always had over Scotland, the ba' game became more and more one-sided. A long series of defeats for the Wark men resulted in the pitch passing permanently into Scotland, perhaps as an enduring trophy. That might be true. It should be.

Rejoining the tarmac road, I walked west through the sticky scent of rapeseed flowering in the fields beyond the hedge, its yellow brilliance almost blinding. In the distance I could make out my destination, the low, rounded hump of Wark Castle. Like Norham, it was another northern bastion on the Tweed, built in 1136 by Walter Espec, a trusted Norman-French lieutenant of Henry I of England. Often visited by English kings with business on the border, Wark Castle was said to have been the scene of a famous royal moment. In 1349 Edward III bent down to pick up a lady's garter from the floor of the great hall. He recognised it and returned it to the beautiful Countess of Salisbury. When a gaggle of courtiers were heard to snigger, the king smiled and said, '*Honi soit qui mal y pense*' – 'Shame on him who thinks evil of this.' Thus was the Order of the Garter invented. Even though this tale is only slightly more credible than William Webb Ellis's exploits, it is a good

story with at least a hint of authenticity. The insignia
worn by the knights who became the first members of
the Order of the Garter is essentially the Cross of St
George and they have individual pews in St George's
Chapel at Windsor Castle. Even though it may be seen
as a quintessentially English institution (with a French
motto), its precepts of chivalry and the bonds of a band-
of-brother knights link it to the growing fascination with
the Arthurian legends, and especially the fourteenth-
century poem *Sir Gawain and the Green Knight*.

I turned up a narrow lane off the tarmac road and
walked past a new house that had been given the name
of Bailey Cottage. In 1136 Walter Espec had built a
version of the classic Norman motte-and-bailey castle,
one with a high mound with a keep on top and a much
larger, defended, enclosed area below it. Next to a play
area with swings was an encouraging sign for 'Wark
Castle, Part of the Flodden 1513 Ecomuseum', the latter
not something I'd come across on my travels. Beyond
was a row of what might have been council houses and
some cottages to my right, but around the play area and
the car park were half a dozen new houses, one of them
large and imposing. Beside it was a busy building site, a
cleared area perhaps waiting for another big house.

Further uphill, towards the mound of the motte, was
a grass-crested track that looked promising. I wanted to
climb the mound to see what Walter Espec saw. Castles
are usually built on vantage points, to be in commanding
positions, to look out over the surrounding countryside
and be seen from it, flags flying from its towers, signals
of authority. I knew that, like Norham, Wark was built

to guard a ford over the Tweed and that it too would look north to Scotland, scanning the horizon for signs of approaching trouble.

By the side of the track I met the first line of defence, the first prohibition. A sign that read 'Private Land. No access without permission. No Parking'. OK, fair enough. We have occasional problems with walkers at our farm thinking that Scotland's 'right to roam' legislation allows them to go wherever they like. But a map next to the baffling Ecomuseum sign had indicated a path along the high bank of the river. I could find no one to ask about permission and so I walked down to my right, towards the Tweed. Through the trees, I could see two islands, and the channels between them were likely the Wark fords, which the castle guarded.

Taking pictures of the motte and the rubble core of its long cast-down walls, I passed a cottage (no one seemed to be at home) and found a newly strimmed path. It led to a steep stile over an ivy-covered wall and I saw that its middle tread had been broken off and was hanging by a nail. Very difficult to climb, stretching my ancient hamstrings, it was greasy and green with what looked like algae. Clearly it had discouraged others.

Once I'd scrambled over, with a few grunts and expletives, and squeezed through a kissing gate that would only open a few inches, I came on a narrow corridor, the grass once again recently strimmed. Why? For whom exactly? Behind another 'PRIVATE' notice there was more detail – a lot more detail. Attached to the fence was another sign, all its letters emphatically capital:

PLEASE READ
THIS IS NOT COMMON LAND
THIS IS NOT OPEN ACCESS LAND
THERE IS NO PUBLIC RIGHT OF WAY
THEREFORE
THERE IS NO 'RIGHT TO ROAM'
FUCK OFF.

OK, I made up the last line. But that was the message. The whole thing was very confusing. Why had the paths been strimmed if they were so difficult to access? And why all this ill-disguised anger? I had the sense of some statutory obligation very grudgingly discharged. The 'right to roam' reference seemed to hark back to a face-to-face dispute and be a reminder that Wark Castle's role in keeping out the Scots had not faded into history. I know that an Englishman's home is his castle, but this was miles over the top.

To the left of the narrow corridor that led up towards the base of the ruined motte was a barbed-wire stock-fence and to my right what looked like an electric fence. On our farm we enclosed a fifty-seven-acre park, with about a mile of this to keep frisky bullocks off my neighbour's land, and we nailed yellow warning signs on all the strainer posts. There were none here and I didn't feel like finding out the hard way if the top wire was hot. Unworried by the fences and all the prohibitions, dozens of rabbits skittered around the field beyond. They seemed very tame, and a young one ran around my feet for a few moments before it remembered to be frightened and scrambled under the stock-fence. I supposed that the signs and defences I had passed meant they encountered few human beings.

I could see very little of the motte, even though the path took me close. It was heavily overgrown and I saw recent falls of masonry at its foot. I wasn't tempted to climb the fence. God knows what that would have triggered. Klaxons, floodlights clanging on, armed guards appearing from nowhere. I could see that the steeply sloping faces of crumbling rubble might not have been safe and there was no winding path visible from where I stood. Instead I walked down to a stone stile over a low wall, and the most deeply worn steps I'd ever seen, and made my way back to the middle of the little village.

Passing behind the motte, which was larger than it seemed, I saw what looked like an information board hidden behind the dried-out canes of last summer's willowherb. The path that might once have led to it was very overgrown and had clearly not seen the tread of visitors for a very long time. Half a dozen beech saplings, each about ten feet high, barred the way. When I finally thrashed through and reached the board, it was almost completely blank, with only a few faded words and phrases. Years of winter rains and summer sun had washed and bleached out whatever it had had to say about the castle.

I was mystified. Wark Castle was important, just as important as Norham, which was well looked after and much visited. Why was this site so pitifully neglected and so aggressively defended? Later, I checked and the castle is on the National Heritage List for England and in the care of Historic England. Perhaps their resources are impossibly stretched. The village, the new houses and the building work were all located where the castle's bailey had once been. Perhaps the community simply didn't want visitors or archaeologists poking around their property. Perhaps an Englishman's home really is his castle. His castle, nobody else's.

I unshouldered my rucksack and sat down on a bench near the play area and stretched out my legs. Time to feast on the pies from the Cornhill Village Shop and enjoy some fizzy water. Having spent some time pondering, I ate the delicious, (very) spicy pie first and then managed half of the chicken and mushroom. I'd have the rest later.

The road to where the border comes out of the Tweed and heads south towards the Cheviot Hills was arrow-straight and not very long. As I made my way to the hamlet of Carham, I wondered if Roman engineers had directed my steps. The faint traces of the ditching of marching camps, temporary defences dug by an army on the move, had been detected at Learmouth near the Ba' Green, at Mindrum and now at Carham. Perhaps a road linked them. No more than half a dozen houses, a church and a farm steading, the village is tiny. Cars take ten seconds to get through it. But a thousand years ago it was significant.

By the tenth century, the old kingdom of Northumbria, once ruled by kings who called themselves *Bretwaldas*, Britain-Rulers, found itself squeezed in a political vice. To the south, Alfred's Wessex dynasty had steadily grown powerful and Athelstan's reach extended up the length of England. At the Battle of

Brunanburh in 937 he defeated an alliance of Celtic and Viking kings and absorbed much of Northumbria into his realm. To the north, the macMalcolm dynasty was ruthlessly ambitious. Somewhere in the Perthshire glens in 1005 Malcolm II ambushed and assassinated his cousin, Kenneth III, and made himself undisputed king of Alba, Scotland above the Forth and Clyde. Thirteen years later he wanted to move his frontier further south, to the banks of the Tweed. Malcolm summoned Owain, the last known king of Old Welsh-speaking Strathclyde, to muster his host and bring it to the woods of the narrow valley of the Caddon Water, not far from modern Galashiels. The king of Alba was massing his forces for a descent into the old kingdom of Northumbria.

Malcolm knew that the fertile farms and villages of the Tweed Valley would enhance the revenues of his growing realm and as the war-smoke of hundreds of campfires billowed over the oak trees by the Caddon Water, the kings and their captains laid their plans.

Scouts had ridden back up the trails by the Tweed to report that Eadulf, Earl of Bamburgh and the successor of the old kings, had reached the river near Cornhill at the head of a force of spearmen. Malcolm and Owain hurried to meet him, to engage Eadulf as quickly as they could and, crucially, to choose their killing ground. In the eleventh century, battles were usually contested by forces of spearmen on foot, who formed themselves up in shield-walls before advancing. 'Rim to boss!' was shouted by their leaders, as they locked shields and poked out their spears beyond them. Sometimes a second rank pushed their weapons through to make a more dense, bristling front.

When armies clashed, they pushed and hacked at each other with swords, axes and long knives, as well as spears, shouting insults over the tops of their shields, the stink of sweat, often of mead or beer, and of blood ever present. Because most men are right-handed, raising or pushing a weapon with that hand, a pair of shield-walls locking together often produced a curious effect. Almost every man in the line, because he was right-handed, tended to seek the protection of the man on his right. This reliance made him push his right-hand man both forward and sideways. Precisely the same tendency affected the opposing shield-wall, and this will have made both sets of combatants move in an anti-clockwise direction on the battlefield. A bit like a scrum wheeling in rugby.

Reliable right-hand men were very important and it's the origin of the phrase. It may also be why best men stand to the right of the groom at wedding ceremonies.

The battle at Carham was likely fought on one of the haughs by the Tweed, either north of the church at Carham or to the west. Malcolm and Owain's army probably crossed at the Wark fords. Battles were often fought at or near convenient places. The greatest danger to a shield-wall was outflanking. That may be what happened at Carham. The Scottish army was almost certainly larger and its king will have wanted an open killing ground so that they could form a longer line, get around the Northumbrian shield-wall and roll it up. Later chroniclers, such as Symeon of Durham, wrote that there was great slaughter that day; if Malcolm's Highlanders and the Strathclyde men got in behind the Northumbrians, there could have been only one outcome. Inciting each other to *freagarrachan*, to rage-fits, the northerners climbed over the wrack of dying and screaming men and drove those still upstanding into the drowning river or lifted them wriggling into the air on their spear-points. Symeon exaggerated wildly when he wrote that 'all the people who dwelt between Tees and Tweed were well-nigh exterminated'. What he meant was that there was great carnage at Carham, and that the power of the Scots king now reached over much of the old kingdom of Northumbria.

Once again I found history in a box, a red telephone box with a sign that claimed it was 'The World's Smallest Visitor Centre', and that it commemorated the Battle of Carham in 1018. Clearly no one from Carham had ever been to Branxton. Perhaps in this small but growing network of minimising the importance of history and literally belittling the death of men in battle, I was missing something. Like Doctor Who's policebox, these old telephone kiosks might have been time machines. If only I could find the switch or the right button to press, then the music of Ron Grainer's BBC Radiophonics Workshop would begin. I would be teleported back to 1018, the shield-walls and the wheeling scrummage of death by the Tweed.

The door was as stiff as the kissing gate at Wark, but once I had squeezed into the box, there it was! A button. 'Please press to hear about the Battle of Carham.' I pressed, closed my eyes and waited for Ron's weird, wobbly underwater music to begin. But nothing happened. Even after several presses, prods, jabs and expletives. I looked around for more possibilities and all I could see were some maps and lists. But where the telephone directories used to be shelved, there was a stack of white envelopes. I picked one up and found that it contained a free book, a complimentary copy of *Carham 1018: The Battle, the Border and the Dawn of Two Nations* by Clive Hallam-Baker, with a foreword by Lord Joicey.

This was more like it. Time travel of a kind, I supposed. On the back of the book was a list of questions under the heading 'The Battle of Carham': 'When was it fought? Who commanded the Northumbrians? How did it fix the border along the Tweed? Why did it presage five hundred years of border warfare? Why is this little known battle more significant than Flodden?' Below a photo of a shield-wall of battle re-enactors, who certainly looked the part, was the tag-line, 'Carham – An Enigmatic, Isolated Hamlet that Conceals an Event of Vital Importance'. And below this was the reason for publication – a logo, 'Carham 1018–2018', the thousandth anniversary, and there were thanks to the Battlefield Trust and the National Lottery Heritage Fund.

This was stirring stuff. I walked through the gate into the churchyard and sat down on the parched grass with my back to a wall that had been warmed by the afternoon sun. After an introduction and a chapter disposing of the potentially problematic issue of 'When was the battle fought – 1016 or 1018?' (if the author had concluded it was 1016, the thousand-year commemoration would have been held two years too late, and what would have happened then? Would the National Lottery have demanded their money back?), Mr Hallam-Baker begins Chapter Eight, 'The Battle', with a disarming sentence: 'Little, in fact nothing, is known about the battle itself . . .'

After that shaky start, he recovers and goes on to propose that the Battle of Carham did, indeed, take place at Carham. Then in the narrative, history moves on beyond 1018, and five-hundred years of border warfare, peace eventually descending, and after the Union of the Crowns in 1603 the penultimate chapter is entitled, 'Things Settle Down'.

Carham's parish church is beautiful. Very simple, with a nave and a well-proportioned square bell tower, it sits in a graveyard on a small plateau above the Tweed. Beyond it is the Holm, an area of haughland in a loop of the river, the probable site of the battle. The present church was built in 1790 on the footprint of much earlier buildings. Sometime in the late seventh century, a small wooden cell or chapel was constructed by monks and dedicated to St Cuthbert. At that time Northumbria extended far to the north, to the shores of the Firth of Forth, and the Tweed Valley was part of the heart of the kingdom. Cuthbert's exemplary life came to be a powerful element in its identity, how some Northumbrians saw themselves at the time.

As a young man, the saint took holy orders at the monastery of Old Melrose, now in Scotland (partly as an outcome of the battle at Carham). Cuthbert became Bishop of Lindisfarne and was revered as England's greatest native saint. Durham Cathedral guarded his relics until the Reformation and the great patrimony of the prince-bishops was constantly enriched by gifts given in his name. When the border began to settle on the Tweed in the east, those who lived on its southern banks remembered Cuthbert and spoke of themselves as the *Haliwerfolc*, an Old English compound that means 'the Holy Man's People', the English. It is a very early and clearly paradoxical definition.

It may be seen as ironic that Cuthbert was born, raised and ordained in what is now Scotland, but that's not really the point. Above all, he was a Northumbrian, an identity now – and wrongly – attached only to those who live south of the border.

Ten years ago I worked with Professor Jim Wilson of Edinburgh University, an authority on ancestral DNA. We looked closely at demographics and maps of the Borders, both sides, and found that we could see the watermark of an underlying identity expressed in surveys of DNA – and in my own ancestral DNA. The analysis is straightforward. My Y chromosome DNA, a small part of my genome, which is passed on down the generations only through the fatherline, originated in southern Sweden and northern Denmark. Sampling indicated that there were significant numbers of men in south-eastern Scotland and north-eastern England who also carried this marker. Such historical records as exist claim that the Angles who established the kingdom of Northumbria came from that part of Scandinavia, the place where the marker is most common in the world, where it has mutated the most and therefore where it originated. I was triumphant, more than proud, when I discovered that I was a Northumbrian and that I had many DNA cousins, no doubt many times removed, on both sides of the Tweed.

From Carham Church I walked down to the river that runs through my people's history and wondered if Cuthbert, that solitary and vulnerable man, carried my marker. I hope he did. I would be honoured. The Tweed loops lazily southwards and then turns west to where the Carham Burn trickles into it and the border moves towards the Cheviot Hills and the watershed ridge. It would be mostly uphill now, and occasionally down dale, very different and much harder going than the flat land beside the river.

Day Six

The Whispering Land

'Last night I dreamt I went to Manderley again' must be one of the most beguiling opening lines in English literature. With one simple and brilliant sentence, Daphne du Maurier draws the reader into the story of Rebecca, a character who does not appear in the novel. But rather than reading it, I heard it first.

When television sets became cheap to rent in the early 1960s, our family seemed to move from reading to watching. Virtually every evening we caught the early BBC news, then a current-affairs programme. *Tonight* was hosted by the genial Cliff Michelmore and it featured memorable, even eccentric, reporters such as the pork-pie-hatted and goatee-bearded Scotsman Fyfe Robertson, or the suave Alan Whicker, with Derek Hart, and Geoffrey Johnson Smith, as well as topical calypsos from Cy Grant. Around these nightly staples were shows like *Hancock's Half Hour, Sergeant Bilko,* a very scary drama called *Quatermass and the Pit* and much else. But perhaps most memorable of all were the old black-and-white Ealing and Hollywood films the BBC played on rainy Sunday afternoons. As grey skies gathered over the rooftops in our street and raindrops pattered on the windows, that was when I heard Joan Fontaine utter the first line of *Rebecca* and I was hooked, hypnotised, drawn into another world.

She went on to say:

It seemed to me I stood by the iron gate leading to the drive, and for a while I could not enter, for the way was barred to me. There was a padlock and a chain upon the gate. I called in my dream to the lodge-keeper, and had no answer, and peering closer through the rusted spokes of the gate I saw that the lodge was uninhabited.

No smoke came from the chimneys and the little lattice windows gaped forlorn. Then, like all dreamers, I was possessed of a sudden with supernatural powers and passed like a spirit through the barrier before me.

My mum gave me the novel to read, saying, 'It might be a bit too lovey-dovey for you.' Long ago I lost her precious book, an edition from the *Reader's Digest* Book Club, I think, but I have another copy by me on my desk. When I started to read it again, I found myself walking with ghosts once more down the driveway to Manderley.

'I had not thought the way so long. Surely the miles had multiplied . . .' When the invisible dreamer, Joan Fontaine (I couldn't get her cut-glass accent out of my head), came to the ruined house, she began to recall the past:

Light came from the windows, the curtains blew softly in the night air, and there, in the library, the door would stand half open as we had left it, with my handkerchief on the table beside the bowl of autumn roses.

After a few moments of reminiscence:

A cloud, hitherto unseen, came upon the moon, and hovered an instant like a dark hand before a face. The illusion went with it, and the lights in the windows were extinguished. I looked upon a desolate shell, soulless at last, unhaunted, with no whisper of the past about its staring walls.

And finally, there was a resolution: 'We would not talk of Manderley, I would not tell my dream. For Manderley was ours no longer. Manderley was no more.'

After only four pages I recall being mesmerised, unable to stop reading, hungry to know what happened next, what had happened to ruin the great house on the cliffs above the roiling sea at Manderley. And once again, I had to force myself to put down the book. Du Maurier's genius was to use a powerful sense of place, her genius for *loci*, for places of spirits, and to do much more than set the scene or locate the action of the novel. Using the details of the overgrown driveway, the ivy in the moonlight clinging to the ruins of the house, reclaiming it, she hides secrets, covers the past with fallen trees, choking it with weeds, grass and moss. In *Rebecca*, Manderley is more than the frame for the story, it is the story, a place full of meaning and memory, an enormously powerful character.

After *Rebecca*, I read *Frenchman's Creek* and once again du Maurier worked her magic, as she described another house in Cornwall. Navron, too, is ruined, but by shifting seamlessly between the present and the seventeenth century, she brings the setting back to life.

'When the east wind blows up Helford River the shining waters become troubled and disturbed and the little waves beat angrily upon the sandy shores.' That is the first sentence. As the nightjars call in the shadows of the light midsummer nights, the tale begins to unwind. In the first few pages, du Maurier writes of an unnamed twentieth-century yachtsman who takes his dinghy to explore the upper reaches of the Helford River.

> He is alone, and yet – can that be a whisper, in the shallows, close to the bank, and does a figure stand there, the moonlight glinting on his buckled shoes and the cutlass in his hand, and is that a woman by his side, a cloak around her shoulders, her dark ringlets drawn back behind her ears?

Magical.

★   ★   ★

Walking can be self-hypnotic. As I made my way from Carham down to the haughland by the Tweed on another spring morning of bright sunshine after night rain, I found myself soon in a rhythm, on good ground, and nothing but a few hundred yards of flat riverbank in front of me. The water shimmered, a pure cobalt blue against the bleached white of the exposed shoals of stones, and on the far side of an old channel that had once carved out an island, a small herd of cows lay on the sweet grass, corralling their calves in a protective circle.

At seventy-two, I have lived a biblical span and seen the world change faster than at any time in history. And seen my life change, too. Born and raised only five miles from where I was walking, I cycled and wandered through this landscape as a boy all the summer days long and I know I was made by the early experiences I had here. I found places to escape to, places forbidden to me, places I could hide, places where I thought I could be myself, alone.

Muirside House was grand, Georgian and very private. Dense rhododendra hung over a high stone wall on the Moss Brae and a locked iron gate barred the entrance for all but the intrepid. Rustling through the bushes on a school holiday summer evening, long after the time I'd been told to be home, I came to the edge of wide lawns planted with solitary copper beeches and green oaks. Beyond them rose the dark mass of the house. Perhaps there was no one there. Running from tree to tree, hunched over like a ten-year-old commando, I was soon close enough to be sure the house was empty. Walking, upright, not running, more confident, I crossed the gravel forecourt and looked up at the high windows and wondered. And suddenly a light went on. Then another. I turned and ran like the wind, crashing through the rhododendra in the half-dark, across the Moss Brae and all the way home – where I saw the relief on my mum's face a moment before I suffered the wrath of my father and his raised hand.

My dad came from a line of single parents, mothers who managed to bring up a child without the help of the father. Consequently he had no role model, not much idea of how to be a father himself. My dad never showed any physical affection for me that I can remember, although he must have cuddled me as a baby and a toddler. I have a photograph taken on the doorstep of our prefab. My big sister, Barbara, sits on one side and my dad is holding me. I must have been on the point of walking. But when I grew older, my main memories of him are tinged with fear. My dad hit me, and I was scared of him, always very wary in his presence, not sure what would cause him to shout at me or worse. That was not unusual in our street, or for my generation. Other dads hit their sons; teachers used the tawse, a leather strap, to punish children.

When I was older, bigger and able to fight back, my dad took to deriding me. At school I enjoyed history ('What's the bloody point of that?'), studied Latin and Greek ('Useless waste of time') and I was cast in school plays ('Christ Almighty!'). Even when it became clear that I could play rugby well, my dad found that difficult too. He wanted to, I think, but I can't ever remember him encouraging me, and when the South of Scotland selectors came to watch me play, he knew but didn't tell me and I called off with a slight injury I could probably have fixed with some treatment. Goodness knows what contradictory emotions churned in his heart, but mostly they caused him to lash out.

I knew that my mum and my grannie (who lived with us) loved me, and that sustained me. When I left school, I meandered through university, made some accidentally good decisions and was very lucky. In 1976, I found myself unexpectedly in charge of the Edinburgh Festival Fringe and made a success of it. Very quickly I became part of Scottish public life. I was asked for my opinions by journalists, taking part in panel discussions on TV and issuing press releases, even though I was only twenty-five. And in other roles since then I have been publicly visible for more than forty years. Scotland is a small country so that's not difficult if you have something to say or contribute.

I always intuited that I'd come home to the Borders and end my days in the places where I had begun them. Looking back, I think now that these familiar landscapes and their detail, their secret places, are still an anchor for me and always have been. Sadly, it is now unusual for a child born in a prefab with nothing, with few advantages, to find themselves in leading cultural roles. Education was my stepladder and now it is too expensive for most young people who begin life in my circumstances. I somehow found the confidence to make some sort of mark and I think that came in part from the places I knew when I was a child, what was my country, and, in my imagination, mine alone, places where I sent down roots. And on that sunny morning on the banks of the great river, walking past the dozing cows and their calves, I felt myself content and secure in that landscape. If I listened, waited and looked around, I knew it would whisper its stories to me.

English side or Scottish side? I had come to where the Carham Burn trickles into the Tweed and Scotland begins. The drought made it easy to hop from one country into the other. Having walked up to where the road to Kelso runs, I had to decide which side I would walk. The Pathfinder showed no path on either bank of the burn and it seemed that my entire journey south to Yetholm and the foot of the Cheviot Hills would be along the edges of fields. There would be many fences to climb and dykes to scramble over, and a lot of map reading if I wanted to walk along the thick black line of the border and see both sides of the story.

Also known as the Reddenburn, the Carham Burn once marked an international frontier, something easy to forget. It was the site of a trysting place and some heated argument. At York in 1237, the border was first formally defined when Alexander II of Scotland and Henry III of England had their seals affixed to a document. In return for certain estates in Cumbria and Northumberland, Alexander renounced his wider claim to the north of England. While Berwick remained in Scotland, the line of the border was fixed in the midstream from the mouth of the Tweed until it reached the Carham Burn. That was clear enough and largely undisputed. The anomaly of the Ba' Green emerged much later. But where the frontier abruptly turns south there were arguments over what was and still is some of the most fertile and well-drained land in the north of Britain. From where I was standing, trying to decide which side of the burn to walk, I could hear the echoes of loud disagreement. Here is Hugh de Bolebec's highly partial account of what happened in the summer of 1245. It is a letter to Henry III.

I and the knights of Northumberland met the Justiciar of Lothian, David Lindsay, the Earl of Dunbar, and many other Scottish knights at Reddenburn. Six English and six Scottish knights were elected as a jury to make a true perambulation of the march between the two kingdoms, and in particular between the lands of Carham (in England) and Hadden (in Scotland).

The six English knights, with one accord, immediately set off along the rightful and ancient marches between the two kingdoms, but the Scottish knights entirely disagreed and contradicted them. I and the Justiciar of Lothian thereupon decided to elect a second jury to reinforce the first. Once again the English knights agreed on the boundary and the Scots dissented.

Since the Scots had thus obstructed the business, I took it upon myself to empanel a third jury, this time of twenty-four English knights, who declared the true and ancient marches on oath. But when they started to make a perambulation of this line, the Justiciar and his fellow Scots forcibly prevented them, and stopped them carrying out the perambulation by threats.

I chose the English side. It might be more peaceful. To the east of the bridge over the Carham Burn, where Hugh de Bolebec and his knights had gathered seven centuries ago, there was an open field entry and a ten-yard-wide swathe of unplanted land before the rows of barley began, something that looked odd to me. On the Scottish side, the farmer had sown his crops right up to the very edge of the field and there was no room to walk. As I would discover, this wasn't an example of Scots thrift wringing every last grain of corn out of the land and the well-off English not bothering.

There was no path through the lush and long grass and the great variety of green weeds I trampled on, some knee-height. One of them, I have no idea of its name, even smelled green as I waded through it, like the savoury scent of freshly shelled peas. The overnight rain made for very wet walking and my beige boots quickly grew dark chocolate brown. I felt in the right boot that the damp was beginning to get through. Disappointing. The English farmer had left just enough room at the edge of his planting for there to be a narrow, muddy track and like a geriatric tightrope walker I tiptoed up it towards a low ridge. For some strange reason the final row of planted barley was yellow, as though it had withered or been sprayed. To my right the Carham Burn trickled through a deepening declivity, making the border very emphatic. A gauzy sun strength-ened and I began the usual sequence of peeling off layers down to a cotton shirt.

All around me I heard birdsong trilling and piping. A row of ancient hawthorn trees wore a sugar-dusting of white blossom and at last I found a narrow path through the high grass and weeds, one made by animals. It led me to a surprise. At sometime in the recent past, the Carham Burn had been dammed behind a low concrete wall with an iron sluice gate set in the middle. A very picturesque pond had filled up behind it but before I began to walk out on the wall to investigate, I saw a swan sitting on her nest under the shadows of the thorns on the far side. She looked stern, and so instead of poking at the edges of her pond, I walked in a wide circle around it. I noticed that the nest was a substantial structure of small branches, as well as twigs. More unlikely bounty from Storm Arwen.

A cooling breeze riffled across the barley on my left, the swaying movement like a wind on the sea, the green waves softer, more gentle. Tramping uphill by the side of the fence I began to daydream again. Over the blossoming trees along the border I could see the farm of Nottylees and the fields around it. On both sides of the burn the land was the same, the soil dark brown, the weeds and thorns all blown by the same winds and watered out of the same grey skies. It was the people and their stories that were different. Even though Hugh de Bolebec, a Norman Frenchman by the sound of his name, and his twenty-four knights walked the same ground as Justiciar Lindsay and his men, and were about the same business, the Englishmen sounded exasperated and the Scots thrawn, even aggressive. Seven hundred years later, P. G. Wodehouse wrote that it was never difficult to distinguish between a Scotsman with a grievance and a ray of sunshine.

Scots think and write differently about the land, even though the soil, the insects, animals and plants on either side of the border are not different. Much further north but just as fertile and also watered by great rivers, the fields and farms of the north-east lowlands of Scotland were home to James Leslie Mitchell. He grew up in the Mearns in the opening decades of the twentieth century, a country district between the Grampian Mountains and the North Sea to the south of Stonehaven. He soon left to pursue a career as a writer. From the unlikely setting of Welwyn Garden City, almost as far away from the Mearns as it is possible to be on the long island of Britain, Mitchell remembered the land and he made it the main, the motive character in his brilliant novel *Sunset Song*. Writing as Lewis Grassic Gibbon, he began not with a dream but a map of Kinraddie, a collection of farms associated with an old estate. Chris Guthrie, his heroine, lived on one of them, Blawearie, and the Song, the main narrative, opens with images of her and the land.

Below and around where Chris Guthrie lay the June moors whispered and rustled and shook their cloaks, yellow with broom and powdered faintly with purple, that was the heather but not the full passion of its colour yet. And in the east against the cobalt blue of the sky lay the shimmer of the North Sea, that was by Bervie, and maybe the wind would veer there in an hour or so and you'd feel the change in the life and strum of the thing, bringing a streaming coolness out of the sea.

What brought this glorious, atmospheric passage particularly to mind was the cycle of droughts we've suffered at our farm and across the Tweed Valley over the last year. They are nothing new, surely, but their cause likely is. Carbon emissions were not at the front of Chris Guthrie's mind; it was more the cycles of the land, and the weather that nourished and buffeted it.

> But for days now the wind had been in the south, it shook and played in the moors and went dandering up the sleeping Grampians, the rushes pecked and quivered about the loch when its hand was upon them, but it brought more heat than cold, and all the parks were fair parched, sucked dry, the red clay soil of Blawearie gaping open for the rain that seemed never-coming. Up here the hills were brave with the beauty and the heat of it, but the hayfield was all a crackling dryness and in the potato park beyond the biggings the shaws drooped red and rusty already. Folk said there hadn't been such a drought since eighty-three and Long Rob of the Mill said you couldn't blame *this* one on Gladstone, anyway, and everybody laughed except father, God knows why.

It's hard to think of two novelists more different than Lewis Grassic Gibbon and Daphne du Maurier, but that's not the point. Both make the land and its buildings central to their stories, set as they are at either end of Britain. Difference is to be expected. It's how they write about places that matters, the cast of their imaginations, and how the land plays on their minds and memories.

Grassic Gibbon, raw and elemental, and yet familiar and warm. His people have the earth of the Mearns grained into their hands. Du Maurier is in love with the mystery of the thing, with atmospheres, clouds over the face of the moon, shadows and the romance of the land. I am not asserting necessarily that one is quintessentially Scottish and the other a central part of Englishness, like Agatha Christie's St Mary Mead, but they are very different and characteristic. Because England is very crowded by comparison, with the vast bulk of its population living in cities and large towns, and the roads and other transport links regularly choked, the land can seem invisible, at best obscured, busy with people looking for a break, a breather. In Scotland there is much more room, less than a twelfth of the population on more than 30 per cent of the landmass of Britain, and most of them live in the large towns and conurbations around Glasgow and Edinburgh. On all my walks over the years of writing about this place, I've met very few people and since I left the road at the bridge over the Carham Burn, I had seen no one, and heard no engine noise, not even in the distance.

Beyond the swaying, waving barley field was a few acres of managed pasture that had been recently grazed and was nothing like as wet as where I'd been walking. I turned back to look at the widening vista to the north and saw what I thought was a lark fluttering in the updraughts. Should I be ashamed to say that I recognised its silvery, liquid song from the last few notes of Ralph Vaughan Williams' *The Lark Ascending*? Probably. I love birdsong but can only be sure about honking geese (and

I know there are many sorts), crows cawing, swallows twittering, owls hooting, wood pigeons woo-hooing and the lovely notes of the blackbird in the bushes by the track. I have my bedroom window open between about April and October unless it's raining and I hear the blackbird and the woodies each morning.

A line of taller trees curved away to my left and, looking at the Pathfinder, I realised that this was the line of the old railway from St Boswells in the heart of the Borders to Berwick by the sea. All that stood between me and climbing up the embankment was an electric fence. One set up to keep cattle back, it would give me a hell of a belt if I brushed against it. But, hallelujah, the farmer had made a gate, a coiled section of the hot wire with an insulated plastic handle attached that could be lifted out of a keeper to break the connection and allow me to pass through unbelted. Good man.

The old trackbed seemed intact. With a grassy crest between two black cinder tracks, it looked as though it was still used by wheeled vehicles, probably tractors and carts. I'm old enough to remember steam trains whistling and chugging along it, taking trippers to the North Sea and its beaches. In the spring of 1964 Mr Goodall, our Latin and Greek teacher, led a holiday expedition of pupils from Kelso High School to go youth hostelling in the western Highlands and we made the entire journey by train in less than a day, door to door. At Kelso station, a steam train from Berwick-upon-Tweed puffed in. 'Change at St Boswells for Hawick, Carlisle and London Euston,' shouted the station master before blowing a whistle, and at the rear of the train the guard waved a green flag. The carriages shuddered, the iron wheels clanked, we shoved our rucksacks up into the netting shelves above the upholstered seats in the third-class compartment and the journey began. Having rattled into Edinburgh Waverley, we changed for Glasgow Queen Street, where we caught a tight connection to Fort William and on to Morar, the white sands below the mountains and the endless evening horizon of the Atlantic stretching out to the west. I've never forgotten it.

Now only ghost trains run along the trackbed. When I walked east for a few yards and reached the bridge over the Carham Burn and the border, I realised how many links there were after three hundred years of union between England and Scotland. It struck me how difficult it might be to police what could become an international frontier once more. The governing Scottish National Party lost the independence referendum in 2014, but Britain's exit from the European Union two years later supplied a pretext for holding another one soon. If that reverses the result of the first, then old railway trackbeds will become a problem, particularly if Scotland rejoins the European Union as an independent nation and an international frontier complete with customs checks, long queues of lorries, paperwork and barriers needs to be set up. The border seems very porous. Perhaps a modern version of the criminal society of the sixteenth century, the age of the Border Reivers, will return.

I'd been walking for more than two hours and the sun had grown brighter and stronger. Time for a hat.

And, it turned out, time for a blaze of floral glory. When I crossed the railway trackbed and entered another field of barley instead of a wide green margin, there was a great swathe of uncultivated land, several acres in the corner that was protected by a shelter belt of pines. Red and white campions grew everywhere, lighting the morning with their pure, rich and vivid colours. There is surely no fresher, more perfectly natural colour than the petal of a young flower. Bees buzzed from bloom to bloom, all of them fresh, probably brought out by the recent overnight rain and warming mornings of sun. As I tiptoed through the field of flowers, I realised that this was no corner-cutting but the result of a deliberate policy. Later, I discovered that DEFRA, the old Ministry of Agriculture, Fisheries and Food, had brought out a new scheme designed to encourage local nature recovery, tree planting and the restoration of wild landscapes. 'Make Space for Nature' was the mantra, and although red campions were nowhere mentioned, they were already emblematic of this new scheme in action. Farmers were being paid to carve out and set aside these beautiful enclaves, seen by very few people, and all was being done in the name of reducing carbon emissions to net zero by 2050.

But only in England, it seemed. Devolved government in Scotland means that the Environmental Land Management Scheme stops dead at the border. That was why I had been able to walk up the English side, although I didn't realise it at the time. The new scheme had made room. I looked out to the west, to Scotland, and could see no red or white campions or any other

wide patches of wild flowers. The only colour that was
not green came from fields of yellow rapeseed. All of
which is surely crazy. Climate change will not stop at
the border. Carbon emissions do not turn back at road
signs. These are international, global problems that
need cooperation, coordinated action, global solutions.
In Scotland I discovered that there is the Agri-
Environment Climate Scheme. I read that it was more
livestock-based. Perhaps there are areas across the rest
of Scotland where space is being made for nature and
where wildflowers bloom, but there seemed to be none
at the border. Where is the common sense to make
common cause, or even a local plan that champions
campions?

My map showed the border beginning to wander as
it moved away from the Carham Burn and closer to the
old railway trackbed. It was as though Scotland had
taken a bite out of England. From a railway cutting, the
border suddenly turned sharp left and then ran due
south in a straight line. On my right was a deep ditch
dug to mark it very clearly. Another glance at my map
reminded me of the reason for this strange zig-zag.
Across the Scottish field to the west of the ditch was a
shelter belt of pines called the Duke's Strip.

The adoption of James Small's swing plough and other
innovations towards the end of the eighteenth century,
a period of change that came to be known as the
Agricultural Revolution, changed the look of the land
profoundly. The old open rigs gradually disappeared,
fields were enclosed and the outbye, the old commons
of summer grazing used by farming communities,

towns and villages were grabbed by surrounding lairds and lords. I was walking through what was once Wark Common, land used by the villagers on the banks of the Tweed to pasture their beasts in summer, gather fuel and harvest forage for the winter. Place names on the Pathfinder remember it: Wark Common Farm and Wark Westcommon lay to the south. English lords and landowners seized most of it after an Act of Parliament was passed in 1799, but on the Scottish side the Duke of Roxburgh showed how powerful and influential he could be. The area of Wark Common he claimed lay on the English side of the border. So he had the border moved. And the deep ditch was dug for the avoidance of any doubt.

The ground began to climb and ahead was a tall thorn tree, foaming brilliant white with blossom. I came on a track beyond it and noticed a change in the colour of the soil from a dark loam nearer the river to a russet ochre on the higher ground. It was a good place for an ambush.

As a boy, I don't remember much in the way of toys – maybe a cap gun and its smell of cordite as the hammer exploded the tiny dots on the roll with a sharp and satisfying crack. The landscape, the lanes, fields, streams and woods were our playroom and as an Apache chief, Geronimo, I reckoned this track was the right place to ambush Kit Carson, or Davy Crockett, King of the Wild Frontier and his friend, Fess Parker, maybe Wyatt Earp and his brothers Virgil and Morgan, or the Cisco Kid. There was plenty of cover for my braves behind the bushes, down in the border ditch.

Another track led steeply uphill and I noticed that it had been metalled, the stones and gravel peeping through the grass. At the top of the rise, near the Duke's Strip, I turned to look north over the Tweed Valley. The vista was vast. I could make out Great Dirrington Law rising above the lower ridge of the Lammermuirs beyond Duns, the three Eildon Hills near Melrose, and eastwards I saw the land dropping down towards Berwick and the sea. I remember meeting an old man who had once been Provost of Kelso at a viewpoint high above the town. It was another sunny summer's day long ago and the town below seemed drowsy in the heat. There was a haze over the farmland beyond it. He waved his stick at the view and said, 'Aye, son, there it is. The Inhabited World.'

The border ran straight, south-east, for about a mile towards a B road that linked the upcountry farms in both Scotland and England. In the distance I could see a faint powdering of blue across a green field near Wark Westcommon Farm. On my right, Scotland was being sprayed. With long wings on either side, a tractor pulled a tank of fertiliser through a field of what might have been barley. The first human being I'd met that day waved at me from the cab as he swung the great contraption around like a swing bridge and drove away up the dreels.

It was flax, the field of powdery blue, its flowers just come into bloom. I took a photograph with my phone camera and checked later. At the same time as the Duke of Roxburgh was pushing the boundaries, a great deal of flax was grown in the Borders. It was also called lint and place names mark where it grew: Lintmill, Lintlea and Linthill. Flax was processed for the production of linen and it was big business, employing many people. Having been soaked in ponds to soften it, the plants were shredded into fibres as they were pulled through a heckle board. These looked like the beds of nails I had read about as a boy in Arthur Mee's *Children's Encyclopaedia*, marvelling and wondering why Indian fakirs wanted to lie down on them. This laborious and boring work was usually done by groups of men in heckle sheds and often the long days were relieved by readings. The men paid for someone to read newspapers to them and so became uncommonly well informed about current affairs. When hustings were held at elections in the early nineteenth century, candidates did not often enjoy it when hecklers shouted questions at them.

Rather than fibre for weaving linen, I suspected the flax had been planted for two other reasons: to make linseed oil and as part of the Environmental Land Management Scheme. Beyond the road I saw what I thought might be an entire field of red campions. Against the delicate blue of the flax flowers and near the yellow rapeseed and green barley, the contrasts were wonderful, the homely geometry of the fields making the English countryside look like a giant sunlit Mondrian.

Having scrambled up a bank, careful not to trip on the tough stems of wild raspberries, I was glad to be walking on a solid road even if it was only for two hundred yards. Not having constantly to look where I was going was a welcome break. Once I'd crossed two more fields, keeping the border fence on my right, I arrived at another stretch of road and the white line in the middle marked the old frontier. It led me up to Pressen Hill Farm before turning south once more. The contour lines of my map were beginning to bunch; a reminder that much of the second half of my journey would be uphill.

At a triangular wood named, like so many others in hunting country, Fox Covert, the border followed the road for a hundred yards before, unaccountably, plunging into the trees. Like so much woodland I'd seen, it had been badly thinned by Storm Arwen, with trunks leaning at drunken angles against upright survivors, like men outside a pub after closing time on a Saturday night. At the southern edge of the trees I had a very awkward climb over a ramshackle gate above the burn that the border followed. At the top of the rise beyond I saw the Cheviot horizon for the first time. It didn't seem much closer. I would have to climb up Bowmont Hill. It was only six hundred or so feet high, but its steep flanks made it look like a green version of the Eiger. A straggle of old trees marked the border line.

What I didn't reckon on was a gully that led to another Fox Covert, very steep on both sides. Horsey as well as hunting country, the remains of a cross-country course of rustic jumps were strung out along the floor of this little valley. A horse might have been handy since I was finding climbing up these slopes more and more challenging.

Enclosed fields planted with barley or flowers or both were giving way to more open pasture, as the land began to undulate, its sweeps and curves accentuated by the sinuous lines of shelter belts. The dense, dark green of the trees and the lime-green grass seemed a picture of harmony and peace. But when the north wind brings wind-driven winter rains, the ewes would retreat to the margins, huddling together for shelter under the over-hanging branches. Animals in the open hate the sting of the cold rain and I noticed that Storm Arwen had thinned some of the strips of protecting pines.

When I reached the foot of Bowmont Hill, I crossed the fence to the Scottish side. The high pasture had been grazed billiard-table flat, exposing the contours, allowing me to pick the best line, often a diagonal. I like to think I am reasonably fit, if a little creaky, but my hamstrings were beginning to twang as I forced one foot in front of the other. Still, I kept insisting to myself, over the hill was a downslope and at the bottom the road to Yetholm, to a large glass of cold something (a cold pint of shandy with all its bubbles began to dance in front of my eyes like an apparition) and a late lunch. But most of all I prayed that my map reading was right and there wasn't another summit beyond.

Glory be, there wasn't. I sat down, dumped my ruck-sack and took off my hat to let the breeze dry my matted hair, and drank the last of my water. The views were long and hazy. It was past midday and the sun was directly overhead. Puffs of cloud clustered over the long hump of Cheviot and I could make out the distant white dots of grazing sheep on the flanks of the hills on the far side of the Bowmont Valley. Looking at the land below, the sweep of it and the patterns of hedges, lanes and field-ends reminded me of early childhood. Playing amongst the banked-up shaws of potatoes in our back garden, I made miniature worlds. US Cavalry forts were mounded out of the brown, loamy earth, a stalk of straw planted for a flagpole and twigs made a stockade. To mark the trail across the plains from the lettuce patch, I laid out rows of small pebbles and, with a broken cup, made a bridge over the Rio Grande.

Looking down on the Inhabited World is a reward for climbing up into the high country, and the Tweed Valley below me has always seemed a place apart. I sat in the sun on the foothills of its southern rampart, the Cheviot Hills, gazed across to its northern bounds, the windy moors of the Lammermuirs, west to the hills of the Ettrick Forest and east to the moat of the North Sea. The dizzying speed of modern communication, both geographical and electronic, has not dented my sense of this self-contained, hill and sea-girt landscape, nor made my love of it any less intense. There is nowhere like it. The Borders is not England, despite its history and many ancient bonds with the south. But sometimes I think it is not Scotland either. Perhaps I should remember that when considering the nature of English nationalism.

*   *   *

With a few sub-vocal noises, I stood up and steeled myself for the last lap.

For about forty young cows in the field below, my approach was the most interesting thing that had happened that day, probably that week. When I reached the fence, they cantered over to greet me. Like pigs, boisterous young bullocks are not to be trifled with. Another unwelcome and weary detour. I climbed over a drystane dyke, ducked under the single wire of another electric fence and finally reached the road. That was where my Pathfinder ran out, reaching the edge of the sheet, but I knew the way from there to Yetholm. What I didn't know was how long it was. I'd imagined half a mile. It was almost two miles. By the time I reached the Border Hotel in Kirk Yetholm they had stopped serving lunch but kindly made me some cheese and tomato sandwiches. I was almost too tired to eat them, but the pint of shandy was like nectar. The bubbles were indeed winking at the brim, the glass cool against my cheek.

Day Seven

The Sheltering Hills

'The track is my boundary,' said the farmer, as he switched off the engine of his little electric pick-up and trailer. 'It follows the border.' He smiled. 'It's not Scotland, but you can walk where you like. Doesn't bother me.' I'd crossed the Bowmont Water at Yetholm Mains and walked past what looked like four council houses to arrive on the banks of the Shotton Burn. It flows down from the Cheviots and since the twelfth century has marked the line of the frontier. I looked up from the flat valley floor to where the hills began to rise steeply, even abruptly, like geography drawn by children. 'I'll leave the gates open. Don't need to shut them behind you. I'm coming back that way. One needs mending anyway. It's on the list.' Nudging his grey-muzzled old collie along the seat, he smiled and turned the ignition key. 'Have a good day.'

The track by the Shotton Burn was well made, fully metalled and flat for the first half mile. A good, gentle start under a cloudy-bright sky for what I knew would be the most taxing day yet – the steep climb up into the hills. The map showed contours rising sharply from 120 metres to 320 in less than a mile. My plan was to make the journey along the watershed ridge, where the border mostly runs, in shorter stages. No sense in rushing and risking a pulled muscle or a turned ankle. If, God forbid, that happened, how the hell would I get down off the hills? Except with great and painful difficulty. In any case, before I started climbing, I had a quest to complete, one that might prove to be a key to another world. By the side of the Shotton Burn, in flattish ground, the map noted in the olde-worlde font they use for historic locations the site of St Ethelreda's Chapel. I wanted to see if I could find it.

According to the farmer, local antiquarians hadn't had much luck, but he went on to say something intriguing. When he first took on the farm, the boundary track had, for no apparent reason, skirted around a rectangular area by the burn. 'Just follow the track and you'll come to where we straightened it out.' I wondered if there had been a memory of sanctity there, perhaps a graveyard.

Keeping the Shotton Burn on my right, I walked past some magnificent, lush-leaved hardwoods – beech, oak and chestnut – and came to a strange, atmospheric place. Between the burn and a high, dense stand of over-hanging trees, the track wound around a singular, flat-topped rocky outcrop. I immediately felt I'd seen it before. The grassy crag looked very like the *Torr an Aba* in the centre of Columba's monastery on Iona. I'd been there recently and thought it seemed like a natural pulpit, the place where Scotland's great saint would have preached and blessed his people. When I climbed up, I found I could see much more than from down on the track: long vistas to the north and the Bowmont Valley, and south to the mass of the Cheviots. In the much misunderstood and mysterious centuries of the Dark Ages, when Britain was changing, forming and emerging, Christian worship often happened out of doors. Perhaps the faithful gathered at the foot of the crag to listen to the word of God, just as crowds had come to hear Jesus speak and preach in the bright, sunlit early days in the Holy Land. But there was no room below the crag, no flat ground by the side of the burn to build a chapel, and I walked on.

The border turned eastwards and the landscape began to open up to high moorland pasture. By a last line of hardwoods there was a closed gate, what might have been the boundary of the farm. Scattered by the fence were a dozen big stones. When I turned some of them, I found they had been worked, one side faced and squared; another had been chiselled on all its faces. In the dyke, white with lichen, I could make out more cut stones, some worked much more than a drystane dyker would have needed to. When I pushed aside the long grass, more came to light. A track led diagonally up to a flat terrace above the burn and, again, despite not having gained much altitude, the wide vistas opened up once more, as Creation unfolded. But I could find no visible trace of St Ethelreda's Chapel, not one stone left standing upon another. All that remained was a change in the vegetation in one place, a large patch of nettles and other weeds instead of grass. Perhaps that was all there was, the ghost of the church of an ancient, half-forgotten saint, lost in the windswept hills.

The little chapel was still standing at the beginning of the thirteenth century, when the clerks at Kelso Abbey noted in their records that it lay 'in Schottun, beside the place of Colpenhope [a lost name that might have survived in Countrup Sike, a stream that runs down the border line for a few hundred yards] on the river just as it descends towards the chapel of St Edildrede, the virgin'.

Slightly better known as St Aethelthryth, or much easier St Audrey, she was a seventh-century virgin queen. One of four saintly daughters of King Onna of East Anglia, born sometime around 636, Aethelthryth was packed off to a reluctant dynastic marriage with Tondberct, Prince of the South Gyrwe, a kindred who lived in the watery wastes of the Fens. The new princess managed to extract a promise that she would be allowed to remain a virgin and be faithful to her vows of chastity, although how that worked for a dynast presumably anxious to see his dynasty continue is anyone's guess. In the seventh century the sea reached much further south than the shores of the Wash, and the land of the Gyrwe was a tidal patchwork. The Isle of Ely was an island. It would be a place that became very important in the strange story of Aethelthryth.

But before we get lost in a tangle of unfamiliar, unpronounceable and half-forgotten, far-flung names, it's important to take a step back in an attempt to understand clearly why a chapel was built in the foothills of the Cheviots and dedicated to a princess of the Fenlands, a long way to the south. And also to understand something of the ancient granularity of a deeper English sense of self, one component of a series of regional identities that have been re-emerging into the light over recent decades.

Some of the earliest layers of sediment, of a sequence of historical processes, rely on a vanishingly scant number of written sources and a collection of unprovable assumptions salted with a generous shake of common sense. Archaeologists have discovered that Roman Britain died away in the fifth century after political and administrative ties with the empire were severed. Towns were deserted, villas abandoned and a new society was gradually formed. Recently historians have attempted to demolish or heavily modify an accepted sequence of events but their efforts have more to do with the academic rituals of a succeeding generation's wish to reject the conclusions of their predecessors. As the great historian of Europe and Poland Professor Norman Davies once told me, 'many academics spend a career attempting to murder their fathers'.

It seems to me that little or no new evidence has been well enough marshalled to change the widely understood sequence of events that took place after the end of the Roman Empire in Britain and the much later coming of first the Vikings/Danes and then the Normans. It begins with a period when immigrants sailed the North Sea from southern Scandinavia, north-west Germany, the Low Countries and, to a lesser extent, from northern France. This may have been prompted by severe coastal inundation, driving people from their settlements on the shoreline. Between 470 and 520, a trickle grew into a flood and Old English began to be more widely adopted in the east of England. Writing in the early eighth century, the great monastic historian Bede of Jarrow called this the *Adventus Anglorum,* the Coming of the English. He does not say anything very much about the native British or the fact that immigrants from the west were also crossing the Irish Sea. Once numbers (and intermarriage – it is likely that most immigrants were men) had reached a critical point and Old English had more or less supplanted Old Welsh (and probably what is known as Late Spoken Latin), powerful lords like Ida at Bamburgh began to assert themselves, take royal titles and make kingdoms.

This second phase became known as the Heptarchy, the time of the Seven Kingdoms, a model adapted by George R. R. Martin for his *A Game of Thrones* novels. The political map of the fictional Westeros has more than a passing resemblance to Dark Ages England. Northumbria, Mercia, East Anglia, Essex, Kent, Sussex and Wessex were all clear entities by the early decades of the seventh century. The first three were combinations of Anglian kindreds who had originated in southern Sweden and Denmark, many from an eastern area called Angeln, the root of the name of England. And they were also my DNA ancestors. According to Bede, the remainder were all Saxons from north-western Germany and the North Sea coasts to the south of the Elbe. He also mentions a sprinkling of Jutes from Jutland, and it seems that there were others from the Friesland archipelago and elsewhere.

The final phase of the formation of Anglo-Saxon England was its gradual unification. It gained momentum under Alfred the Great and his resistance to Danish incursions at the end of the ninth century. Athelstan, the grandson of Alfred, was the first king of all the English between 927 and his death in 939. His writ ran the length of the country, even including southern Scotland. While all of this consolidation was taking place, native Old Welsh-speaking kingdoms survived in Wales, the West, the North and in Cornwall.

Leaving aside for the moment quibbles about the unlikely tidiness and apparent inevitability of this long, half-millennium process, it is clear that the Anglo-Saxon period forms an important part of an overall sense of English identity, as well as an emerging series of regional variations. Alfred is the only English king to be deemed Great, and parts of his story, the burning of the cakes at Athelney and the defeat of the Danes, are widely remembered. More powerful is the notion that the Anglo-Saxons were, and perhaps still are, the English, and vice-versa. They gave the nation its name, originally Englaland, and its language. And when William the Conqueror, 1066 and all that, came along, the English became the underdogs, the underclass, the working class, ordinary people. Compared to the over-dogs, the wine-drinking Norman-French lords who decapitated Anglo-Saxon society and hid behind their high castle walls, the beer-drinking English became the salt of the earth, the yeomen of England, John Bull, the backbone of the nation. These vague notions began to harden in the nineteenth century when Britain, largely the English, began to acquire a vast empire, the greatest the world has ever seen.

Hereward the Wake: Last of the English was an enormously popular novel published in 1866 that turned a
Fenland rebel into a national hero. It sold in huge numbers,
and film and TV versions were made well into the twentieth century. I remember a particularly vivid BBC TV
series made for children and broadcast on Sunday afternoons that starred Alfred Lynch as the hero of the English
fightback. From the Isle of Ely, where Aethelthryth
founded a convent in the seventh century, Hereward led
resistance to William the Conqueror and his French-
speaking Norman oppressors. Almost unreadable now, it
was written by Charles Kingsley, a vicar in the Church
of England who championed working-class causes,
helping to fund and found labour cooperatives and
working-men's colleges. He also wrote *The Water Babies*,
an enduring bestseller that sold well as late as the 1960s.

Kingsley was an Anglo-Saxonist, espousing a set of
ideas that promoted a Germanic/Norse racial identity
for England. More, he believed that the Church of
England was 'wonderfully and mysteriously fitted for
the souls of a free Norse-Saxon race'. Even more remark-
ably, Kingsley held that the ancestors of the Anglo-Saxons,
Norse peoples and Germanic peoples, had actually, physically not metaphorically, fought alongside the god Odin
and that Queen Victoria was genetically descended from
him. Many seventh-century Anglo-Saxon kings claimed
the same lineage. Prominent intellectuals vigorously
promoted these ideas. The Liberal peer Henry Bulwer
believed that it was 'in the free forests of Germany that
the infant genius of our liberty was nursed'. Thomas
Arnold, the pioneering educationist and historian,

attempted some cultural synthesis: 'Our English race is the German race; for though our Norman fathers had learned to speak a stranger's language, yet in blood, as we know, they were the Saxon's brethren both alike belonging to the Teutonic or German stock.'

Crackpot stuff, especially a belief in the existence of a pagan god from a vicar and a canon of Westminster Cathedral. But it was all widely credited. These notions of racial superiority were not thought to be eccentricities in the nineteenth century, and they are the unmistakable ancestors of the evil ideologies that drenched Europe in blood in the twentieth.

This way of seeing the English as a superior race requires inferiors, the 'other', those who pale by comparison. One of the recurring themes of Anglo-Saxonism was contempt for what Kingsley, Thomas Carlyle, Thomas Arnold and others saw as the Celtic peoples of Britain. This was particularly noticeable in the Scottish Lowlands, where people increasingly identified with the Teutonic world and the superiority of the Anglo-Saxons. Gaelic-speaking Highlanders were characterised as a lazy, weak and inferior race who babbled a primitive language and suffered from what they themselves called '*miorun mor nan Gall*', the great ill-will of the Lowlander.

These attitudes persist. I witnessed them first-hand in 1989 when the Conservative government surprised everyone by announcing a substantial fund for the production of television programmes in the Gaelic language. Some of these were to be broadcast at peak time on ITV. At that time I was director of programmes at Scottish Television and, at one meeting, I was compelled to deliver a warning about what I saw as naked prejudice against the Highlanders and Islanders we would be working with in making this raft of new productions. We were all used to being thought of as peripheral, unimportant, even quaint, by the London-based TV companies and we should not be treating the Gaels in the same way, passing on the same prejudices. 'We all think we are patronised by London. Let's not have Glasgow patronise Stornoway,' I said. I am not certain that message hit home as much as it should have.

The English sometimes saw and still see the Welsh in the same way. In 2005 the journalist and restaurant critic A. A. Gill launched a tirade, calling the Welsh 'loquacious, dissemblers, immoral liars, stunted, bigoted, dark, ugly, pugnacious little trolls'. Had he said as much about Black or Jewish people, there would have been a prosecution. In the event there was little more than a chorus of grumbling west of the Severn. The Welsh and the Gaels were used to such treatment. These racist attitudes persist in Britain, rumbling like an unwelcome base note under the debates about devolution and also matters of identity.

Recently cultural references long hidden inside the indiscriminate characterisation of England and the English as Anglo-Saxon have begun to emerge. The Heptarchy has become more than a historian's label and taken on new life. At the border crossing at Berwick, the ancient Northumbrian royal colours of yellow and purple flew beside the dual carriageway, and by chance I came across an even more pungent set of cultural references, some surprising memories and celebrations of Mercia, the kingdom of middle England.

The throbbing traffic of the M6, its frequent road-works and tailbacks, and its standard service stations can numb travellers, remove almost all awareness of the landscape they are driving through. To me, Sandbach had only ever been an unusual place name on a road sign at Junction 17. But in the late spring one year it became a destination. One of my wife's horses was due to compete in the Premier League Dressage at Somerford Park Farm, an excellent facility near Sandbach, and we booked a hotel in the town.

The little place turned out to be a complete revelation, steeped in the story of Mercia. Almost within earshot of the drone of the motorway, its medieval centre has been miraculously preserved. The irregular square or market place is not tarmacked or even cobbled but set with smooth river-stones somehow embedded but definitely not flat. Pleasing tufts of grass poke through and there is even a scattering of daisies. Almost all of the pubs and shops are very old and festooned with strings of small Union Jacks and portraits of the queen in celebration of the platinum jubilee, and off the square are narrow lanes barred to wheeled traffic of any sort. It seemed to us like a world apart, a place from another time, another England, a medieval town built on top of a Saxon settlement, preserving its shape.

In one corner, surrounded by a phalanx of concrete bollards topped with explanatory plaques, stood something utterly remarkable, jaw-dropping. Two tall stone crosses sat in massive, stepped-stone sockets, missing only their tops. More than twelve centuries old, the shafts carried beautifully carved biblical scenes and representations of animals, still clearly identifiable. Like most early crosses, they would have originally been painted in bright colours. The plaques told me that the long shafts and the missing crosses at their tops had once also been adorned with metalwork and embedded with precious stones. Tradition links their making with the coming of Christianity to Mercia and its kings in the middle of the seventh century and also associates them with the ancient bishopric of Lichfield, founded in 669. In the seventeenth century, iconoclastic Puritans tore the crosses down and the carved blocks were dispersed – but not forgotten. George Ormerod, a local antiquarian, reassembled them in 1816.

Around the cobbled square and its two spectacular monuments, the twenty-first century crowds in, with a huge supermarket, its car park, and a mall of new shops and flats above them. But memories of Mercia have not been forgotten. The pagan King Penda, who defeated Christian Northumbrian armies, gives his name to Penda Way. And beyond that I saw a police car. In 1967 four county constabularies formed themselves into West Mercia Police. Old and once-powerful English identities are coming back into the light, and awareness and curiosity are following the revival of the old names.

Others have been lost entirely. Probably in the second half of the seventh century, Northumbrian clerks compiled a fascinating document. Known as the Tribal Hidage, it is a tribute list that noted the size (and therefore value) of thirty-five kindreds in early Anglo-Saxon

England. It omits Northumbria (because Northumbrian kings saw themselves as Britain-Rulers, tribute-takers not tribute-payers) but includes the remainder of the Heptarchy – Mercia, Wessex, Sussex, Kent, East Anglia and Essex – as well as many others.

For four kindreds, the Tribal Hidage is their sole appearance in recorded history. No one knows who or where the Herefinna, Noxgaga, Hendrica or the Unecungaga lived. They have left no mark on the land and no scrape of a quill on parchment or vellum. The Jutegaga were probably the Jutes noted by Bede and they settled in the Meon valley in Hampshire. Tondberct, Aethelthryth's unwelcome husband, ruled the South Gyrwe of the Fens and his neighbours were the North Gyrwe, above them the Spalda (whose name has survived in the town of Spalding) and the East and West Wixna to the south. Perhaps the most arresting kindred name in the lists of the Tribal Hidage was that of the Wreocensaete. Theirs was a large territory to the west of Mercia and it bordered the lands of the Old Welsh-speaking peoples. It is probably present in the place name of Wrexham and the singular hill called the Wrekin that rises above the Shropshire plain, but in fact it has a Roman origin. Another cognate name, Wroxeter, derives from the Latin version of Viroconium. It means the place of the Man-Wolves, the Werewolves. The story behind that sounds more than intriguing, but it is probably buried too deep.

The world described by Bede and the Tribal Hidage was the world inhabited by Aethelthryth, the virgin queen commemorated on the windy hillside I was climbing. There are modern echoes close at hand. The Merse, the fertile countryside I'd passed through north of the English border, is directly cognate to Mercia, its particular meaning of borderlands linked either to Wales in the west or Northumbria to the north. And the virgin queen almost certainly passed close to where her chapel would be built. When Prince Tondberct died in 655, Aethelthryth sought seclusion on the Isle of Ely, where she founded a convent. But in 660 her father pledged her to Ecgfrith, the heir to the great and expanding kingdom of Northumbria. He was only thirteen at the time and she was about twenty-four, and so Aethelthryth continued her life of prayer and devotion and travelled north to the nunnery at St Abbs on the Berwickshire coast. It had been founded by her aunt, Aebbe. But when Ecgfrith became king in 670, she feared that her virginity might be in peril and fled south to take refuge at Ely again. She died there in 679.

One of the certain signs of sanctity was the miraculous preservation of the corpse of someone who had given their life to the church and when Aethelthryth's was found to be uncorrupted, she was immediately revered and made a saint. In the seventh century, this could be done without reference to the papacy. The sisters at Ely sought an appropriately grand sarcophagus for what they hoped might become a shrine and some of them travelled to the ruined Roman town of Grantchester, a place they called 'a small, abandoned city'. Amongst the ruins, they found a marble coffin. This episode was emblematic of another component of Englishness, one that I would soon walk through and wonder at.

Splendid this rampart is, though fate destroyed it,
The city buildings fell apart, the works
Of giants crumble. Tumbled are the towers,
Ruined are the roofs, and broken the barred gate,
Frost in the plaster, all the ceilings gape,
Torn and collapsed and eaten up by age.

These are the first lines of an elegy known as 'The Ruin', written in either the eighth or ninth centuries in Old English. It is a powerful, even lyrical, reminder that Anglo-Saxon society grew and expanded amongst the remains of another – the grandeur that was Rome.

Those who crossed the seas to settle in eastern England, and even as far north as the foothills of the Cheviots, could scarcely avoid noticing the marks that the Romans had left on the landscape. For much of the four centuries of Britannia, forty thousand soldiers had been stationed in the province, a very large proportion of the entire imperial army, almost an eighth. Soldiers spend 90 per cent of their time not fighting and instead their commanders sometimes embarked on enormous building projects. The largest Roman monument in the empire lies only twenty or so miles south of the border line. In 122, the Emperor Hadrian commanded the construction of a wall from the North Sea coast to the Solway Firth to act as a frontier, a limit to an empire that had been expanding quickly, perhaps dangerously quickly. The wall would also be a barrier to uncontrolled traffic and access. Its scale is vast and its impact spoke of the power, the reach and strength of Rome. The soldiers painted the wall white and on sunny days the ramparts would have dazzled and dominated the landscape. It was an unmistakable statement.

By the time Britannia was cut adrift from the empire in the early fifth century, the wall garrison had become overwhelmingly local, and perhaps even hereditary. Here is an observation from Procopius that sheds some light from across the Channel. He was a sixth-century historian based in Constantinople:

> Roman soldiers . . . stationed on the frontiers of Gaul to serve as guards . . . handed down to their offspring all the customs of their fathers . . . Even today they are clearly recognised as belonging to the legions to which they were assigned in ancient times, and they carry their own standards when they enter battle . . . And they preserve the dress of the Romans in every particular, even down to their shoes.

At Birdoswald, on the western end of the wall, a powerful lord converted the fort into a power base sometime in the later fifth century, building a hall for his warriors and retainers out of a granary. The walls still stood and the arched and castellated gatehouse lay directly in front of the new hall. Along the rest of Hadrian's Wall, surprising evidence has come to light that shows parts of it were refurbished and defended into the eighth century. Archaeologists have found no evidence of abandonment at several major forts and a considerable amount of material, such as brooches and pins of both native and Anglian design, as well as much else. It appears that the garrisons slowly mutated into the warbands of local lords; the fortifications were maintained, and all were fed and sustained by a *territorium* that was cultivated and protected. Uniquely in post-Roman Britain, Hadrian's Wall was a concentration of groups of armed men and it seems that these were slowly absorbed into the expanding kingdom of Northumbria. This core of military capability may be what made the successors of Ida so quickly powerful.

Buildings interpreted as churches have been found at the forts of Vindolanda, Birdoswald, Housesteads and Corbridge. As the imperial religion, Christianity was another legacy of Rome and the growing number of abbots, priests and missionaries in the north, many of them literate, was a network that to some extent replaced the imperial administration. The prestige of saints Cuthbert, Aidan, Wilfred and others further sustained the notion of Northumbria as a successor, as its kings basked in the afterglow of the empire.

Just as enduring was the vast network of roads the legions built, a web of communication that held the province together. Dere Street ran from York to the shores of the Firth of Forth and beyond. It struck north directly through the Cheviots and I hoped soon to walk along part of its length. Its hard, metalled surface survived centuries of winters, with little or no maintenance, and armies tramped along it well into the Middle Ages.

There seems little doubt that the new Germanic settlers consciously lived in the shadow of the empire and in time they would come to borrow some of its ancient glory in their political structure and rituals. In the west, amongst the Old Welsh-speaking kindreds, Rome's legacy still survived. Carlisle endured as a working town into the later seventh century. When St Cuthbert visited in 685, he escorted Ecgfrith of Northumbria's new queen (the replacement for the unwilling Aethelthryth), Eormenburg, and showed her a working Roman fountain. It implies a surviving acqueduct, a piped water supply and drainage. In the twelfth century, the chronicler William of Malmesbury saw a large stone building in the centre of the town, with an inscription to Mars and Venus on the entablature, and he marvelled at the surviving paved streets.

The kindreds and kingdoms of the Celtic west still saw themselves as citizens. Stones inscribed in Latin in Wales in the sixth century paid tribute to a man who was 'an example to all his fellow citizens'. Another spoke of someone who was a 'citizen of Gwynedd and a cousin of Maglos the Magistrate'. Many of those commemorated bore Roman or Romanised versions of native names. The surviving Welsh name for Wales itself, Cymru, comes from *combrogi*, those people who shared a common frontier, the citizens. Late Spoken Latin took some time to disappear and the sole surviving text of the sixth century, *De Excidio Britanniae, On the Ruin of Britain*, was written by Gildas, a northern cleric. Possibly based in Carlisle, he had access to books and his plagiarisms showed he was aware of the literary heritage of Rome.

The principal and most enduring legacy of the empire was Christianity, the official religion since the time of

Constantine the Great in the early fourth century. It survived in Galloway, and the missionary work of Ninian spread the word of God wider. Ireland sent Columba to the Hebrides in 563 and others followed in his wake, sailing their curraghs up the Atlantic shore. In Wales, David and a host of other saints kept the lamps of the faith alight. It was mostly from the west that missionaries came to convert the pagan Angles, while Pope Gregory I sent Augustine to the south of England to found his great abbey at Canterbury in the Saxon kingdom of Kent. And in the swirl of the winds across the Cheviots, prayers were chanted in St Ethelreda's lonely chapel and men and women lifted their faces to the big skies above the hills to seek their salvation.

I've been very interested in post-Roman Britain for a long time. After the links with the disintegrating empire in the west were severed, it seemed to me that there followed a time when Britain was forming, identities coalescing, new languages spoken and shifting, enduring cultural influences like the Church beginning to establish themselves, all of them taking on distinctive characteristics. The fact that surviving written records for the fifth, sixth and seventh centuries are vanishingly scant has given this period the name of the Dark Ages. I like mysteries and puzzles, and I'm comfortable with messy and imprecise answers to complicated questions. The older I've become, the more suspicious I am of certainty. And so as I tramped onwards from the patch of nettles that might or might not mark the site of St Ethelreda's Chapel, I found myself thinking not of answers so much as patterns, patchworks, how the near-invisible shifts and disruptions of the Dark Ages came to inform notions of Englishness and Scottishness.

Beyond the gate and the scatter of worked stones beside it, I skirted the steep banks of the Countrup Sike and passed close to a wide foxhole in the open meadow. Or it might have been badger-shaped. What surprised me was its boldness. The hole or sett, clearly still in use, had not been dug in any sort of cover, in a wood or a bushy patch of scrub, not even in long grass. It was the home of a top predator, one not afraid of any other in the landscape, including human beings, those at the very apex of the food chain. Which was unusual, given the vulnerability of hill lambs.

I reached another metal gate, this one new and its keeper-post carrying encouraging signs. A solid yellow arrow pointed to a public footpath (not marked on the Pathfinder) and another had a silhouette of a walker and under that was 'Access Land'. It was all very positive, cheery and complete nonsense.

The new gate would not open because the curved hook at the end of the shiny chain was so securely set in the keeper that it could not be shifted, not even after a few blows from a stone borrowed from the dyke. Once I'd climbed the gate, I found a series of new fence posts (the tops had been trimmed off them with a chainsaw and were lying in the long grass) supporting a run of barbed wire. Perhaps this was the beginning of the promised public footpath; perhaps it would run beside the border dyke. That would be handy, especially since I could see a herd of cows grazing about a hundred yards away, many with this year's calves at foot, an unpredictable combination.

It turned out to be a very short footpath. After about twenty yards, it ran straight into a high and well-built dyke, this one topped with electric wire. I had to unsling my rucksack and crawl under the barbed wire. Very rough and tussocky pasture made it hard-going. The grass was so long and dense that each step was very tentative as I made a long diversion around the herd of cows. Being sure to make no eye contact, head down, I gradually left them behind as the terrain began to climb.

After a time, altitude thinned the grass and I heard the most beguiling, melodic noise. Somewhere immediately below my feet was a spring, and the water gurgling out of it sounded like the tinkling of the notes struck by high-pitched keys on a piano. I knelt down and parted some wiry stalks of marsh grass to find a tiny stream of bright crystal water running over some pebbles. Not brown or peaty, it seemed to fountain out of the earth with some force and that was how it made its music. The water was very cold and it tasted of something, perhaps lime. Somewhere under the hills above me was an aquifer of pure sweetness.

When I reached the corner of the wide pasture, I came on a consumption cairn, a pile of massive stones that had been laboriously levered up out of the ground and somehow shifted to the margins. The sheer muscle power needed – and surely ponies were involved – must have been immense. The border dyke turned almost due south. Another much longer, and therefore much dafter, 'footpath' fence ran beside it. This one was narrower, and ferns and bracken completely obscured the ground. No doubt the barbed wire had discouraged the cows from grazing down the lush growth. If I had ducked under it, followed this mad footpath, lost my footing and my balance, my first instinct would have been to grab the barbed wire. Completely barmy. And none of this would have been cheap, considering the logistics of getting men and materials up to this location. I stayed on the pasture and began to climb up towards much higher ground, to the saddle between Coldsmouth Hill and Burnt Humbleton.

Waist-high bracken made walking on the English side difficult. Across the dyke, Scotland looked much more appealing, the grass well grazed, although I couldn't see any stock, sheep or cows. In any case, walking through this bit of England would have soon become impossible. A dense Sitka wood blocked any progress. As I made my way slowly up the steeper ground, I resisted the temptation to turn and look at the views opening to the north. It was just as well. Longer grass and big, toadstool-like tussocks meant I had to keep my eyes on the ground directly in front of me. If I hadn't been concentrating, I might have stood on one of the most perfectly beautiful creatures I have ever seen.

Almost completely hidden in the long grass was a new-born roe deer fawn. Curled in a circle like a sleeping cat, it lay absolutely still, not even flicking its ears at the flies. I caught sight first of the white spot markings along its little back and then looked down to see its head resting on its hind-quarters. It was looking directly at me. Towered over by the shadow of a giant creature, the wee thing's heart must have been hammering. I moved away quickly, only stopping a few yards uphill to take a snap with my phone camera before carrying on as quickly as tired legs would allow. Somewhere in the dense Sitka wood, the baby's mother will have been watching, her heart also racing.

Though the saddle between the two hills seemed not to be far away, the slope leading up to it grew ever steeper and my pace slowed. I found myself pushing off one foot to another with my hands on my knees. I turned to look back at the sweeping vista to the north, across the Tweed Valley, towards the Lammermuirs beyond, thirty miles distant. Immediately below me there was no movement, only the flutter of birds and the piping trills of their songs, and I reckoned the roe deer doe was still watching me from the cover of the Sitka wood and she would wait until I was out of sight before returning to her little one in the long grass.

There was a welcome breeze up on the saddle and I stopped for a sip of fizzy orange juice, an Italian brand I'd found very refreshing. On the slope on the far side, bracken had grown up to the height of the border dyke, but when I crossed back into England I found animal paths made the going easier. Even when progress seemed blocked by Storm Arwen fallers, there were gaps where dead and brittle branches had been broken off – by what? Badgers, foxes? There was clearly a community of wildlife up here in the hills, one that suffered little interference from and only rare contact with human beings. Once the Sitka woods were behind me, the border dyke ran through open pasture and paths soon appeared, first the St Cuthbert's Way, and then later the Pennine Way, both very welcome.

I was searching the horizon for another ancient monument to sanctity. The Pathfinder showed Eccles Cairn a little to the east of the border. The name tells its story. Eccles is from the Old Welsh *eglwys*, which in turn is a borrowing from the Latin *ecclesia*. It carries the meaning of a gathering rather than a church building. The pile of stones is not large, but where it was built is breathtaking, dramatic. Under the vaults of a huge sky, there were long, shimmering vistas in all directions. A hazy, opal sun lit the hills, but a cooling wind blew in over the long hump of Cheviot to the south. Like a sleeping bear, its mass as much as its height dominates the undulating landscape. To the west, I could make out Staerough Hill and some of the houses of Kirk Yetholm peeping out from behind and below it. The name has a Norse feel to it and might be cognate to the root word for a star.

The most unexpected vista from Eccles Cairn was to the east. I could see the rounded summit of The Bell and just beyond it the slopes of its neighbour, Yeavering Bell, a high place that I'd visited twenty years before. At the cairn, I found myself looking through a window into history, a clouded, uncertain story of cultural synthesis, of how the British became the English.

King Oswald's Bernicia, unconsciously remembered by the purple and gold flag of the Percys that flew over the A1 near Berwick, was originally a native British kingdom. Known as *Bryneich* or *Brynaich* in Old Welsh, it meant 'the Land of the Mountain Passes'. Since at its zenith Bernicia had extended over the sweep of the Tweed Valley and the Northumbrian plain, I had never understood that derivation. Not until I stood by the Eccles Cairn, looking at its panoramas. I realised I was surrounded by mountain passes, steep-sided valleys that led travellers down from the Cheviots. Below me was the valley of the Halterburn, beyond it the Bowmont Valley, to my right the College Valley, and curling around the far side of Staerough and leading to Yetholm Mains, Shotton and beyond, was the valley of the River Glen. It flows between the foothills of the Cheviots and Housedon and Coldside Hills before meandering across the billiard-table flat landscape of the plain. I was looking at the core of the old British kingdom of *Bryneich*/ Bernicia and its network of fertile mountain passes.

The farming landscape was different fourteen centuries ago. Most prized was well-drained ground, where crops would flourish and sheep, cattle and goats could graze. Flat land often flooded and was boggy for most of the year. The string of little valleys around me that reached into the Cheviots had been densely populated in prehistoric times, and the evidence for that can still be seen in the patchwork of cultivation terraces, settlements and hillforts meticulously noted on the Ordnance Survey and Royal Commission guides. At the head of the Bowmont Valley the Pathfinder shows cluster after cluster of ancient farmsteads. Where only the bleat of sheep can be heard on the lonely hillsides in the high valleys now, thousands of people once lived. This was a continuity of dense settlement that reached into the historic period and, by chance, it was recorded and preserved.

The Old Welsh-speaking kindreds who farmed in the hills organised their holdings according to the *maenor* system. Its structure survived for much longer in early medieval Wales, and it has also hung on in both name and form into the modern period in the Manor Valley near Peebles. Overseen by a *maer* (a term that lives on in 'mayor') at a mains farm, a *maenor* was made up of thirteen farms in upland areas and its spiritual, parochial focus was the *eglwys*, the *ecclesia*, the church. In the *Scottish Statistical Account* of 1845, there were thirteen farms in the Manor Valley (there are twelve now) and an ancient church almost certainly dedicated to St Gorgian, an obscure Syrian martyr who died sometime around 350. It is as though the old landholding system was frozen in time. There exist toponymic remnants of *maenors* in many places in southern Scotland, but one was perfectly preserved and probably had its early centre, its spiritual focus, where I was standing, at Eccles Cairn. It was not a church but an ecclesia in the old sense, a gathering place. And it was no longer called a *maenor*.

In 655 Yetholmshire belonged to King Oswy of Bernicia. It was a connected string of thirteen farms, stretching from Sourhope at the head of the Bowmont Valley down to Shereburgh, Attonburn, Clifton, Staerough, Yetholm, Yetholm Mains, Halterburn, Shotton, Mindrum and three more farms to the east whose names no longer appear on the map. The *maenor* had become an Anglian *scir* or shire, and its shape was preserved because Oswy gave it in its entirety to the bishops of Lindisfarne in thanks for his victory over the pagan king, Penda of Mercia, and their clerks were careful to write down the details of what the Church now owned. Even when the border began to settle on the Shotton Burn, the old *maenor* retained its integrity. King David I of Scotland granted it to a Norman knight, Walter Corbet, in the twelfth century and he retained ownership of the four farms that inconveniently found themselves in England.

When I first climbed Yeavering Bell, I thought I would come across a blank, nothing more than a rounded, grassy hill with wide views to the north. But instead I found clear traces of dense settlement and fortification. There was a tumbledown drystane dyke encircling what were really two summits and a series of heaps of stones, the remains of a huge prehistoric hillfort built around 1500 BC. Much cast down now, the old walls had once been very thick and high, and I could see traces of what had been gateways. My research later told me that behind the formidable fortifications there might have been as many as a hundred roundhouses, perhaps a settlement of five to six hundred people. I remember wondering what winters must have been like. Everything, including essentials like firewood and water, needed to be brought up the hill, and that suggested the fort as the base of a powerful lord whose status was exalted in every way.

Political power eventually moved down to the foot of the hill, to a wide terrace of high ground above the little River Glen. In the 1950s archaeologists began to excavate there and they made spectacular discoveries, finding the remains of an important royal centre dating to the seventh century and perhaps before, a place Bede of Jarrow called Ad Gefrin. It is an Old Welsh name, and a rare use of a native British name by the great historian of the English. Yeavering derives from Gefrin and it means Goat Hill.

Over many summers of digging and recording finds, the archaeologists came across the outlines of remarkable buildings. Under what are undulating green fields now grazed by sheep, they found great feasting halls of the sort described in the epic poem *Beowulf*, a huge cattle corral, the only pagan Anglo-Saxon temple yet found in Britain, and a unique structure known as the Auditorium. Resembling a section of a Roman amphitheatre and wedge-shaped, it seated a sizable number where they could listen to the voices of status and power, and perhaps the word of God. At the narrow end of the wedge, kings or their proxies would have spoken. In a non-literate culture, laws, instructions or important news could be communicated here to all concerned so that there could be no dubiety or argument. Roman amphitheatres still existed at York and Chester, and whoever designed the Auditorium, probably in the middle of the seventh century, had probably seen one or the other. The Auditorium was a clear case of Anglian kings once more borrowing the authority and prestige of Rome.

What surprised the archaeologists was the tiny number of Anglian artefacts found at Yeavering; only a few shards of pottery and bits and pieces of metal brooches. It may well be that Ad Gefrin kept its Old Welsh name in Bede's history because it was already an established native British royal centre, the capital place of the kingdom of *Bryneich* or Bernicia, fed and supported by the produce of a nearby *maenor*, what became Yetholmshire. Other near-contemporary sources appear to suggest this, as they speak of Ida of Bamburgh in the mid-sixth century 'joining' his coastal kingdom 'to *Berneich*'. This may have been a more or less peaceful fusion. An Anglian warrior elite joined forces with a native British warband to make a new and wider polity, one that eventually expanded into the glittering kingdom of Northumbria ruled over by *Bretwaldas*, Britain-Rulers.

Yeavering was seen as important, a vital power centre, by King Penda of Mercia. When he attacked Northumbria in 650, his army made straight for the royal settlement at the foot of the Cheviots and burned it to the ground. Later in the seventh century, according to Bede, the halls, the great corral and the Auditorium were abandoned and a new royal compound was built at Millfield on the edge of the plain.

The story of Yeavering is uncertain, even mysterious, but it suggested to me not only that these windy landscapes, now very lightly settled, off most beaten tracks, were once centrally important in the politics of early Britain, the time of the Dark Ages. This story also offers hints that the Anglo-Saxon takeover was not always a takeover but may have been a settlement. The fact that early history was chronicled by Englishmen perhaps obscures an altogether more tangled skein of cultural processes.

When I walked down from Eccles Cairn to the border dyke, I discovered the closing stages of a much longer journey than the one I was on. The Pennine Way begins in Edale in the Derbyshire Peak District and for two hundred and sixty-eight miles, it snakes up the hilly spine of England before crossing the border where I was standing. The longest trail in Britain, it comes to an end at Kirk Yetholm, only a couple of miles to the north. Outside the Border Hotel, which offers a free drink and a certificate to all who complete, there is a modern version of a cairn. Against the gable end is piled a heap of discarded walking boots, poles, old rucksacks and a sense of achievement, maybe relief or a muttered vow of 'never again'. The hotel marks the end of the great trek and when I was passing through on my way to Yetholm Mains and the border, drinkers at the outside tables applauded two tired walkers as they came down the hill from Halterburn. Maybe the pile of old boots is more than a memorial to blisters and tired legs, more the end of a secular pilgrimage.

By the dyke, the Pennine Way path continues eastwards and I found travelling in the opposite direction to most people much easier. My Pathfinder showed a steady climb up to the Schil, at six hundred and one metres the highest I'd been above sea level so far. Below me lay the steep, wooded slopes of the upper College Valley, and on the far side the sleeping giant of Cheviot. The sun was quickly westering, but I reckoned I'd have time to get a little closer before turning back and walking down Halterburn to Yetholm.

Green and pillowy, the Cheviots are most definitely hills and not mountains. The jagged crags and tumbling screes of the great Highland ranges are very different, daunting and, for me, to be admired rather than climbed. But when I came to the edge of the Hen Hole, I looked down on drama, a sudden chasm, a gash in the hills. Near-sheer cliffs hemmed in the source of the College Burn, forcing it to race and cascade over the shelving ridges of grey rock formations. It made me shiver.

I'd come a long way since my exchanges with the farmer at Shotton and I decided to ignore a sign that pointed uphill, only one and a quarter miles to the summit of Cheviot. Steps by what had become the border fence had to be retraced and although the wind had dropped and the sky was open, my legs were telling me that enough was almost enough.

Day Eight

Distant Thunder

Marching was much on my mind, not only the business of putting one foot in front of another, but also the march of time. The Pennine Way follows the border fence along the Cheviot watershed after Eccles Cairn and it leads to an even older set of marks left on the hills. I reckoned it might take an hour before my own march fell in step with the march of ancient time.

It was a crystal morning of high summer, the sun brilliant in a cloudless sky. I had been rummaging around and found a wide-brimmed straw hat and a high-collared tennis shirt to protect my neck and head, and below knee-length shorts my legs were slathered with sun block. The sole negative on that glorious day was a heavy rucksack, full of bottles of water. I suppose I could have cupped my hands and drunk from the trickle of springs or burns, but being on the watershed and after weeks of drought, there might not have been many. And anyway, the more I drank, the lighter my pack.

The path was good, the gradients few, the vistas long and clear, and as I fell into a steady pace my thoughts began to drift in the warmth. Marching, the metronomic thud of boots on parade ground tarmac, is something I remember from growing up in the 1950s. Still in the long shadow of the Second World War, stories about soldiers seemed to be everywhere, and not just the cinematic heroics of *The Dam Busters* or *The Guns of Navarone*. National Service took two years out of the lives of young men in Britain until its end came in 1963, and TV series like *The Army Game* and *Bootsie and Snudge* were very popular. The first of the Carry On films was *Carry On Sergeant*, released in 1958. My big sister took me to see it at the Roxy Cinema, our palace of dreams. On lurid, red-painted brick walls hung huge photographs of Ava Gardner, Alan Ladd, Jayne Mansfield and Rock Hudson. They all looked as though they had jaundice, but they were tanned, Hollywood, worlds away from the black-and-white lives of reluctant young soldiers.

There was a lot of marching in *Carry On Sergeant*, as conscripts were bellowed at by a sergeant-major, but the shared experience of National Service and of a recent war meant that jokes found the ready laughter of recognition. Most of it sailed over my head. But despite the slapstick, the amateurism and the apparent lack of discipline, I knew that this was the British Army, the men who had defeated the evil of Hitler and brought peace to Europe after five years of slaughter and destruction. The Germans had been seen off, the French had been useless, surrendering after about five minutes, and the Italians had thrown away their rifles and run for the hills. But not the Bulldog British. We did not flinch, oh no; not even Charles Hawtrey or Kenneth Williams.

These attitudes may have been formed by events that

took place in the Second World War, several generations in the past, but they are enduring, if not indelible. *The Simpsons*, the American cartoon series much enjoyed by younger people, ran an episode in 1995 where a character described the French as 'cheese-eating surrender monkeys'. When France refused to join the coalition to invade Iraq in 2003 and support the USA in the United Nations, the phrase gained wide currency, and French fries were renamed Freedom fries.

My instinctive pride as a little boy was reinforced by the widespread culture of war comics, with characters like Battler Britton (most interestingly, the full name and title of this fighter ace was Wing Commander Robert Hereward Britton) and other Royal Air Force, British Army and Royal Navy heroes. And although there were occasional slips when (especially American) characters talked of England fighting the Nazis, it seemed to me then that my dad and many of his contemporaries had served in the British forces, the army of the whole of Great Britain. He had been in the Royal Engineers and our neighbour across the road, Angus Taylor, had fought at the savage Battle of Kohima against the Japanese in India. The Second World War was Britain's finest hour.

When I sat down, very reluctantly, in Miss Brown's class at the Inch Road Infants School in the late summer of 1955, I remember staring at a large map of the world pinned to the wall. It was covered in patches of red, some of them huge, like Canada, Australia, South Africa, India, and Northern and Southern Rhodesia. Out of date as it must have been, this map represented an enormously powerful symbol. The British Empire was vast, the greatest there had ever been, and even though India had left in 1947, and Canada, Australia and South Africa were effectively independent (nevertheless the title of dominions seemed to carry overtones of residual ownership and lots of Canadians, Australians, South Africans and Indians had fought on our side in the war, when we stood alone-ish), it still seemed to be ours, red and British. Buff Kyle brought a coconut to school one morning. It still had its husk on it and he said his big brother had taken it from a tree in India, or maybe Africa, while he had been on active service.

Change happened very quickly indeed, as the map was drained of its red patches. Malaya became independent Malaysia in 1957. Ghana left in the same year, and by 1967, just before I left school, more than twenty former colonies had been granted self-government. It was an extraordinarily rapid process, mercifully mostly bloodless, and it was baffling. But the empire was gone in less than a generation; the red patches on the map were history. Where was the British army, what had we been fighting for? Britain's sense of itself was transformed overnight. Of course as a teenager I wasn't aware of that so much as a general drift in our status. The world, so recently red, was now dominated by two superpowers, with vast and dangerous nuclear arsenals, and who could put men in space. Britain played third fiddle to the USA and Russia, and the Europeans and their Common Market were travelling in another direction, without us. As General de Gaulle said 'non' and 'non' again, where were we now? What were we?

It was baffling. We had won the war. Stood alone. Defiant. Even the disaster at Dunkirk had somehow become a triumph in our own version of history. The White Cliffs of Dover, serenaded by the ever youthful Vera Lynn, were our southern rampart and we were determined to defend them. But who was 'we'? That turned out to be changing, too.

In the summer of 1966 England defeated Germany, again. At Wembley Stadium in the final of the World Cup. Bobby Moore's team beat the West Germans four goals to two after extra time. As Geoff Hurst broke away down the left wing in the last minute of play, the BBC commentator Kenneth Wolstenholme uttered the famous words: 'There are people at the side of the pitch. They think it's all over.' A moment later, when Geoff Hurst scored, Wolstenholme added, 'It is now.'

After a decade watching the empire disintegrate, England had beaten the world, become the best football team, and much-needed national pride had been restored to part of Britain. Only the Scots had the temerity to remind triumphant England football fans that they had defeated only part of Germany; East Germany was still part of the Soviet Bloc. Matters were made much worse when Scotland came to Wembley, the scene of that World Cup triumph, in 1967. In one of the most stylish performances ever seen, they demolished England, the 3–2 scoreline flattering the hosts. It was a timely reminder that Great Britain comprises four nations and not England plus three colonies, little more than historical footnotes. The largest of them, even in its pomp, could be humbled. But England had ruled the world of football, for a time. It was all very confusing.

A year later, in the late summer of 1968, a sequence of shaky, self-consciously amateurish graphics, with one set of arrows tipped with swastikas and another opposing them with a Union Jack attached, seemed to joust on our TV screens. Accompanying this and the marching column of soldiers that followed was the voice of Bud Flanagan. His song wondered about the German threat to 'old England', and it signalled a clear shift of identity. England? Old England? What? I picked up on that immediately and so did my parents, as we watched the first episodes of *Dad's Army*. So it was England that had won the war? What about the Scots, Welsh and Irish regiments, never mind all the Commonwealth and Allied servicemen? What about the crazily brave Lovat Scouts piper Bill Millen, marching up and down on a Normandy beach in 1944 playing the bagpipes as battle raged around him? What about my dad, Angus Taylor, and all the other dads in our street? Didn't they win the war, too?

And yet I remember my mum and dad laughing at the pomposity of Captain Mainwaring, the weak bladder of Private Godfrey and the antics of all the others. The series was a brilliant play on nostalgia of all sorts and obviously it didn't take history very seriously. But in retrospect I think it signalled change. More than thirty years after the war, and more than fifty years ago, it was part of a general mood shift. *Dad's Army* seems to me now to be a powerful, persuasive and pervasive definition of post-war Englishness, the characters and the setting of Walmington-on-Sea clearly representative of a different interpretation of history, and not only the history of the Second World War.

The structure of the series, both in terms of plot and character development, as well as the source of much of the excellent comedy, is built on a clear sense of the workings of social class. Arthur Lowe's Captain Mainwaring and John Le Mesurier's Sergeant Wilson lead the platoon of Home Guard volunteers because of their civilian status in Walmington-on-Sea. Mainwaring is the local bank manager and Wilson his chief clerk. In contrast with their comrades, both men speak received pronunciation, usually a residue of a private education. Frank Williams' character, the Revd Timothy Farthing, is also an RP speaker and his verger, Mr Yeatman, constantly and cringingly refers to him as 'Your Reverence'. The others in the platoon, with the possible exception of Private Godfrey, are all portrayed as working class, deferential and as more than implied social inferiors.

In the second verse of the title song from *Dad's Army*, a Mr Brown commutes daily on the train to town, to London, probably to be something in the city, before returning, ready to face the Nazi hordes when they attempt to cross the Channel. The bowler hat, the rolled umbrella and the copy of *The Times* are all part of a familiar snapshot of the middle-class London commuter in the tellingly titled 'Home Counties'. It's a quintessentially English image. The Home Guard are, of course, all volunteers, and although some, like Corporal Jones, have seen active service, their actions and attitudes arise from a plucky amateurishness as the bowler is replaced with a tin helmet and the rolled umbrella with a rifle. This set of attitudes is perhaps better defined by comparisons. The heartless, ruthless Nazis were little more than murderous automata who obeyed orders without question and never seemed to laugh, except of course at the misfortune, or worse, of their enemies. The sense of 'we are not like them' was very important and made more real by different attitudes to war. The pluck of the underdog would win through, good humour and humanity would trump the grim and soulless efficiencies of the Hun. The amateur would triumph over the professional because they were nicer, good chaps, people who kept their word.

Vague, wispy, unquantifiable, almost uncatchable stuff, I know, and all of it is no more than a set of interpretations, a collection of impressions. But as with St Mary Mead, a sense of place and the settled order of clearly defined social class was important in the world of *Dad's Army*. It was necessary to anchor the fiction and set it in a credible, imaginable English context of the small and comprehensible place. Maps of Walmington-on-Sea can be bought on the internet, even though most of the filming for the series was done in BBC studios. Exterior locations in various towns were used, and Thetford, some way inland in Norfolk, featured often. The map shows St Aldhelm's Church and hall, where the Home Guard had their headquarters, a pier, Captain Mainwaring's bank and a few other locations. But unlike St Mary Mead, there are very few details. The map-makers have essentially pieced together Walmington-on-Sea from what they saw on television.

They did that to meet a demand. Viewers wanted to believe in a southern Brigadoon, a comforting version of life in an England that almost existed, a place on the White Cliff ramparts that was prepared to fight to preserve Englishness. Even though *Dad's Army* ended in 1977, the series retains a huge following, and since episodes are constantly repeated, its ageing fanbase is constantly replacing itself. It represents a powerfully attractive version of recent history that revolved around nostalgia and longing – a longing for a time when England was at its best, standing alone, sure of its values, and most attractive. And even though it was at war, it was at peace with itself.

*   *   *

I'd made my way west but needed to check my exact position for reasons of personal safety. The larger, uselessly double-sided Explorer map (far too big to be used out of doors – which is, of course, exactly where you would want to use it) marked England as a 'DANGER AREA'. 'If red flags are flying, do NOT enter', shouted a sign. I made sure I stayed close to the border fence, ready to hop over into the sanctuary of Scotland at any moment. Because I could have been shot at, but not as any sort of intruder or invader.

The Otterburn Army Training Estate lies immediately to the south of where I was walking. Established in 1911, it is a vast area, ninety-three square miles of mostly high moorland used as a firing range for artillery. More than thirty thousand soldiers are trained each year in the operation of AS-90, or Gun Equipment 155mm L131. When I looked this up, the technical information was bewildering but the photographs showed what looked like a big tank. The difference between it and the Shermans and Panzers of the Second World War is that the AS-90 can fire shells more than fifteen miles. One could have come whistling out of the clear blue sky at any moment. Possibly. The M270 Multiple Launch System is also hauled up onto the high moorland and it needs an open range of eleven by two miles to test fire. That is why such an enormous area is needed and why it is sensible to pay attention to red flags. The ammunition is live and signs become even more unequivocal: 'DANGER. Do NOT touch any military debris. It may explode and kill you.'

With the baleful return of war to Europe, and the attempted destruction and invasion of Ukraine, it gave me some surprising comfort that these weapons were tested and the skills to use them acquired at Otterburn, right on the border. I'm not certain if it is ironic, coincidental or apposite that Ukraine is the Old Slavic word for 'borderlands'. Perhaps some Ukrainian soldiers were being trained not far from where I was walking.

Otterburn was chosen as a suitable site for artillery ranges not only because it is remote from population centres and arterial roads but also because it is moorland – relatively poor, bleak land. As I made my way west, it occurred to me that views to the south and north are counter-intuitive. Green, fertile, rich, roses-round-the-door England only begins twenty or so miles beyond the ranges, whereas the supposedly colder, poorer north is nothing of the kind. On that sunny morning up on the watershed ridge, the Teviot and Tweed valleys looked lush and productive. Far in the distance I could make out the three Eildon Hills, the place the Romans knew as Trimontium. Below the hills flows the Tweed, and its biscuit-coloured cornfields and green pastures broaden out towards the sea.

As the Pennine Way turned to take me almost due south, the air was still. No wind blew and the silence closed in around me. I began to listen for echoes, the faint sound of men marching, the remote, rhythmic thud of the hob-nailed sandals of ten thousand Roman soldiers. Perhaps I'd be able to make out their marching songs, the jingle of cavalry harness, the creak of ox-carts, the blast of trumpets and the roared orders of centurions. Sometime after AD 79, the empire came north. Gnaeus Julius Agricola, the governor of the province of Britannia, led his men into the Cheviot Hills to invade Caledonia. And when the path rejoined the line of the border, I found myself walking in step with the legions, the men of the II Augusta, the IX Hispana and the XX Valeria Victrix. On the far side of the fence I could make out the line of a ghost road, a Roman road that had been built almost two thousand years ago.

Dere Street runs from the great fortress at York to the fort and port at Cramond on the Firth of Forth and from there to the Antonine Wall and probably beyond.

In the Cheviots its line is wonderfully well preserved and when I reached Gaisty Law I could see where the road bed had been shelved into the flanks of the hills, grassy versions of the spectacular autostradas built in the Alps by modern Italian engineers.

I spent some time tramping around an area of tussocky long grass by the border fence. My map insisted that near Brownhart Law was the site of something that had made these windy hills far less remote. The footprint of a Roman signal station was, I had been assured, easy to see on the ground – perhaps if you were a bird – but I couldn't find it. Nevertheless, archeologists much more skilled than me were certain that a tower had been built, and I could see why that spot had been chosen. The distinctive, conical hill of Ruberslaw could be clearly seen about twelve or thirteen miles to the north-west. There was definitely a Roman signal station on its summit, and from there messages could be sent to Eildon Hill North and then taken down to the commander of the great fort and depot at Trimontium on the banks of the Tweed.

There must have been an answering signal station to the south, a link in the chain that led to York, but I couldn't see where it might have been built. On bright days like this, sending messages would have been straightforward. A polished, shiny metal disc could catch the sun and, in a Roman version of Morse code, simple, rapid communication was possible. At night and on very dull days fires might have been used in a similar way. Only mist and heavy rain would have silenced the signal stations.

Just as a network of roads was built to draw the provinces of the Roman Empire together, a string of these installations relayed important intelligence quickly over long distances. It has been estimated that the commander at Trimontium could get a communication to York within an hour and receive a reply an hour later, if weather conditions were good. Not until the telegraph was invented in the nineteenth century did military intelligence catch up with Roman standards almost two thousand years before.

I gave up my search and walked on towards the Ends of the Earth. On an 1885–1900 edition of the Ordnance Survey, a complex of Roman marching camps and fortlets at Chew Green was labelled *Ad Fines*, literally 'the Limits', but it appears to have been fanciful, a name not conferred by the legions. Shame.

Nestled in a kink in the modern border, the telltale geometry of Roman fortification was unmistakable. From a distance, I could easily make out the long, straight ditches and banks of the camps, dug by thousands of soldiers. Whenever a Roman army stopped to overnight, precisely the same routine was followed. In the heavy packs carried by legionaries and auxiliaries were either entrenching tools or wooden stakes. Once a site had been selected and paced out, a well-honed procedure swung into concerted, coordinated action. Guarded by patrolling detachments of cavalry, watching for threat, men began to work quickly. With mattocks, they dug ditches and piled the upcast inside them. This was tamped down tight, and on top, others either drove in stakes to make a rampart or tied them together into spiky star shapes. The layout of each marching camp was identical. From four gates halfway along each wall two roads intersected at the *principia*, the command post, and in the same places as the night before, soldiers pitched their leather tents. Rows of these were set back from the inside of the freshly dug earthen banks so that they were beyond bowshot, the likely range of attacking archers. In particular the Romans feared night attacks and so each century of legionaries had a pre-arranged muster point always in the same place, so that as they scrambled to buckle on their armour and pick up weapons, they could find their comrades in the dark and form up. Gates were always heavily manned and passwords used.

At Chew Green, the transformation of a slightly sloping hillside would have been magical – had any native scouts dared to approach close enough to watch what was happening. Within two or three hours a camp would have been created as though out of nothing. The site was chosen by Agricola's advance guard because it commanded wide views but was also well watered. Nearby ran the headwaters of the young River Coquet and also Chew Sike. Water was required for cooking an evening meal, and men, horses and probably oxen needed to drink. Under a watchful guard, animals will have been led in relays down to the streams.

The camps are difficult to date, but the earliest was almost certainly dug by Agricola's army. A much smaller and later fortlet was built in one corner and it may have been garrisoned up until the end of the second century. Chew Green is where Dere Street reaches the Cheviot watershed before descending to the Kale Water and thence to the Tweed Valley. The signal station at Brownhart Law was manned and operated by soldiers from the fortlet. Its banks and ditches have changed little over almost two millennia. Still high and deep, their remoteness has protected them from disturbance. I sat down on the innermost bank to enjoy a gentle breeze, drink much-needed water and enjoy my sandwiches.

To the west I could see the outline of another camp, one that may have been dug as a depot for the work gangs of soldiers who made Dere Street. Also known as the Great Road or The Street, its construction must have been a tremendous labour. Once surveyors had pegged out its line, soldiers quarried and broke up stone to make aggregate, while others chiselled rough kerbstones and dug side drains. In cross-section, Roman roads were slightly curved to allow rainwater to drain off into the ditches. Holes could easily become puddles and as a cartwheel juddered into one, aggregate was splashed out and the surface would begin to disintegrate. Although soldiers did frequently march along them, Roman roads were not built to make troop movement faster and easier. They were principally supply routes used by carts, usually pulled by plodding oxen, that carried food and materials for garrisons. Riders could also move more quickly and more safely along roads than over rough country.

For two miles I'd walked in the shadow of the legions and marvelled at how the surface they laid down had survived the rains, snows and frosts of two thousand winters. Dere Street continued to be used by armies long after the end of the empire in the west. Medieval soldiers marched its length and cattle drovers herded their beasts along it. It became known as the Gamelspath and a small medieval village of the same name grew up amongst the ruins of the camps and forts. It may have been a resting place for drovers before they took their cows on through the hills and down to southern markets.

Following the line of the Roman road, the Pennine Way turned south from the line of the border. I had worked out that four or five miles' walking would take me past the edges of two large forests before I reached the main inland border crossing at the Carter Bar. There, the A68 from Edinburgh takes traffic down to the Tyne Valley and beyond.

After Dere Street and Chew Green and all the history and richness that swirled around them, I had mostly barren hill country and difficult walking to negotiate. There was no path in the shadow of the trees and I found myself following the sinuous lines of sheep-walks as I made my way westwards. Even though the ground was uneven and tussocky, and the luxury of the well-beaten Pennine Way, sadly, behind me, the grass had been grazed down and my pace was good. Instead of marching feet, I began to listen to marching music. Somewhere at the back of my childhood memories, hidden behind all the bad behaviour at school (I was a habitual truant and a practised liar to both teachers and parents), there was the faint, piping sound of men whistling. It's a sound I don't hear any more, but when I was young, men whistled while they walked and worked. I helped on a big milk round for the Co-op and the driver of the electric float, Tommy Pontin, wearing his army battledress jacket and navy beret, whistled all morning as we clanked empties into the metal crates and dinked full bottles on doorsteps. Distant at first but approaching quickly was a tune I remembered from the 1950s. In fact, I found I could whistle the first few bars.

'Colonel Bogey' was a march tune featured in the brilliant David Lean film *Bridge on the River Kwai*. Released in 1957, it told a story of Japanese cruelty and inhumanity, as British prisoners-of-war were forced to build a railway and a bridge in the Burmese jungle. When the ranks of emaciated soldiers were marched out to work in the baking sun and intense heat (the whole film seemed drenched in sweat), they whistled 'Colonel Bogey'. Its jaunty theme was given lyrics and, long after the end of the Second World War, we used to sing them, but only when no adults were within earshot.

> Hitler has only got one ball.
> Göring has two but very small.
> Himmler is rather sim'lar,
> But poor old Goebbels has no balls at all.

Unofficial propaganda, the lyrics of the march more than implied that the evil Nazis were really cowards, not possessing enough balls.

As I followed the border fence, the repetitive tune became like an earworm. The only way to drive it out was to find and sing something else. Heard only by the sheep and whatever creatures lurked in the shadows of the wood, I decided not to hold back, even though I cannot sing to save my life. My grannie could. When my dad and my mum went out to work on a Saturday morning (the five-day week was still in the future then), she used to switch on the radio. On the BBC Home Service was Uncle Mac's *Children's Favourites*. They seemed to play Burl Ives's 'The Ugly Bug Ball' on a loop and, as she peeled potatoes in the kitchenette or darned a sock by the sitting room window, my gran used to belt out the lyrics, easily drowning out Burl.

One of the other musical staples of the show seemed like a good way to shut down 'Colonel Bogey' as I tramped through the high pasture.

> I love to go a-wandering
> Along the mountain track,
> And as I go, I love to sing,
> My knapsack on my back.
> Fal-de-ri, fal-de-ra
> Fal-de-ri
> Fal-de-ra-ha-ha-ha-ha-ha
> Fal-de-ri, Fal-de-ra
> My knapsack on my back.

As a five- or six-year-old, I thought the 'Fal-de-ra-ha-ha-ha-ha-ha' bit was something only sung by girls. But there I was, almost seventy years later, singing 'The Happy Wanderer' as loudly as I could, leaving the shadow of the English forest and turning north towards a huge plantation on the Scottish side.

On the BBC Home Service at lunchtime on Saturdays, *Two-Way Family Favourites* linked up service families in Britain with our forces posted overseas. I always imagined the British Army of the Rhine hunting down Nazis in hiding and generally helping to tidy up the mess, but in fact their role was mostly to deter the Cold War threat of Russian invasion. There were also dedications to other soldiers, airmen and sailors who had been posted much further afield. It felt to me that Britain was still helping to police the world then, that the empire was still real and that war might break out at any time. Reassured by the caramel baritone of Burl Ives and a few bars of 'Colonel Bogey', the British Army would protect us and all of our friends around the world. I think that sense of being actively defended, with garrisons in Germany, Singapore, Aden and elsewhere, made us feel more British, more united by shared values, and we somehow expressed that by supporting those posted abroad. Our boys. They were the front line and we were what they were protecting.

In order to avoid Leithope Forest, I'd climbed the border fence into England near its southern edge. It was another vast and dark commercial plantation, most of it the quick-growing Sitka spruce imported from Alaska. If their succulent tips are not nipped off the seedlings by hungry deer, Sitkas can grow four to five feet in a year in the right conditions. That and their hardiness are what make them such an attractive crop. Woods can be harvested after only thirty-five to forty years.

When I reached the western limits of the forest and walked out onto Wooplaw Edge, a wide panorama opened out over the Tweed Valley. But my focus was much closer to hand. I could hear traffic, as cars and lorries climbed up the A68 to the Carter Bar and the border crossing. There was a piper playing and in the nearer layby a snack and drinks van seemed to be doing brisk business. But I postponed a welcome cup of tea and made my way down the northern face of the watershed ridge to read a stone.

Surrounded by a fence, a chunky, dumpy memorial carries this oddly set-out inscription:

ON THIS RIDGE
JULY 7TH 1575
WAS FOUGHT
ONE OF THE LAST BORDER FRAYS
KNOWN AS
THE RAID OF THE REDESWIRE

Anyone who looks this up in standard texts or online will be told that the last battle between England and Scotland was fought on this wide piece of open ground. To outsiders, to people who know and understand too little of the history of the Borders, that might seem like a plausible full stop in our shared history of hostility. But, in fact, it is a very misleading assertion. The truth is much more interesting.

A very old man had ridden up Redesdale from Northumberland on 7 July 1575 at the head of a considerable contingent of English Borderers. Sir John Forster was as old as the century and yet his authority was undimmed and his famous irascibility unmuted. As Lord Warden of the English Middle March and based at Bamburgh Castle, the old man was a Borderer to the soles of his riding boots and he had grunted, cursed and complained his way up to the Carter Bar to settle a few arguments.

For all of Sir John's long life, North Northumberland, Cumberland, Dumfriesshire, and the Teviot and Tweed valleys had been understood as different, unique, a place apart. The marches of Scotland and England were, in fact, a largely criminal society controlled not by either the Crown or the courts but by powerful families such as the Scotts, the Kerrs, the Maxwells, the Armstrongs, the Grahams, the Carletons, the Fenwicks and Sir John's own Forster kinsmen. Loyalty lay not with the kings of Scotland or England but with the heidsmen, the chiefs of the great surnames. Interlocking alliances between these families and their cadet branches largely ignored the border and took little interest in any national policy.

Scottish kings found it very difficult to impose their will and, far distant in London, the Tudors could do little better. Instead, the monarchies cooperated to create a unique institution, the march wardenries, in an attempt to impose order and the rule of law. Sir John Forster's Middle March was answered by the Scottish Middle March. Based at Berwick, the English East March was mirrored by the Scottish East March and, with a headquarters at Carlisle Castle, the English warden of the West March attempted to cooperate with the Scottish warden of the West March. In the middle was an anomaly. For the wild and largely lawless valley of Liddesdale, most of it in Scotland, a keeper was appointed by the Scottish Crown to dispense and enforce justice.

The system rarely worked as it should have. The Scottish march wardenries were usually filled by the heidsmen of the Maxwells, the Scotts and the Humes, most of them steeped in criminality. While the English Crown had a more secure control over appointments, men like Sir John Forster often ignored the authority of the Tudors and ran their march more like a mafia don than a royal official. He cared little for diplomacy or nationality and it was said of him that he 'knew too many Scotsmen'.

The realities of the self-governing criminal society on both sides of the border were well illustrated in the summer of 1547. At Pinkie near Edinburgh, what was in fact the last battle to be fought between England and Scotland had some reluctant participants.

The heidsmen of the Scotts, Humes, Armstrongs and other Scottish families had felt compelled to show willing and bring their men to join their king's army, and Carletons, Milburns, Forsters and Fenwicks had marched north with the English host. As battle was joined, the Scots Borderers managed to manoeuvre themselves directly opposite the English families. But someone was watching them, wondering what was going on. A sharp-eyed observer noticed that both sets of Borderers carried much more identification than simply the St Andrew's and St George's crosses sewn onto their coats 'back and front'. Coloured kerchiefs had been tied like armbands and letters embroidered on their bonnets. The national badges had, in fact, been attached so loosely that 'a puff of wind might have blown them from their breasts'. Even more suspicious, the observer saw that men in the opposing ranks of English and Scottish Borderers were talking to each other – as a furious battle raged around them. When both sides realised they were being watched, they engaged in a pantomime version of hand-to-hand fighting, making an exaggerated show of running at each other, and 'they strike few strokes but by assent and appointment'.

The reality was that the Borderers had turned out at Pinkie to be seen to have done their duty, but they were determined to get through the battle unscathed, whichever way it went. And, at any moment, they might have decided to change sides. It was quite simply not their fight; nothing to do with them and their interests. The dynastic aspirations of Henry VIII and the ambitions of the anti-English faction in Scotland mattered very little to these men and their leaders. Loyalty to their surnames was everything, and Scottish and English nationality came a long way second.

When Sir John Forster at last dismounted on that summer morning on the Carter Bar in 1575, he had several hundred, perhaps more than a thousand, English Borderers at his back. Accounts spoke of 'a flock of five hundred Fenwicks' mustering on the ridge, but that might have come from a poetic love of alliteration rather than sound arithmetic. Close to where I was standing, by the Redeswire Stone, Sir John Carmichael, the Keeper of Liddesdale, was waiting with a smaller band of men.

A force approaching from Jedburgh, ten miles to the north, was expected, but it was late.

A Truce Day had been set. These meetings were in essence outdoor trials attended by the accused and their accusers, each of them supported by hundreds of their kinsmen and allies. As such, they were highly combustible affairs, and for that reason strict formalities were followed. By tradition, the English warden rode forward into Scotland, accompanied by a few lieutenants. When Old Sir John Forster reached the border ridge at the Carter Bar, he rode down and asked the Keeper of Liddesdale if the peace would be kept until sunrise on the following morning. This generous allowance of time was important because it allowed men to ride safely home without worrying about pursuit. When Sir John Carmichael called out that he agreed to the peace or truce, both men held up their hands as a sign that both contingents could safely come together. The English riders kicked their ponies on down the slope to the flattish area surrounding the Redeswire Stone.

By the simple and sensible mechanism of the English side choosing six Scots and the Scots choosing six Englishmen, a jury was empanelled to hear cases and pass judgements on disputes. All went well on that summer's day until Old Sir John was asked by the clerks if he had, as had been promised, brought Harry Robson of Falstone with him, a man accused of wrongdoing, details of which are now lost. At the previous Truce Day, Forster's deputy, Sir George Heron, had undertaken to produce Robson and the case was held over. There was uneasiness. Perhaps the Scots suspected that the

English warden was hiding something (he probably was) when he said that Robson was not with him, and Forster may even have been complicit in whatever this man was accused of (he probably was). Tempers frayed. Perhaps strong drink had been taken. Insults were traded.

Most vocal was Old Sir John. Directing his ire at Carmichael, the Keeper of Liddesdale, he pulled rank, pointed out he had been warden of the English Middle March for twenty years, and what did the Scottish upstart know of the border and its people! Nothing! Forster even cast more than aspersions on the young man's parentage. 'Fye! Fye!' shouted the Scots. 'Comparison! Comparison!' The war of words suddenly escalated, as frayed tempers snapped. The Tynedale men, amongst them the flock of Fenwicks, loosed off a volley of arrows and some of Carmichael's men were killed or wounded. There is more than a hint that this fracas was deliberately fomented by Forster to divert attention from his likely collusion with Harry Robson of Falstone and whatever crime he was accused of.

But his calculated ploy almost immediately went badly wrong. As the Scots were driven down the slope, they blundered into the late arrivals from Jedburgh and their numbers were quickly swollen. As the Scots turned and fought back, Sir George Heron was killed and prisoners seized, including Sir John Forster. After the English contingent had fled, the Scots made it a day and rode down into Redesdale to steal about three hundred cows.

Queen Elizabeth I was furious. Relations between England and Scotland across various matters were delicately poised and the fracas in the Cheviots was more than embarrassing. The Scots were quickly persuaded to release their prisoners, but Lord Killigrew, the queen's ambassador, attended a commission of enquiry held at Berwick. 'The English warden was not so clean in this matter as he could wish,' he reported to London. But Elizabeth was merciful and left Forster in post, and he continued to serve both her, and himself, for another twenty years. The old man died in 1602, in his bed, older than the turbulent sixteenth century on the border, an age that he personified as a quintessential reiver heidsman.

The significance of the Raid of the Redeswire, as it came to be known, was neither military nor even diplomatic. It signalled the beginnings of a long end for an old way of doing business across the border. By the time James VI of Scotland became James I of England, the reiving centuries, the riding times, the criminal society of the borderlands, was already fading. It was unique; a period when family counted for far more than nationality, when a society and a huge part of the landmass of both Scotland and England disregarded central authority, constantly cocking a snook, and its leaders were tough, independent men, hard-riding and as durable as the windy hills they knew so well.

The reivers have not been forgotten. Their legacy is woven into modern society, into the rhythm of the years. Each summer the Borders towns hold festivals called common ridings and they remember the past as huge mounted cavalcades ride around the bounds of the commons and the important places in local history. As part of the Jethart Callant's festival in Jedburgh, there is a ceremony held at the Redeswire Stone and someone is asked to give an oration. Twenty years ago I was honoured to do that, but before I could begin, the past had to gallop up the slope towards me. Carrying the town standard, snapping in the breeze, and followed by his mounted supporters, the Jethart Callant roared what his ancestors roared on the afternoon of 7 July 1575, when the Scots were retreating down the hill.

'Jethart's here! Stand firm and sure, for Jethart's here!'

Just as English identity is granular and sometimes intensely local, Scotland's is by no means uniform. The legacy of the Border Reivers is still very much alive in the Teviot and the Tweed valleys, long memories kept and celebrated in the annual common ridings and the tradition of the ballads, a canon constantly added to. The border is not like the rest of Scotland; it has many cultural ties and similarities, perhaps more, with the communities of English Borderers, who live immediately to the south. Their shared history in the riding times is not forgotten. The existence of the thick black line sometimes distorts that picture.

It was early evening by the time I walked up to the A68 and the border crossing at the Carter Bar. The piper had packed up and gone home and I was much dismayed to see that the snack bar had closed. On the western side of the road, the border climbed up to Carter Fell and my Explorer map told me that after traversing pathless bare hillsides it disappeared into dense woodland. First the trees of the Wauchope Forest crowded on each side and then the vastness of Kielder Forest, the largest wood in Britain, much of it dense regiments of Sitka spruce, enveloped the line before it was swallowed up by the Newcastleton and Kershope forests.

I'd read accounts of previous journeys along the border and none of them had much that was encouraging or good to say about the next twenty or so miles. In 1926, James Logan Mack published *The Border Line*. Over six summers in the early years of the twentieth century, the Edinburgh-based academic walked in the opposite direction, from the Solway shore to the North Sea. The great forests had yet to be planted, but nevertheless Logan Mack found the section between Kershope and the Carter Bar very difficult: 'This region cannot be called beautiful; its chief charm, if indeed it has one, is its utter desolation.'

Well. Not encouraging, but worse was to come. Parts of the route were, he believed, dangerous, and his comments are made all the more credible by his dry, academic style. Logan Mack was not exaggerating about what he found when he reached a place on the border known as Hobb's Flow, where the Kielder and Newcastleton forests now meet.

> In a wet season its passage should not be attempted, and even in a dry one the traveller is not free from the risk of being engulfed in the morass. While I have crossed twice in safety, I do not advise that this route be followed, and he who ventures into such solitude should keep to the west and circle round on higher ground.

OK, I hear you, Mr Logan Mack, I hear you. No more escapades. The Explorer map shows the area at Hobb's

Flow as open ground but surrounded by dense forestry. If I had to seek better ground, that would likely have meant going into the trees. They are usually planted so close together – to maximise yield – that it can be impossible to make progress. And in that case the uniformity of these woods is such that it would be easy to become disorientated and lost.

I'd also read an excellent account of a much more recent journey from west to east by Ian Crofton. Like Logan Mack, he had had a difficult time on the same terrain. At one point it took him two and a half hours to walk one and a half miles. And he also camped in the forests as he made his way towards the Carter Bar and more open country.

As I gazed up at the fells, their south-eastern flanks now in shadow as the sun began to dip, I was not encouraged. What, if I did follow these two pioneers, would I learn by tramping between the trees and avoiding dangerous morasses? And I hate camping. And my wife would never allow me to stray beyond the range of a mobile phone signal. I have a slapstick habit of falling over and sometimes injuring myself while not looking where I am going, thinking about something else, looking around, taking wrong turnings, cursing the new maps, not paying due care and attention.

I decided to go around the featureless forests and meet the border as it emerged from their shadows at Kershopefoot. From there I'd follow it down the Liddel Water, and then on to Gretna, the Solway shore and journey's end.

Day Nine

The Lost Bounds

Kinmont Willie Armstrong was not a Scot or an Englishman, although he sometimes pretended to be both, one or the other, and most often neither. Above and before anything, he was an Armstrong and a Borderer. Like Old Sir John Forster, he lived a long and eventful life, rode forays for fifty years and never hesitated to promote the interests of his family, his surname and his allies. In the early sixteenth century, the Armstrongs accepted pensions from Henry VIII's exchequer as 'assured Scots', supporters of the English king's dynastic ambitions. In 1542, while little more than a boy, Kinmont Willie fought at the disastrous Battle of Solway Moss, when the Scots army was cut to pieces – but he was on the English side, the right side to be on at the time. Cementing local bonds, he married the daughter of his neighbour, Hutcheon Graham, and arranged for his sister's betrothal to his wife's brother. Kinmont's daughter became the wife of another ally, Thomas Carleton, deputy warden of the English West March and constable of Carlisle Castle. That relationship was later to prove absolutely crucial. When James IV of Scotland led a small army to deal with the Maxwells in Dumfriesshire, Kinmont Willie arranged a classic Armstrong ruse. To avoid confrontation and likely capture, the Maxwells were led, perhaps blindfolded (friendship had its limits), into that impregnable fortress, the Tarras Moss, a vast, boggy and treacherous wilderness in the hill country east of Langholm. The web of obligations, favours and alliances woven by the Armstrong heidsman was to prove his salvation.

★   ★   ★

'DAMAGED BRIDGE' warned a roadside sign, as I turned off to cross the Liddel Water and go from Scotland into England. Was this a clumsy, lumbering metaphor for the state of the British union? Both still worked but needed some repair. The bridge extended the metaphor by turning out to be narrow, needing to be negotiated with care, rather than obviously falling apart. On the eastern side of the river there seemed to be a few yards of no-man's-land before another sign announced the beginning of England. Looking back over my shoulder, I could see no answering sign for Scotland. Instead, travellers were welcomed to the Scottish Borders. Above the message was the logo of the council of the same name, a stylised drawing of a reiver, complete with steel bonnet, a spear and a pony that might have been rearing up before galloping into the charge. I'm not at all sure about the message that sends. A symbol of violence above a message of welcome. Welcome to what, exactly? The story of the reivers is unique, fascinating, but is it encouraging for tourism? Family holidays, visits to the sites of criminal acts, murder, executions, feuds and blood-soaked conflicts?

I wanted to look at one of these. Tourneyholme was a meeting place where Truce Days were held at the western end of the border and I knew it lay close to Kershopefoot. Once I'd passed the Welcome to England sign, I walked up past some well-set houses surrounded by the colours of high summer at their fullest burst. Flowers seemed to be everywhere. On the roadside by a white house there were more than twenty large pots of yellow, white and red blooms. I recognised geraniums and begonias in all their glorious abundance. Tall, mature woodland shelters the handful of houses from the bleak hills behind and the dark regiments of pines that carpet them, the sterile woods I'd declined to stumble through. Kershopefoot seemed a sylvan, cosy, peaceful place.

'Turniam,' said the old man, when I asked where I might find Tourneyholme. I couldn't place his accent on either side of the border. He had the billowing, roller-coaster vowels of the Northumbrian farmer who laughed when we couldn't get the buowlts in the hails, but he also talked of *yow* for you and *mei* for me, hints of the strong local dialect spoken in Hawick. 'It's just a field,' he said, 'nowt for yow to see.'

He was out for his constitutional morning walk with an elderly Yorkshire terrier who wandered about off the lead sniffing half-heartedly at last night's scent trails by the side of the road. The old man seemed very comfortable, walking beside me with an easy familiarity back down to the line of the border, his arms folded behind his back and a stick he clearly didn't need threaded between them. In the warmth, he wore a cotton check shirt, a pair of tracksuit bottoms held up by braces and what looked like a substantial pair of what might have been outdoor slippers. The village seemed like an extension of his sitting room. 'That's it ower yonder.' He pointed at a gate down a wide path off the road. 'Gan doon a bit and yow cannot miss it.' And with that, and a wave of his stick, he wandered off across the damaged bridge over the Liddel Water, his little dog trotting behind.

A brown sign I'd not noticed said 'Reiver Trail'. Promising. But when I reached the gate, I found a much-neglected information board. It had fallen off its supports and been propped up against a post. When I had cleared away the grass and carefully stamped down some poisonous ragwort, I read:

> You are actually standing in Scotland but just a few feet away is another country . . . But four centuries ago these fields at Kershopefoot would have echoed with the sound of fighting, with disputes often ending in murder.

I'd found Tourneyholme, or Turniam, no question. And it was indeed just a field surrounded by high hardwood trees. The fallen information board went on to tell a story of Mary, Queen of Scots' mad husband, the Earl of Bothwell, and an altercation he had with the notorious reiver Little Jock Elliot. It's a good story, but not the best story associated with the field I was looking at.

In 1593, Kinmont Willie, Will Elliot of Larriston and the Armstrong Laird of Mangerton ran a major daylight raid down into Tynedale. So many riders were at their back, probably more than a thousand, that no one dared challenge the reivers. The cover of darkness was not needed. They rounded up more than three thousand head of cattle and began to drive them back over the hills to Liddesdale. Lord Scrope, the warden of the English West March, got wind of what was going on and he instructed his deputy, Thomas Carleton, to lay an ambush. But Carleton's father-in-law, Kinmont Willie, his comrades and the huge herd of stolen cows somehow managed to evade the trap and simply vanished. Pleading innocence but in fact entirely complicit, Carleton reported back that he could not find the Armstrongs, not anywhere. Furious, Scrope sacked Carleton from his deputy wardenship.

There had been few Truce Days in the West March for some time and Scrope demanded that they be revived. Justice had to be seen to be done. A date was set at Tourneyholm, and on 17 March 1596 many men came, including Kinmont Willie. The usual assurances had been given, and at the conclusion of business the old reiver splashed across the Liddel Water to the Scottish bank and began to ride home. On the English side a large party of riders, some of them probably Tynedale men who had suffered in the great daylight raid, walked their ponies at the same pace as Armstrong. There was name-calling, and insults were almost certainly traded across the little river. But as at the Redeswire, ill-humour soon darkened into something worse. Ignoring the Truce Day immunity, the English riders turned their ponies, crossed the river, laid hands on Kinmont Willie Armstrong and took him to Carlisle Castle, where he was held prisoner.

There was an immediate uproar. Walter Scott of Buccleuch, the Keeper of Liddesdale, wrote to Lord Scrope, demanding Kinmont's release. He received no reply. Buccleuch wrote again. Still no reply. Finally the Keeper went over Scrope's head and sent a letter to Sir Robert Bowes, Elizabeth I's ambassador at the Scottish court. The English queen was old and frail by this time, and there were delicate matters around James VI's succession to be resolved. Bowes wrote to Scrope insisting that laws had been broken and that Kinmont Willie should be 'enlarged', or released. No reply. Lord Scrope had in his custody a man who had tormented him and his predecessors and he was damned if he would simply let him go. Behind the reassuringly massive walls of Carlisle Castle, he was defiant as well as silent. Matters, it seemed, would not go well for Kinmont Willie Armstrong.

Walter Scott of Buccleuch sent out a series of secret messages. On 7 April at Archerbeck, near Canonbie, about half a mile from the border on the Liddel Water, a meeting was set. Buccleuch, his close kinsman, the immensely experienced and fearless Auld Wat of Harden, and Gibbie Elliot of Liddesdale waited and talked over what might be done, about how they might rescue Kinmont Willie. After a time, Thomas Carleton and his brother, Lancie, arrived with Andrew Graham and two of his men. It was a meeting that reflected Kinmont's web of contacts, both English and Scots, all reivers to their blood and bone, and they had come together, united in their desire to deal with Lord Scrope, an outsider who had broken their code.

Carlisle Castle was near-impregnable and not even a huge force of thousands of riders could hope to take it.

They had no cannon or any other equipment and no knowledge of siegeworks. Buccleuch argued for a small, experienced elite force. Much better to go to Carlisle with only eighty or so of the very best men they could hand-pick. Auld Wat would be a seasoned, unflappable second-in-command. There would be a band of Elliots led by Gibbie, and no one could persuade Kinmont's four sons to stay at home. That was enough.

The English Grahams would look after security. The raiders would cross their land, moving quietly in the darkness, and the Graham scouts would sweep the countryside in front, making sure that they did not blunder into another party, or were observed by someone who might turn and gallop to Carlisle to warn the castle garrison. Most important were the skills of Ebby's Sandy Graham. The Englishman knew a way to get Buccleuch's men into the castle undetected.

At Archerbeck, Auld Wat, Buccleuch and the Carletons went over every detail, the whole operation, how to get out as well as in. Once they had Kinmont Willie on a pony, they agreed on a precise route back north. This was vital. Ambushes needed to be set for any pursuers. Through a trusted go-between, Willie Kang Irvine, the Johnstones of Dumfriesshire agreed to lie in wait in places with good cover.

Knowing Carlisle Castle and its garrison very well, the Carletons agreed to supply intelligence and do what was necessary if and when Buccleuch and his men broke in. Thomas and Lancie told the others that Kinmont Willie was being held in a house in the lower, outer courtyard of the castle. And it was next to an old postern gate in the western wall that opened directly to the outside. There was no need to attempt to get through the well-guarded and well-fortified main gate. The set-up was perfect.

At Archerbeck, Buccleuch and the others talked for four hours and hammered out a detailed plan that all agreed and understood. A date was set. The raid would run on the night of 13 April and all of the chosen men would meet on the day before at Langholm Races. The fun, the crowds and the hubbub would be good cover, as well as a reasonable, innocent motive for men to gather. The Carletons were insistent. There could be no delay. Scrope was capable of anything. And complete secrecy was vital.

It was raining when Willie Kang Irvine rode to the racecourse, splashing over the ford of the Esk. After he had sought out Buccleuch and was reassured that the raid would run that night, Willie wasted no time and rode west to warn the Johnstones to prepare to set their ambushes. When the racing came to an end and gloaming descended, the chosen men saddled their ponies and, in small groups so as not to attract attention, slipped quietly out of Langholm on the Carlisle road.

By the time they reached the banks of the River Eden as it curves around Carlisle, the weather had closed in. It was raining heavily and very windy. To avoid detection by sentries posted on the bridge before the castle, Buccleuch led his men around to the west. They would have to get across what was probably a rain-swollen river, swimming their ponies in the night. One of the riders later said, 'It happened to be very dark in the hindnight [after midnight] and a little misty.' It was good cover, but very dangerous.

There were no casualties, and once all the riders had crossed the Eden Buccleuch divided his force. Most took up a position by the west wall of the castle, their lances couched, watching for movement, waiting to see if the garrison on the walls had spotted them, ready to deal with any that sallied out of the Irish Gate. Meanwhile, a handful of riders dismounted and went with Ebby's Sandy Graham up to the postern gate. As quietly as possible, with his crowbar, mallet and chisel, he removed the stone from the wall that acted as a keeper for the bolt. And they were in.

There was no cry of 'Who goes there?'. No resistance of any kind. Later, Lord Scrope claimed that the heavy rain and wind had driven sentries inside, or they had fallen asleep. Or they had been bought by Thomas and Lancie Carleton.

Kinmont Willie was quickly found, roused, bundled out of the postern gate and onto the back of a spare pony. They rode hard for the river, but there was no pursuit; no alarm was raised as Buccleuch led his men into the chill waters of the Eden, to the far bank, and north to Scotland and safety.

A great deal is known of the detail of this raid because it was followed by an almighty row, an enquiry and repercussions. It was also valedictory, a last hurrah, a brilliantly planned and executed example of the skill, guile and courage of the reivers, men who in the 1590s and long before had ignored nationality, cared only for family loyalty, and come together to right a wrong and defeat central government – on both sides of the border. But the men who followed Buccleuch through the black darkness of that rain-soaked, misty and windy night must have sensed that their world was fading.

The end, when it came, when James VI became at last James I of England, was brutal and brief. In a concerted police action between 1603 and 1610, thousands of reivers were rounded up and enough of them hanged, drowned in murder holes, deported or ennobled to rid the border of its endemic criminality. Walter Scott of Buccleuch took ship for the 'Belgic Wars' with two thousand men to fight as mercenaries in the Dutch war of independence against Spain. The Grahams were deported to Ireland and on market days notorious thieves no longer strutted the streets of Hexham or Hawick.

But these men and their riding times are not forgotten, and two emblematic moments in the history of the USA are a striking memory. When President-Elect Richard Nixon was inaugurated on 20 January 1969, he was flanked by the Revd Billy Graham and former President Lyndon Johnson. All are the descendants of Border Reivers and all have the square-jawed, stern faces of determined men, men who might have ridden to Carlisle on a rainswept night to see their version of justice done. And when, the following year, Neil Armstrong rode the moonlight as his ancestor, Kinmont Willie, could never have done, when he reached out and touched the moon, it was the greatest raid ever run.

★   ★   ★

'This is the old trackbed, isn't it?' When I walked back from Tourneyholme to the road that led up into the village, I met the old man and his dog returning from their constitutional. I'd decided to follow the track of the Waverley Line as far south as I could. It ran very close to the border, the midstream of the Liddel Water, and it was as close as I could get without using a canoe.

'It is,' he said. 'Yow here to see what Beeching chopped?' He spat out with some venom the name of the man who had recommended the closure of the line more than fifty years ago. It turned out that the old man had worked for British Rail as a linesman. His job had been to walk a section of the route and check for problems or obstructions. 'Seven miles, I had. The big tunnel at Whitrope was the safest. Nearly a mile long, but I never saw one stone come out of it. Not one.' He must have used a powerful torch in the darkness. 'Icicles were bad, though. Dangerous.' He held out his hands wide. 'Yow had to watch when you knocked them doon.' In darkness, I bet you did. When I asked him about the state of the trackbed now, he shook his head. 'Damned shame,' said the old man whose job it had been to keep it clear. 'It's aal overgrown. Grass up to your chest. Young trees are the worst of it. Bad, in places.'

When I walked back down to the trackbed, I saw that it led south through a tunnel of trees in full leaf. It looked like a wormhole that would lead me back to another place and another time. There was no sign of the station platform at Kershopefoot, even though the place owed its existence to the railway. But at least a road led to it.

In the depths of the Wauchope Forest, north of where

I began my journey, surrounded by massed ranks of hundreds of thousands of Sitka spruce, is a relic, a boarded-up and tumble-down memory of a time unimaginable to us now. Riccarton Junction was a railway village built in 1862 on what became known as the Waverley Line. It ran from Edinburgh through the Borders to Carlisle. And it was Riccarton's sole link with the outside world. No road led to the village until 1963, when a forest track was laid down. There were thirty houses, a station complete with a ticket office and a waiting room, a grocery shop on the platform because all it sold came by rail, and a school. All the men worked for the railway company. If anyone wanted to go anywhere, they had to take the train. The village was created to serve a junction between the Waverley Line and the Border Counties Railway. It led east to Kielder, the Tyne Valley and Hexham.

In the middle of the nineteenth century, railway-building boomed in Britain and it was a revolution that took place over a very short period. Steam trains made the world move much faster. Before gangs of navvies began the back-breaking pick, shovel and barrow work of making cuttings, building tunnels and viaducts, and laying down thousands of miles of trackbeds, transport was very slow and small-scale, just carts and coaches, almost all of it horse-drawn. Most people walked. With the rapid spread of a rail network all over Britain, bulk goods, post and parcels, and large numbers of people, could be transported much more quickly and comfortably than ever before. Business boomed and the world grew smaller.

At Kershopefoot I could see that the goods yard, the

sheds, stores and the railway track itself, had all completely disappeared, but the station master's house and the ticket office still stood behind a high hedge. A ticket was bought there sometime in the 1930s and it survives in the collection of an enthusiast. Valid for three days from the date of purchase, third class, it was issued by LNER, the London and North Eastern Railway, and it took the buyer from Kershopefoot to Badminton in Gloucestershire via Crewe and Bristol, from one small English village to another.

This sense of connection is very striking. Nowhere was in the middle of nowhere any longer. The British had come closer together than ever before because almost every part of Britain was linked by the web of the railway network. Before the trains came, a journey from Kershopefoot to Badminton would have taken days and been logistically a tremendous undertaking. After 1862, you just bought a ticket, the driver hooted the whistle, the big iron wheels clanked, the carriage couplings juddered and off you went.

And it was not just communities in Britain who moved closer to each other. My Uncle Bill worked on a farm near Hassendean, a small, rural station on the Waverley Line north of Hawick. He told me once that a few years before the outbreak of the Second World War the son of one of the local landowners was on leave from the army. To rejoin his unit, the young man bought a railway ticket at the tiny station. The clerk had no difficulty in selling him a return from Hassendean to New Dehli.

With so much at stake, the early private railway companies competed ferociously, often raising huge sums from investors to build new lines, always hoping to make big profits. But there was also a little sentiment involved. The North British Railway, based in Edinburgh, christened the route through the Borders as the Waverley Line after the series of historical novels written by Sir Walter Scott. Edinburgh's main station had the same name. The new line would cross the Tweed not far from Abbotsford, Sir Walter's famous house. It was also good marketing. Scott's novels were at the peak of their posthumous fame in the 1860s and 1870s and his romantic, heroic stories were in the air as trains trundled down the valley of the Gala Water and on into the heart of the Borders.

Almost a hundred miles long, the new line turned out to be very difficult to construct. The preferred route used the flat ground in the river valleys as much as it could, but it had to traverse two summits. Ten miles south of Edinburgh, Falahill, at the eastern end of the Moorfoot Hills, presented the first obstacle and the line needed deep cuttings and a circuitous route, with gradients that trains could climb at a reasonable speed, and without the need for locomotives at either end. South of Hawick, in the foothills of the Cheviots, was Whitrope Hill, and a long section of the line required a tunnel, as well as a substantial viaduct at Shankend. It was the tunnel the old man from Kershopefoot would walk through with his torch, looking for fallen stones, knocking down icicles in winter. Once trains began to run in 1862, branch lines were quickly built, the most significant linking St Boswells with Kelso and on to Tweedmouth and Berwick-upon-Tweed. I'd crossed its trackbed on my way south from Carham into the Cheviot Hills.

The Waverley Line was never the success the North British Railway hoped it would be. The difficult terrain meant that the journey times were slow between Edinburgh and Carlisle, and passing through thinly populated, rural areas, passenger numbers could be uneconomically low. What just about kept the line viable was goods traffic, especially to and from the textile mills in Galashiels, Selkirk and Hawick. Railway nationalisation in 1948 eventually brought a programme of rationalisation. In 1963 Richard Beeching published his report, *The Reshaping of British Railways*. It analysed traffic volume, compared it to costs, and showed that the section of the Waverley Line between Hawick and Carlisle made substantial losses, with fewer than five thousand passengers a week using it. The numbers on trains from Hawick to Edinburgh were not much better.

There was also growing competition. Before the Second World War shoppers and trippers from Hawick often opted to go to Carlisle and beyond by train. There was no other option. That was how people travelled. In any case, tickets were cheap. My mother, Ellen Irvine (who was born and raised in Hawick), and her sisters often went south. All of them working in the textile mills, they had money to spend and Blackpool was a favoured destination easily accessible by train. But when Dr Beeching's report appeared in 1963, habits of travel for ordinary people were changing fast. Second-hand car ownership was growing in Britain, rising from 31 per cent of all households in 1961 to 52 per cent in 1971. Trains were slow and cars took you from door to door. It seemed that the Waverley Line was doomed to close.

But not without a fight. Protestors rightly realised that the closure of the line and its branches would create what one historian called 'a railway desert', a huge area of Britain with no access to trains, without a long car or bus journey to a station in either Edinburgh, Carlisle or Berwick-upon-Tweed. This in turn would have the effect of making the Borders almost invisible, a place to be travelled through and not to, and only accessible by car, bus or lorry. The economy would consequently shrink as the area slid into the status of a backwater, and it duly did.

The last passenger train was an evening sleeper to London St Pancras that departed Waverley Station on a bitter night in January 1969. There were vocal and vigorous protests at Hawick Station and some of the points on the track had been tampered with. But when the train approached Newcastleton, north of Kershopefoot, the driver suddenly braked. His lights showed up a large crowd on the tracks, even though temperatures had plummeted and it was well past midnight. They had shut and padlocked the level-crossing gates, effectively blocking the route south. Two or three hundred from the village had been led by their minister, the Revd Bryden Mabon, to make a last stand, a grim protest in the freezing darkness of a winter's night. The crowd refused to disperse and eventually policemen arrived, having driven down from Hawick. When they attempted to push back the level-crossing gates, scuffles broke out, the minister was arrested and bodily removed. But it was a stand-off. The crowd flatly refused to budge.

On board the train was the Liberal MP for the Borders

constituency of Roxburgh, Selkirk and Peebles. David Steel had won his by-election partly because he opposed the closure of the line, and he was respected by the protesters. Steel brokered a deal. If the police would release the Revd Bryden Mabon without charge, then the crowd would agree to disperse. They did, and they did. And the last train to run on the Waverley Line rumbled on into the darkness and into history.

Protest never completely died, as fell predictions came to pass. The Borders economy shrivelled, as the textile mills failed to modernise and adapt, and were increasingly priced out of the market by Far Eastern producers and others. Alternative industries came and went, and it became clearer and clearer that a powerful stimulus was needed. After a concerted campaign involving some of those who had protested at Hawick Station in 1969, as well as local politicians, the Waverley Line, renamed the Borders Railway, reopened in September 2015. I had the joy and privilege of being a passenger on the first train to run south from Edinburgh in more than forty-five years. At the terminus at Tweedbank, near Melrose, the late queen performed the opening ceremony on the day she became the longest reigning monarch in British history.

The new line has been wildly successful. Far exceeding all forecasts, more than four million passengers used the Borders Railway in its first three years. There are far too many cars now; the arterial A7 to Edinburgh is a poor, winding, undualled and dangerous road. Parking costs in the city have rocketed. It is now much cheaper, more pleasant and quicker to travel by train.

Before the Covid pandemic shut down the economy,

there seemed to be a build-up of benefits in noticeably increased tourism, as visitors came down to the Borders and Edinburgh money began to travel south to buy better and bigger houses for less. But the real prize would be to convert what is essentially a branch line into part of the British rail network by reopening the section from Tweedbank to Hawick and then on to Carlisle.

Sadly, the Scottish Government is showing little enthusiasm for extending the Borders Railway, consigning the area to remain a branch economy dependent on traffic coming exclusively from the north, from Edinburgh and the rest of Scotland. Perhaps it is an issue of cost and scarce resources. The terrain remains difficult and a great deal of expensive engineering works will be needed. But I wonder if there is also ideology at work here. The SNP government is committed to securing independence for Scotland, but creating a new link with England that will need to be policed may not be a priority. If true, that is more than a shame. Are the economic prospects of the Borders being sacrificed on the altar of nationalism? I hope not.

Builders of railways avoid gradients as much as they can, and the tree-lined trackbed was pleasingly flat, making for easy walking and a decent pace. I met no one on my journey. With the quiet, the solitude was welcome, the sense of the past and the passage of time wrapping itself around me. Occasionally I'd see a steep-sided ravine on either side carrying a stream down into the Liddel Water, but I'd have no impression of walking over a viaduct. What might have been parapets were completely covered in ivy, creeper and willow scrub. When I stopped and attempted to peer over, I realised that I had no idea where the parapet began and ended, and thought better of it. Curiosity might very easily have killed the cat.

Hoofprints in the black mud told me that others came along the trackbed on the older form of transport that the trains supplanted. For some unfocused reason, I found that pleasing. Ahead I could see a splash of sunlight where there was a gap in the tree cover. A roe deer was grazing with her fawn, a little creature but much further on than the baby deer I'd almost trodden on, on the flanks of Coldsmouth Hill. The deer looked up, ears pricked, and then skittered into cover. When I reached the glade, it was as though I'd risen up to the sun and the clean summer air. But I also realised how much the tree cover had baffled sound. The engine noise of a tractor came from my left and, on the right, across the Liddel Water, I could see the road to Newcastleton and hear its traffic as big log lorries ground down through the gears to climb the hills.

It was a rusty oil drum that seemed to supply a thick exclamation mark where the open trackbed suddenly shut down. Beyond it were several tall bushed-out birches that completely blocked progress. A path led uphill to my left and I felt I'd no option but to follow it. This was what the old linesman had been talking about, what had grieved him so much. Out in all weathers, he had performed a crucial service in the cause of safety, as well as doing a job that hadn't paid well. 'Left the railways in 1960. The money was bad. Got an HGV licence.' Maybe it was because I'd been struck by the doggedness of that sort of day in, day out labour, done without help or even company, that I decided I wasn't going to let a few bushes beat me.

Having pushed through the thick lower branches of the birches, I found that the trackbed had been colonised by hundreds of dead and dying saplings. Most had fallen at drunken angles but I found I could snap my way through the bone-dry tanglewood, breaking down branches with my boots. The taller trees at the sides had kept the light from the saplings and the thick aggregate might have prevented them from sending down taproots so that they could drink. It was a strange, grey, shadowy place, this long thicket of dead, leafless young trees.

Ahead I could make out where the wood ended. An old, rusty gate had been lashed to some posts with binder twine, and some lengths of wire stock-fencing stretched across it. Rickety gates and fences are hard, even dangerous, to climb, but at least I could see no barbed wire. Once over, I couldn't make out the trackbed; there was no clear line in the rough pasture that lay beyond the wood. Then I almost tripped over a sure sign. Half-buried in the long grass was a broken section of a concrete sleeper, a relic left behind when the work gangs lifted the rails of the Waverley Line after 1969. I found several at intervals and they reassured me that I was definitely on the right track, in all senses. But the walking was still difficult. More than fifty years since the closure of the line, it was inevitable that not only nature would reclaim it, so would other users. Cattle had been run on the section I was following and they had made a mess, mashing the ground into a squelching morass. Large ring feeders had been set up on the hard standing of the trackbed, but the jostling hooves had created a deep bog. When I reached yet another gate, I found a double string of barbed wire on a high fence. Climbing through a row of concrete posts to one side, almost certainly a relic of the railway, I managed to clamber over a drystane dyke without dislodging anything, although the drop on the far side was an unwelcome surprise. But beyond it the state of the line was much better and I followed it around a long, looping, lazy curve.

Even though I had folded it as small as I could, my stupidly huge Explorer map was still difficult to read. Equally stupidly I hadn't brought the Pathfinders because I was planning to walk a long way and would have needed several. However, I reckoned I'd come about three miles in an hour and a half. My progress had been much impeded by the dead saplings and the number of other obstacles I'd been forced to negotiate. But I hadn't bargained for what met me around the long bend.

A new wooden gate next to a clear-felled patch of forest was unequivocal. 'PRIVATE LAND' read a sign in bold capital type, and under that in a smaller face 'NO PUBLIC RIGHT OF WAY'. The tone was emphatic but not as angry as the signs around Wark Castle. But I was surprised. At the time of the closure of the line, British Rail was in public ownership. I couldn't find out what happened to the trackbed after the rails were ripped up. Did it revert to neighbouring landowners? Did they buy it? Was the price nominal? I decided to unlatch the new gate and press on. I had not met or seen anyone since I left the old linesman at Kershopcfoot, so there was nobody to ask and I wasn't doing any harm or any damage. But after a few hundred yards I realised I might get shot.

The forest I was walking through appeared to be a

giant pheasant coop. Along the margins of the line there were groups of feeders, and in several places I saw large fenced and netted enclosures where young birds were scratching around. Through the trees to my right I could see the Liddel Water and beyond it a big house, probably the centre of the estate I was walking through. Very quickly.

I find the notion of such summary prohibition difficult to accept when it comes to access to land, especially places where history, our story, everybody's story, runs through it. There is an awful lot of private land in England and its owners are perfectly entitled to forbid entry. A recent book, *Who Owns England?* by Guy Shrubsole, quotes some surprising statistics. One per cent of the population owns 50 per cent of England, and that comprises 'a few thousand dukes, baronets and country squires [who] own far more than all of middle England put together'. It is a picture, writes Shrubsole, that has changed little over the centuries. By itself, the royal family owns a staggeringly vast acreage of land, about 1.4 per cent.

In Scotland, there is a misperception, a belief that the picture is different, somehow more democratic. It is not. Half of the landmass of Scotland is owned by four hundred and thirty-two individuals. Arguably, private landownership is more significant north of the border. What is different is the issue of access, and that's probably why big signs saying 'Keep Out' make me feel uncomfortable.

The 'right to roam' legislation enacted by the Scottish Parliament in 2003 allows walkers to cross private land

and camp and picnic there under certain sensible conditions. There are idiots, of course, who abuse these new rights. Our small farm is near a town and has good tracks through it. But more than once we have had people walk through our garden around the farmhouse and, when challenged, some of them claim that the 'right to roam' legislation allows them to go where they please. It does not. The same is true when we have stock in the fields. Walkers can cross, but must give the animals a wide berth, and if they are injured, we have no liability. The worst excess we've had to deal with was a couple who parked their car in the gateway to the track that leads to the farm and the stables, completely blocking access. When I saw the empty and locked car, I assumed the thoughtless idiots had gone walking, but I'd no idea where and I wasn't about to spend hours looking for them. My neighbour kindly came up with a tractor and we attached a chain to the car bumper, dragged it down the half-mile track and into a muddy field and shut the gate. I had to be persuaded not to padlock it.

Despite these incidents, I think the 'right to roam' legislation ought to be extended to England, but I wonder if it ever will be. Scotland has lots of room, particularly in the Highlands, but also in the Borders, where the population density outside the towns is sparse. By comparison, England is crowded and complicated. The potential for misunderstanding, as well as outright abuse, is much greater. Perhaps issues of access could be left to the discretion of individual landowners and a widely accepted code of conduct published. The Countryside Code is very general and talks about attitudes

('Be nice, say hello, share the space'), and it advises people to stick to approved paths and tracks. Perhaps something more specific would help.

Meanwhile I was listening intently for the pop of approaching shotguns and wondering when I could get beyond the pheasant forest. By the side of the trackbed, I could see relics of the railway, a small brick platform and more bits of concrete sleepers. I took my watch out of my pocket and saw it was a long time since I'd had breakfast. I didn't feel comfortable stopping in the private wood and so quickened my pace. By the time I finally came to another new wooden gate with a big 'PRIVATE LAND' sign on the other side, I was famished. Leaving that behind and an older sign, 'NO TRESPASSERS', I emerged into open country, sunshine and a handily eroded bank below a fence that made an excellent seat. I'd come about four or five miles and needed my sandwiches, my sugary fizzy drink and a rush from Cadbury's Caramel Nibbles, the latter close to an addiction. I had picked some wild raspberries in the pheasant forest (theft?) and their tartness went well with the chocolate.

The trackbed swung around past some houses and on into a very overgrown field. A road ran parallel and to get my weary legs going again I opted for the flat tarmac. The wild flowers and high grasses on the verge were alive with butterflies, some beautifully marked, others simply beautiful. I saw a cabbage white flutter into the air, its wings brilliant in the sunshine. Beyond two redbrick railway cottages with a chiselled plaque – NBR 1889 – I passed another thing of beauty: a wide, sloping hayfield with a string of mature hardwoods left in it. It's warming when farmers do that; aesthetics triumphant over a loss of yield. The hay had been cut into long, rich, green piles and a tractor pulled a whirling version of a harrow to both turn it and make fewer and thicker piles. Against the golden yellow of the ground, the colours were splendid. Nearby was the sound of an industrial process. In another wide field, a machine was picking up the cut grass and through a wide spout was filling a high-sided trailer. There were no fewer than five of these trailers, all pulled by tractors, their yellow warning lights spinning on their roofs, waiting to take over once a trailer was full. The speed with which this harvest of silage was being lifted was astonishing.

I walked downhill to Penton Bridge, to where the map told me the Waverley Line crossed the road. If that precise route is used, if and when the railway is ever extended to Carlisle, there will be difficulties. Three big houses seem to stand in the way. I found a passage around them and carried on south to a place I'd visited a long time ago.

Liddel Strength was once a mighty fortress. Hidden by trees on a cliff high above the river and its confluence with the Esk, it is immensely commanding and impressive. Ancient mysteries swirl around its deep ditches and high banks.

The railway line squeezes between the great fortress and the edge of the river cliff, and the views to the north are long. But the geography has been moved. When the builders of the Waverley Line found there was too little room at the foot of the cliff, they diverted the course of the river. That created a kink in the border, like the

Ba' Green near Wark, and there are now two more acres of Scotland that didn't exist before 1862. Liddel Strength is usually described as an English bastion on the Scottish frontier. It was destroyed in 1346 during the reign of David II and its significance withered after that. But, in fact, the story of this remarkable place is much older and it contains faint, gossamer traces of the doings of a man whose name is famous the world over and who has a central role in one of the most significant tales the British tell themselves.

In the early, shadowy centuries of the Dark Ages names are often all that survive, the names of people and the names of their places. Before it was known as Liddel Strength, this extraordinary fortress, with its ten-yard-deep ditches and vertiginous, manmade banks, was known as Caer Gwenddolau. The name has survived, only a little changed, to the south as Carwinley and it appears five times in various versions along the Carwinley Burn before the burn tips into the River Esk. It means the Fortress of Gwenddolau, a man who appears in the genealogies of the later sixth century as Gwenddolau ap Ceidio, a warlord based in the old Roman city of Carlisle. In 573 a bloody battle was fought between his soldiers and the host of Peredur and Gwrgi, princes of Ebrauc, or York. All of this is remembered not in any chronicle but in very early poetry in Old Welsh that has survived in the bardic canon of Wales. Bede of Jarrow ignored the doings of the surviving British kingdoms and makes no mention of the battle. It was fought at a place called Arfderydd, close to the old fortress.

Gwenddolau was killed in a great and bloody slaughter,

but the Battle of Arfderydd, anglicised as Arthuret, is chiefly remembered because it was the first mention of Myrddin, his bard. Unwittingly he killed his nephew, the son of his beloved sister, who was fighting in the ranks of the York princes. This drove Myrddin out of his mind and, as madness overtook him, he fled north into the great Wood of Celyddon, or Caledonia. A poem composed in his voice has these two lines:

> I slept alone in the Woods of Celyddon,
> Shield on shoulder, sword on thigh.

Myrddin's story became well known, and more bardic poetry recorded his prophecies. In the *Armes Prydein Vawr*, *The Great Prophecy of Britain*, it was foretold that the Celtic peoples of Britain would drive the Angles and Saxons back into the sea from whence they came. In a very early version, a line appears: 'Myrddin foretells that they [the allies] will meet.' Britain became known as *Clas Myrddin*, the Enclosure of Myrddin. His name also appears in the tradition of *Y Mebyon Darogan*, the Sons of Prophecy, the great warriors who will lead the combined Celtic host against the English. They knew themselves as *Y Bedydd*, the Baptised, and the Germanic kindreds as *Y Gynt*, the Heathens. It was a contest between light and darkness, between the soldiers of God and the pagan devils from across the sea, and between the Cymry, the inheritors of Rome, and those who would destroy the empire and its remnants. The first of the Sons of Prophecy was Arthur, the warlord.

In the early twelfth century, Geoffrey of Monmouth

wrote *Historia Regum Britanniae, The History of the Kings of Britain*. It tells the first coherent, and mostly fictional, story of Arthur and his attempts to hold back the tide of the Angle and Saxon takeover of England, and it was an immediate publishing phenomenon, very widely copied, and it quickly became famous all over western Europe. Some of Geoffrey's material came from surviving Old Welsh bardic poetry from as early as the sixth and seventh centuries. That is where he came across the story of Myrddin, his madness and his flight into the woods of Celyddon, and his prophecies. The *Historia Regum Britanniae* was written in Latin and Geoffrey Latinised most of the Welsh names. Arturus was simple enough, but changing Myrddin to Merdinus presented problems. Merdinus means Shitty One. And so Geoffrey simply changed it to Merlinus. And Merlin the Wizard, companion and advisor to Arthur, was born.

About twenty-five years ago I wrote a book called *Arthur and the Lost Kingdoms*. Gathering evidence from many sources – bardic, historical, toponymic and linguistic – I argued that Arthur was a real person, a warlord from the kingdoms of *Y Gwyr y Gogledd*, the Men of the North. They composed the very earliest surviving literature in Old Welsh. Another early Son of Prophecy was Owain ap Urien, a king in *Yr Hen Ogledd*, the Old North. But the Anglian takeover of southern Scotland obliterated those traditions and it was long assumed that everything that was recorded in Welsh happened in Wales.

There were, it turned out, many traces of the life and words of Myrddin in southern Scotland: place names and powerful traditions. The great difficulty was that he and Arthur could never have met, since Merlin/ Myrddin was born long after Arthur's death. Geoffrey of Monmouth cared little for such details and, in the interests of telling a good story, he put them together. And what a story.

In the late Middle Ages, the Arthur and Merlin tales faded. But in 1832 Alfred Tennyson published *The Lady of Shalott* and in 1859 *Idylls of the King*. The latter sold a phenomenal ten thousand copies in a week. There were many imitators and the Pre-Raphaelite painters enthusiastically took up Arthurian themes. Chivalry, the Round Table, the righting of wrongs, and the romance and mystery of it all cemented the story of Arthur into British, European and American culture. In 1958, T. H. White's *The Once and Future King* reinterpreted and renewed the legends and inspired the musical *Camelot* and the Walt Disney animation *The Sword in the Stone*.

The enduring popularity of these stories is difficult to understand. Arthur failed to hold back the tide of Angle and Saxon invasion, he was cuckolded by Lancelot, betrayed by Guinevere, duped by Mordred and he died in defeat at the Battle of Camlann. And he may never have even existed. Perhaps the answer is simple. Arthur was a heroic failure, something the British appear to admire. He was decent, chivalric and the name of Camelot has come to stand for a golden age. He was an embodiment of hope over adversity, and somehow came to be seen as the quintessence of Britishness. His Celtic origins and those of his mentor, Merlin, have long been forgotten and Arthur has cast a long shadow over our sense of ourselves.

Day Ten

The Last Day

From the peace of the overgrown old railway line and the ancient mysteries and dramas that echoed around the ramparts of Liddel Strength, I came abruptly to the roar and clamour of the twenty-first century. The traffic on the A7 thunders south to Carlisle, to the M6 and Preston, Manchester and Birmingham, leading deep into the heart of England. Even though the road was straight and visibility good in both directions, the whoosh and throb of cars and lorries was relentless and I had to jog across when a gap appeared. Swinging my rucksack off in a layby, I checked the map. Having walked in leaf-shaded stillness for so long, with only birdsong around me, I wanted to get away from the road as soon as possible but not blunder off in the wrong direction. I was looking for the eastern terminus of the Scots Dyke, the place where the border took a very different turn.

Across Europe most frontiers follow natural features and, with the exception of the Berwick Bounds and the Duke of Roxburgh's bite out of Wark Common, the border between Scotland and England runs along the line of the Tweed before climbing into the Cheviot Hills and marching along the watershed ridge. Having emerged from the darkness of the great woods, it runs along the Kershope Burn, down the Liddel Water and the Esk to reach the racket of the A7. Then it suddenly changes, striking almost due west in a straight(ish) line across open fields. What became known as the Scots Dyke is fascinating. A purely political creation, it was the first manmade frontier in Britain since AD 122, when the Emperor Hadrian commanded a wall to be built. Its remains lie only ten miles to the south.

The dyke divided an area that truly existed between Britain, that was neither England nor Scotland. For generations, the English and Scottish wardens of the West March ignored what was called the Debatable Land. About fifty square miles, it stretched from the Solway shore in the south to the edges of the treacherous Tarras Moss in the north, and was bounded by the River Sark in the west and the Esk and Liddel in the east. The wardens ignored the Debatable Land because it was ungovernable. The riding surnames of Armstrong, Graham, Elliot, Nixon, Bell, Irvine and others ruled over their own kingdom. And they were powerful: the Armstrong heidsmen could put three thousand men in the saddle in a morning. If substantial outside forces from either kingdom threatened to overwhelm even those numbers, the reivers could quickly spur their ponies northwards and disappear into the dangerous, trackless wastes of the Tarras Moss and wait for a government army to grow hungry.

But by 1552 the wardens had had enough. So long as

the lawlessness was confined to the Debatable Lands and its environs, it could be tolerated. When it began to spill over too often, action was taken. The Scottish and English governments appointed two commissioners from each side and agreed that the French ambassador in Edinburgh should have a casting vote in the likely event of disagreement over where the frontier might run. Henri Cleutin, Monsieur d'Oysel, appears to have adopted a direct, no-nonsense approach. Running west from the banks of the Esk, a straight line should be drawn until it reached the River Sark. The land to the north would fall within the realm of Scotland and the southern section would become part of England. Armstrongs and Elliots would become subjects of the Scottish Crown (and their responsibility), while Grahams and Bells would become Englishmen (and would be expected to obey the laws of England). Simple.

And it was. In theory. Work gangs appear to have started digging two parallel ditches at either end, piling the upcast between them to make a bank, a defining, unmistakable, unarguable border. An entertaining myth interprets a wiggle in the middle as an attempt by each side to carve out a few more square yards, but the reality was that a perfectly straight line was made impossible by patches of boggy ground. What was known as quickset or thorns were planted in the ditches to discourage crossing the bank and at each end stones bearing a Maltese cross were erected. It was first known as the March Dyke but eighteenth-century map-makers renamed it the Scots Dyke, the implication probably being that it was built to keep the Scots out of England.

On an overcast, damp and humid morning, it looked to me that the dyke and its immediate surroundings had been designed to keep everyone out. At first I couldn't get near it. The owners of a hotel that sits only a hundred yards into England had kindly allowed me to approach this remarkable monument through their grounds, but I could not find a gate. Not for the first time that day, I had to climb a barbed-wire fence, very slowly. Very carefully. Pulling the snagging barbs out of the crotch of my jeans was a delicate matter requiring good balance, patience and dexterity. None of which I possess. Swearing, I am good at.

Once over, I found myself in a meadow of long grass, heavy and soaked by overnight rain, but beyond it I could see the Scots Dyke. Or rather the line of the dyke. It is buried deep in a three-and-a-half-mile-long strip of dense woodland, what would turn out to be a formidable barrier – from every direction. Having climbed a second, mercifully lower barbed-wire fence, I found myself at the eastern terminus of this manmade frontier. It is marked by an oddity. On a small, slippery, algae- and moss-covered platform, surrounded by post and rail fencing, stood what looked like a wooden tombstone. With a hole near its tapered top, it also had the feel of a standing stone. Down one of its edges, I could make out some carved lettering, most of it wind- and rain-worn, indecipherable. Except for one phrase: 'giftie gie us'. It's part of a poem by Robert Burns and part of a much-quoted aphorism.

Oh, wad some Power the giftie gie us
To see oursels as ithers see us!

Oh, would some power give us the gift,
To see ourselves as others see us!

The lines are from the poem 'To A Louse, On Seeing One on a Lady's Bonnet at Church'. The sense of it is how horrified the pious lady would have been if she knew a parasite was wriggling around on her hat, probably having come from her scalp – and that everyone but her could see it. It's a good phrase that all of us would do well to remember, but the reasons why it had been carved (presumably by Scots) on the wooden marker escaped me. To see ourselves as the English see us? Does it sound like a bit of handwringing, ever so 'umble contrition for annoying our neighbours for several centuries? I hope not.

Beyond this enigmatic monument, the shadowy wood of the dyke stretched out through green fields on either side. There was a path that wound around obstacles and fallen trees, but it became quickly clear that Storm Arwen had ripped through this strip of woodland with extraordinary ferocity. Mighty trees had fallen, their root boles tearing up huge masses of earth that left deep holes filled with rainwater. The great wind had come from the north-east, for all the fallers had come down on that axis, and the eastern side of the wood was much more badly affected. Fences, deep ditches and old hedges running across the line of the frontier added to my difficulties and it soon became impossible to move forward along the border line. Sideways was the sole option.

I climbed a third barbed-wire fence into a wide field of well-kept pasture. There was no stock I could see, but the ground had been recently grazed, probably by sheep. There was none of the mess cows make at gates, poaching the ground, shifting about, standing and staring vacantly at nothing, anything, the very definition of bovine. Despite being soft underfoot, a rare condition in this summer of drought, there were no spiky clusters of marsh grass or many weeds, except for at the margins. Beyond yet more barbed wire was another big field recently cut for hay or silage, its bright green shoots of new grass just showing through the pale yellow of the cut. Compared to the tangle of the wood, it was easy walking and soon the traffic noise of the A7 faded behind me, big skies opened up and I could make out the silhouettes of the northern hills in the distance.

Making my way in the shadow of the trees of the Scots Dyke, it struck me they were a very effective screen, much higher than the original ditch, much more emphatic. In suburban housing estates, those anxious to enjoy as much privacy as possible often plant hedges of quick-growing cypress or thuja on the boundaries of their gardens. Here was a gigantic, eighty to a hundred-foot-high, three-and-a-half-mile-long hedge that prevented Scotland and England from invading each other's privacy. Except for occasional half-gaps where trees had come down, it was impossible for me to see through to England at all.

After about a mile of fence-climbing and field-walking,

I came to the most formidable barrier of all. In a deep, steep-sided declivity, the Glinger Burn flowed through the line of the dyke from Scotland down into England. Marked on the Pathfinder as a burn, I imagined I'd be able to throw my rucksack over (thereby committing myself) and hop across from one grassy bank to another. In reality it was much more substantial than a mere burn, deeply pooling in places, the water black dark under the overhanging trees and far too wide for all but an Olympic long jumper. And he or she would have to be surefooted. There was no pit of soft landing sand on the far side. The burn ran across wide shelves of mossy stones and through deep gaps between them. If I had found a narrow place where I might leap across, my landing site looked distinctly skiddy and dangerous. I'd got almost to the end of my journey without mishap and I wasn't about to start taking risks now. Coming closer to the bank, I thought I'd walk upstream to look for shallows, places where I might get across without the water filling my boots. As I climbed a fence, I put up a little flock of a dozen or so wrens. Some fluttered above me to settle on the branches of a willow that hung over the burn. With their tip-tilted tails and butterfly-like movements, wrens make me smile. I'm old enough to remember them on farthings, the smallest bird on the smallest coin.

Realising that I couldn't get safely across the Glinger Burn, I reluctantly left the line of the border and walked up to Glenzierfoot Farm. The sweet stink of silage greeted me, as I passed the tall concrete walls of a huge pit. Grass seemed to be a major crop in this part of the old Debatable Land and, far from the sixteenth-century descriptions of a desolate waste, these fields struck me as good, fertile farmland. Of course, modern drainage and good management have improved and expanded cultivation and grazing, but even before the Agricultural Revolution and mechanisation, it will have been valuable, productive ground.

Having turned west again off a single-track tarmac road, I found myself on a bridge over the Glinger Burn. Something plopped into the water as I crossed and a dog barked in the distance. Crossing another recently cut field, I rejoined the line of the border. Storm Arwen had wreaked spectacular havoc. For more than two hundred yards every single tree on the edge of the woodland strip had been knocked down, their root boles ripping up the earth as if a fissure had opened in the ground after an earthquake and the trunks plunging into the wood. Was this an all-too-obvious metaphor for the state of the British union and current relations between the Scottish Government and Westminster? Would another storm flatten the wood entirely and obliterate history? Or would a Trumpian wall be built instead?

It was impossible to re-enter the wood at that point and follow the line of the Scots Dyke precisely. From what I was able to see, peering into the gloom, the bank and its parallel ditches seemed to have disappeared. During the First World War much of the plantation was felled, timber being in great demand, and a railway line built on top of the border bank to make extraction of the cut trees easier. Despite vigorous protests from James Logan Mack that an important historical monument was being destroyed, the felling continued. In places, it looked to me that the old boundary ditches had been cut deeper to drain the fields and the bank had been largely levelled.

I came to a wooden gate into the woodland strip and beyond it lay a plantation of birches, too whippy and young to have been knocked down by the great storm. The last few fields had been uncut and the long grass was soaking wet. While my beige boots had held out and kept my feet dry, what my grannie called my 'breekfeet' were sodden. 'Nicky-tams,' she'd have said. 'That's whit you need, eejit.' These were lengths of leather cord or string that farm workers used to tie up the legs of their trousers below the knee to keep the feet, the bottoms, of their breeks out of the wet and the mud. I was also tired of walking against the grain of the wet grass. The wind from the north-east had blown it down and I had to lift up my feet to avoid becoming soaked right up to the knees. With less than a mile left to the end of the dyke, it would be good to walk its line, if I could.

But as at the beginning of the day, the path through the trees soon ran into more obstruction, more fallers, and beyond them I could see another deep transverse ditch. Why not try the English side? A hazy sun had begun to light the day and beyond the wood I could see a biscuit-ripe barley field, its whiskery heads rippling in what might be a cooling breeze. Only one last barbed-wire fence barred the way.

It was high, and below the string of barbs was wire stock-fencing. Having walked up its line, I couldn't find any gaps or a place where the fence was lower, and there was a continuous bank on the far side that would make climbing over harder. Under a birch with low-hanging branches I could grab onto, I put the toe of my boot in one of the square spaces in the stock-fencing and swung my right leg over. The height of the fence meant that the crotch of my jeans immediately snagged and I had to plant my right heel, not the toe of my boot, on the other side to stop myself from being cut in a very tender place. That made disengaging from the barbed wire difficult and swinging over the left leg almost impossible. So I grabbed the top of the fence post, putting most of my weight on it, and pulled out my heel to turn it around. And the post snapped.

I fell headlong over the other side and part of the way down the bank. But not all of me. The crotch of my jeans was still snagged on the barbed wire. When I toppled over, it ripped the fabric in a three-foot-long tear and left me with one leg still attached to the fence. Somehow I managed to pull hard on the hem of my jeans and rip through that too, as I freed my leg. At fifteen stone, I fall with a thump and was badly winded. Gasping and wheezing, I rolled on my side and got myself on my hands and knees. If I'd had the breath to swear, the air would have been blue. I managed to stand up and, remembering from my rugby-playing days, I bent up and down from the waist to reinflate my lungs. Looking down at my right leg, I saw that the inside of my thigh was covered in blood, the barbed wire having torn long, jagged scratches. And my left hand had several puncture wounds where I had grabbed the wire, trying to save myself as I fell.

With my hankie and some tissues, and using the wet from the grass, I cleaned up the blood as best I could. Still blowing hard from hitting the ground, I walked out from the shade of the trees to the edge of the barley field. But when I looked around to see if anyone was about, anyone who might have witnessed my argument with the barbed wire or heard my swearing when I lost it, I realised that my specs had gone. They must have flown off when I fell. Looking for specs without your specs is awkward. After ten minutes of crawling around in the long grass, the sun glinted off one of the lenses and I puffed out my cheeks in relief.

With the ripped leg of my jeans flapping behind me in the welcome, cooling breeze, I walked along the wide margin of the barley field, grateful that no one was around. I might have felt differently about being on my own if I'd suffered serious injury, broken something or worse, instead of looking like an idiot. I realised I must have been feeling better if I was worrying about what I looked like. Anyway, young people seemed to favour pairs of jeans with tears in the legs. Did they come pre-torn, or was it a DIY job? Whatever, I urgently needed another pair and no doubt the Gateway Outlet Village in Gretna could supply them. I pulled my watch out of my pocket, mercifully undamaged in the fall, and reckoned that it had taken me two and a half hours to travel the three and a half miles of the Scots Dyke. I was close to its western end, perhaps two fields away. After that, it was a five-mile walk on easy tarmac to a new pair of jeans.

I heard the piou-piou call of buzzards and looked up to see them gliding on the updraughts above the tangle of the gloomy wood, searching the ground for movement. Ahead there was more of the wild world. Three roe deer looked up from their grazing. The two adults jumped the fence with graceful ease, but I saw that their little fawn was too small to follow them. It fled away from me, along the fence line, and in the shadows of the trees I could see one of the adults running alongside at the same pace. The little one must have got out of the wood to graze and so there must be a way back in. Then it suddenly disappeared. The adult had been directing, leading its fawn to a place where the fence was not so high. I wished I'd found it.

About a hundred yards ahead I saw a double line of trees and a row of telegraph poles. It was the minor road that would lead me south, eventually to the mouth of the River Sark, where Scotland and England stop, where the line of the border spills into the Solway Firth, the place where my journey would end at last. But before I reached the tarmac, one infuriating, ridiculous barrier stood in my way.

Right at the end of the Scots Dyke there was a high and wide metal field gate. The farmer had wrapped the top two rails with tight coils of barbed wire, winding the strands so close that it was impossible to put a hand on the gate. It was also chained and padlocked. What was going on? On the Scottish side of the border I'd seen none of this sort of thing and yet from the Berwick Bounds to Wark Castle and the pheasant-infested woodland on the old Waverley Line, England had been repeatedly disfigured by PRIVATE! KEEP OUT! And this was the worst, the most vicious example.

The hedge of thorns was too thick to push through. I could see no other gate and I certainly wasn't going to climb back into the dangerous woodland of the dyke. By the side of the bristling, barbed gate was about six inches of wooden rails nailed to the thick gatepost and another hidden in the hedge. I managed to squeeze enough of the toe of my boot between two of them to get some purchase, and reach a point where I could swing a bloody, bare leg over to the other side. Pushing myself up on the gatepost, too new to snap, I managed to get over with only a puncture wound to a finger and without converting my jeans into a kilt.

Once I'd stopped the fresh bleeding with an already red hankie, I completely lost it, began shouting at the gate, cursing the attitudes it represented. I'd walked the length of an important place in Britain's history that had been all but destroyed by thoughtlessness and made almost inaccessible by defences that might have been found on the perimeter of a prison camp. I kicked the gate and swore a bit more. Our history belongs to us, to all of us, landowners and landless. It's our story and we have a right to know it, to understand it, to visit the places where it happened, not just read about it in books or online. Barriers should be broken down, not raised even higher. Walking down the B road, I passed several gates with barbed wire wound around them and chained with padlocks and swore at them too. The farmer must have a key ring like a jailer in a Dickens novel.

As ever, the peace of the countryside calmed me. I was the only traveller on the road. There was no traffic and I began to enjoy the clumps of wildflowers in the verges. Yellow blooms that I thought at first were poisonous ragwort turned out to be delicate, larger versions of trefoils and I plucked a blossom of meadow-sweet and held its scent close for a moment. At a farm, chickens pecked and foraged in the verge and did not scutter off when I walked by. A mile further on, a sign asked me to slow down for children and horses. Shaded by the broad leaves of an old chestnut where the flies were probably more tolerable, a beautiful roan horse was standing dozing, its ears flicking, the lids of its liquid eyes heavy. It seemed not to have a companion to stand guard and when I stopped at a gap in the hedge, it roused itself and walked over. I tore up some succulent grass from the verge to feed it and the gelding let me stroke its long, elegant nose and pat its neck. Horses are trusting, noble creatures. After the handsome roan and I parted company, I met several cyclists riding in the opposite direction. Did they seem to speed up when they got closer and saw me and my flapping, bloody denim outfit, or did I imagine that?

When I crossed the little River Sark from England into Scotland, there were no signs to mark the border, no welcomes or flags, just a well-made little hump-backed bridge. No barbed wire either. But the buzz I could suddenly hear was not from swarming bees. It came from a line of great pylons, their six arms carrying electricity from Scotland down into the cities of England. In the distance I saw a speeding train on the main line from Glasgow, and the rising hum of the motorway replaced the buzz of the pylons as I walked further south.

When I reached the outskirts of Gretna Green, people

working in their front gardens looked at me as I passed and then quickly looked away. One trouser leg flapping behind me like a flag must have seemed odd (and safety pins were never part of my survival pack in my rucksack) but at least I didn't make the mistake of saying 'good afternoon'. That would have sent them running indoors. When I reached the Famous Blacksmith's Shop, now an extensive tourist attraction complete with the mandatory bagpiper, at least two groups of people pointed at me from the safe distance of the other side of the street. 'I ripped my jeans on a barbed-wire fence, okay! I'm not a crazy person,' I didn't say. A sign at the crossroads made me sag: 'Gretna Gateway Village 1 mile'.

Having walked under the thunder of a bridge carrying the M74, I came to the Marriage Hall. A wedding appeared to be emerging, although it looked unlike any I'd ever seen. The bride was carrying a small dog, the groom had in his hand what looked like a posh shopping bag and people I took to be guests were engaged in a vigorous exchange that was on the point of developing into an argument. When they saw me coming down the pavement towards them, all stopped, looked at me without inhibition, staring, silent, until the little dog barked at me and I stepped off the pavement to walk around the wedding party.

Gretna Green and Gretna are noisy. The roar of traffic, road and rail, seems incessant. The motorway slashes straight through, as does the dual carriageway of the A75 to Stranraer and the Irish ferries, and the main railway lines run roughly parallel. It's not so much a town as a series of busy junctions. Perhaps that's a theme; why so many still join in matrimony, even though all of the historic reasons for being married at Gretna have long ago evaporated.

Forty-seven years after the Union of the Parliaments the border still mattered – to young lovers. The Marriage Act of 1754 set a minimum age of twenty-one for those in England who wished to marry but did not have the consent of their parents. No such restrictions applied in Scotland, and ministers and priests did not have a monopoly on conducting ceremonies. It was possible to become legally married by making a simple declaration in front of two witnesses and thereafter having the marriage dated and recorded. Gretna Green lies less than a mile from the border, and after 1754 breathless runaways arrived from England, and were sometimes pursued.

The local blacksmith, Joseph Paisley, began conducting brief ceremonies in his forge. After a fee had been paid and two witnesses found, he would ask the couple standing on the other side of his anvil, 'Are you of marriageable age?' That is, over sixteen. And then, 'Are you free to marry?' That is, not already married and planning to become a bigamist. The answers to both questions were always yes, and then the blacksmith would bang his hammer on the anvil and the deed was done. For a century, business boomed until an act was passed that insisted couples spend a three-week residency in Scotland before any ceremony took place. Despite this, the anvil continued to ring. Even after the English age of consent was reduced to sixteen, and marriage by declaration was banned, couples still come to Gretna.

It is astonishing how tenacious tradition can be. With its ceaseless traffic noise, the brutal routes of roads and railways seriously compromising any sense of what might be a romantic or picturesque setting, people still want to be married in Gretna Green. Baffling.

Having negotiated the dangerous junction of the A75 and the old A74, the ancestor of the motorway, where there is a pavement on only one side of the road and a blind corner and blind summit on either side, I at last found the entrance to the Gateway Outlet Village. Here, people were much less inhibited. A grossly fat man leaning against his car looked up from his mobile phone and stared at me as I passed. Others moved quickly out of my way. The first shop I came to was Marks & Spencer. Thank goodness. Good old Marks & Sparks. Generous waist sizes. Choice.

I quickly found the jeans rails, picked out the right size (by no means the largest) and headed to the fitting room to discover exactly what 'flexible waistband' meant.

'We've got a first-aider in the store!' Standing by the cubicles, the lady in charge managed not to raise her voice, just.

'I'm fine, thanks,' I said, needlessly pointing to the ripped, flappy leg of my jeans. 'Had an argument with a barbed-wire fence. Lost.' I saw that my boots were covered with tiny yellow grass seeds and I'd forgotten that my breekfeet were still soaked.

'It's no trouble,' she persisted, as I waited for a cubicle to come free. Women who passed me with clothes on hangers pressed themselves against the walls. 'We can call a doctor if you like?'

I smiled. 'It's OK.' I said. 'Looks worse than it is. I expect I'll live.' I squeezed into a cubicle, hauled off my boots and wet, ripped jeans, straightened up and looked in the full-length mirror. And scared myself.

At some forgotten point after I'd fallen, I must have wiped my forehead with my left hand, the hand with all the puncture wounds. Above my eyebrows, up to where my hairline used to be, and on one cheekbone, much of my face was caked in dried blood. And just below my left ear was the track of a bright red trickle where I must have cut myself when I hit the ground.

When I am wearing a particularly ancient and much-loved shirt, with a frayed collar and cuffs and perhaps a button or two missing, and comfortable jeans with perhaps a hole or two and maybe a paint stain, my wife tells me that I look like a homeless man and on no account should I go anywhere or see anyone else. That afternoon I looked like a deranged half-dressed homeless man who had been in a fight and come off worse.

'Thanks,' I said to the lady in charge of the fitting rooms. 'These fit fine. I'll just keep them on.' As if there was any other option. I'd done what I could about the mess on my face with spit and my already bloodstained hankie. 'You don't happen to have any wipes?'

Bless her and Marks & Sparks, she did and handed me a handful, directing me to the nearby customer toilet. She also agreed to dispose of my ruined jeans. ('Recycling.') After I'd cleaned the rest of the blood off my face and combed my hair, I went to pay.

'Hang on,' said the lady behind the till, as I walked away. Was there blood on my neck? She came out and tore something off my backside. I must have flinched. I'd left the labels on. When I got home, I'd never be able to think of a plausible reason for buying new jeans or explain the long scratches on my legs. I'd be grounded, never again allowed out on my own.

'Is there a pub near here?' The lady with my labels was smiling sympathetically at me, as I visualised a pint of shandy, the glass cold and misted, the bubbles winking at the brim.

'Across the main road,' she said.

The pub was busy. One bar was packed with football fans watching and haranguing a big screen. In the bright sunshine, dozens sat at unshaded outside tables (only the British do this) as plates piled with burgers or fish and chips were set down in front of them. Inside the door of the lounge bar was a sign, 'PLEASE WAIT TO BE SEATED'. I waited. A queue formed behind me. There were plenty of free tables. Waitresses were ferrying plates outside while a sullen-faced barmaid pulled cold pints of lager and set them on trays. I waited a bit more. For another fifteen minutes the queue waiting patiently to be seated was ignored. Feeling I should take the lead, I approached the bar. 'Can we just sit anywhere?' The barmaid looked at me blankly, with a slight shake of the head. 'You'll just need to wait.' She pointed. 'Like it says on the sign.' As I walked out of the door, back into the sunshine, it seemed to me they were making so much money that politeness and good service were not needed.

At a petrol station across the road I bought a pork pie, a packet of peanuts, a small bar of chocolate and two cold bottles of fizzy orange juice. On a bench under a tree by a roundabout I enjoyed a very late lunch, on this, the last day of my journey between Britain. It seemed like a long time ago, another age, since I'd crossed the A1 at Berwick and followed the edges of the bounds down to the Tweed.

Back up at the Famous Blacksmith's Shop the piper was having his photograph taken with tourists. I noticed he was holding not his pipes but a half-empty bottle of mineral water. Being an icon was clearly thirsty work. Under a strange sculpture, an arch formed by two giant arms that grew out of the ground and clasped hands at the apex, couples were having their pictures taken. Another sculpture, possibly by the same artist, was a little more explicit. In a tight, almost muscular clinch, a naked couple embraced, their groins unfeasibly close, surely causing some discomfort for the man, always assuming he was enjoying himself.

Like the Gateway Outlet Village, the Blacksmith's Shop was about shopping. I had expected tat and trinkets, but, in fact, the quality of the goods on display was excellent and, so far as I could tell, not overpriced, many cuts above the sort of thing sold on Edinburgh's High Street. I bought a well-produced and well-written account of the history of the shop and the marriage industry, and having visited the food hall I wished I hadn't had my roadside lunch. But the nature of what was on sale didn't surprise me.

Tartan was everywhere, even a wide range of tartan gloves at £9.99, something I hadn't seen before. There were tartan rugs, handbags, purses, wallets, tea towels, scarves, tartan-covered hip flasks, diaries, notebooks, little pots shaped like tartan tammie hats, suitcases and a host of other items. Another tastefully laid-out shop featured many brands of whisky, malts and blends, and packaged in cellophane-wrapped hampers were some of Scotland's famous food brands: the likes of Tunnock's Caramel Wafers and Barr's Irn-Bru.

It was all predictable and depressing, even if the quality was high. The border is about as far away from the Highlands as it is possible to be in Scotland, but here was the appropriated iconography of the clans and the *Gaidhealtachd*. In a place where history happened all around it, momentous events that changed nations, where local identity used to be immensely powerful and distinctive, visitors and shoppers were offered tartan, whisky, bagpipes and the rest of the weary, threadbare images of a Scotland that never was, all of it backed by a familiar soundtrack. When I was in one of the emporia, I heard James Horner's plaintive music from *Braveheart*, a film that put William 'Mel Gibson' Wallace in a kilt and painted a saltire on his face. The Borders has a unique, rich history, but it had been drowned out by a flood of cliché, by hackneyed images from elsewhere. About the old Debatable Land, the haunt of Kinmont Willie Armstrong, where Merlin fled into the forest, where medieval armies and Roman legions marched, there was silence. And outside the Blacksmith's Shop on a tall white pole flew the obligatory saltire flag, bookending my journey from Berwick.

Scotland, and especially the Scottish borderlands, is so much more than this. And yet, wandering through the shops it seemed to me that a uniform identity was being imposed on us as a consequence of insecurity, something defined not by Scotland's history or cultural traditions but by a need to be as different from England as possible. And nowhere is more different than the bens and glens of the Highlands, the hollering, charging, tartan-clad clansmen of the *Gaidhealtachd*. They even speak a different language, no matter that it is all but dead, and the songs are sad and wistful, romantic and plangent, and different. Or loud. Bagpipe music is unmistakably Scottish. It is impossible to imagine the massed pipes and drums marching down the main streets of Walmington-on-Sea or St Mary Mead. It would be like fingernails on a blackboard.

Sitting in the shade outside the shops with a cup of tea and a consoling piece of shortbread (something that would not be on the banned list of Scottish kitsch; scones, too, are exempt), I wondered what the equivalent of Gretna Green on the English side of the border might look like. How would visitors to England be welcomed? What stories and images might prompt the production and sale of gifts and souvenirs? Are there shops such as these at other places of entry, like Dover or Folkestone? I wasn't at all sure about the answers to any of these questions. Perhaps England is already well enough known; perhaps such things are not needed?

London seemed to be a cultural focus of a wider identity. The great tourist attractions of the Tower of London will no doubt trade in items to do with Beefeaters and all the history and ceremony around it. The monarchy is a magnetic focus for the tourist trade and its merchandise. But much of the attraction of London is less to do with Englishness than because it is one of the few truly international cities, a world city like Paris, New York, Rome and Berlin. Great architecture, the National Gallery, concerts at the Albert Hall, famous shops like Harrods and Harvey Nichols, and the National Theatre are all, in fact, international.

It's how the English see themselves that interests me and I've argued that fiction as much as fact or history supplies important elements in the patchwork of Englishness. At Gretna, it struck me that unlike Scotland's sense of itself, it has little to do with its immediate neighbours. England is simply too big, too rich and too powerful to care what the Welsh, the Irish and the Scots think. The so-called Celtic nations simply don't matter much. France, Germany, Spain and Italy have had a far greater influence, as the Brexit referendum showed. The Frogs, the Huns, Spics and Wops might even have been seen as a threat to English identity, as they attempted to submerge it within a United States of Europe. Despite that remarkable spasm in 2016, I don't believe that the English will impose a uniformity of identity on itself in the way that Scotland appears to be doing. I think there will emerge a mosaic of strong local clusters of cultural traditions and a new recognition of distinctive histories. And all will react against London's dominance. Tyneside, Yorkshire, Manchester and Lancashire, Cornwall and the Midlands-Mercia are already asserting themselves. The spectacular opening of the Commonwealth Games in Birmingham in 2022, with its snorting animatronic bull, the display of all the famous cars manufactured in and around the city, the music of Edward Elgar and the great ethnic diversity of the region showed very vividly how such identities can be constructed. A petition demanded that the bull should be displayed permanently in the centre of the city as its symbol. And it was.

I hope similar opportunities present themselves in Scotland. The sticky, cloying inauthenticity of tartanry not only corrupts and traduces the glorious culture of the *Gaidhealtachd*, it hides and sometime buries the richness of our local identities. My journey only strengthened my views on this. No one has any right to shoehorn me or anyone else into a uniform sort of Scottishness. No one can tell me I cannot be British as well, that I can't also identify with Miss Marple and Captain Mainwaring, with scruffy William Brown as well as Old Sir John Forster, Eric Liddel and Walter Scott of Buccleuch.

When Gaelic speakers meet someone they don't know, they don't ask them where they are from, where they live or what they do. Instead they say, '*Co às a tha thu?*' It means, 'Who are your people?' Those and many more, they are my people, all of them: Border Reivers and farmers on both sides, great Olympic athletes, lady detectives, snooty bank managers playing at soldiers, and naughty English schoolboys. All of them. They enrich my identity, my sense of myself, and they do not dilute it. To paraphrase Walt Whitman, I am large, I contain multitudes and I will not be told who I am or should be. I will continue to find that out for myself.

It was time to walk the last mile, to leave behind the shops and the traffic noise of Gretna, and to make my way down to the mouth of the River Sark. Near the garage where I'd bought my picnic there are streets of new housing too recent for my old Pathfinder map, but one sign told me where to go. Sarkfoot Road led to a boarded-up building that might have been a care home. Beyond its car park and an algae-covered pond was a wicket gate at the top of a gentle rise. Beyond that lay a panorama, the River Sark, the Solway, huge skies and vast vistas to the west. It felt as though I'd stepped through a portal. The sun sequined the sea with sparkling glints and the ebb tide had exposed the featureless flats of Rockcliffe Marsh on the English shore.

I came on a relic. By the muddy banks of the trickling little river were the massive, brick-built piers of a bridge. One of them had collapsed into the Sark. They once carried a railway built during the First World War to service a leviathan, a monster that has left very little trace in Gretna. It was the largest factory ever built in Britain and it supplied the means to kill and wound millions of people.

*   *   *

At 4 a.m. on 9 May 1915, officers focused their binoculars as the early morning light crept across the flat and desolate landscape near the village of Aubers. Having climbed the trench ladders, they scanned the German front line, little more than two hundred yards away, searching for movement, trying to make out and locate enemy positions behind the dense lines of barbed-wire defences. It was very quiet and the soldiers massed in the trenches below spoke only in whispers, not wishing to give any warning of the attack to come.

At 5 a.m. the British bombardment began and the skies rained thunder. High-explosive shells from howitzers whistled over the heads of the men in forward trenches, while field guns fired volleys of shrapnel, trying to blow holes in the German wire. Half an hour later, the bombardment intensified as shells were loaded into the field guns, trained on enemy positions, and more volleys were fired.

When the artillery ceased, whistles were blown and their officers led the infantry attack across no-man's-land. The men of 1st Northants, 2nd Royal Sussex, 2nd Royal Munster Fusiliers and 2nd Welsh Fusiliers would find no cover, as the German machine guns opened fire. The short artillery bombardment had done little damage and before the offensive the British had gathered no intelligence on the much-improved and reinforced German defensive positions. From behind massive breastworks, machine-gun crews poured murderous, incessant fire on the British advance.

The slaughter was immediate and devastating. Soldiers were catapulted backwards, riddled with bullets, as they reached the top of the trench ladders or the parapet steps. Some units were so badly hit that none could advance beyond their own parapet and the trenches behind them filled with the bodies of dead and dying men. It was blood-drenched carnage and chaos. And yet officers were ordered to continue the attack. Three brigades, about fifteen thousand men, attempted to advance across no-man's-land but were cut to pieces by a coordinated, well-organised cross-fire from German machine-gun positions. These were so well entrenched that in all the confusion, smoke and panic of these near-suicidal advances they were difficult to see. Entire lines of men were felled like ninepins by the co-ordinated hail of bullets that spat and zinged through the early-morning air. It was said that the German machine-gunners were so appalled that they shouted at the British to stop, to retreat. But still they kept on coming, ordered forward by their officers, those who had not already been slaughtered as they led from the front.

The few places that had been breached became death traps. Soldiers were forced to bunch. That made them easy targets and so many men were hit that the gaps became clogged with the dead and dying. About a hundred extraordinarily courageous men of the Northants and Munster regiments broke through the German lines, but all were quickly killed or captured. Hundreds more were lying flat on the bare ground in no-man's-land, some so desperate that they used the corpses of their comrades as cover. They were hopelessly pinned down, unable to advance or retreat. By 6 a.m. the offensive had completely stalled. In less than half an hour thousands had been killed or wounded and no ground gained.

Astonishingly, General Sir Douglas Haig ordered a renewed bombardment in the afternoon to be followed by another infantry assault. At about 4 p.m. 1st Black Watch and 1st Cameron Highlanders and other units charged across what had become a killing field littered with bodies, some men still alive, crying out in pain and for help. Within minutes, they had suffered a thousand casualties. The carnage was extraordinary. All along the British Front, men were being shot to pieces as the German machine-gunners raked across their lines.

The Battle of Aubers was a disaster. In a single day, 9 May 1915, the British army suffered more than eleven thousand casualties, most killed or wounded within yards of their trenches. They never had a chance. Five days later a military disaster became a political crisis.

Watching the British attack was a retired soldier. Charles à Court Repington was appalled at the senseless slaughter of his former comrades and his Sandhurst-education and military experience helped him identify the root of the problem. Repington realised that the opening bombardment had been far too brief and had left the well-built German defences largely intact. And the reason for that was a chronic shortage of ammunition. Far too few shells were being produced in Britain. What made his observations incendiary was the fact that Repington was a war correspondent working for *The Times*.

He sent a telegram, part of which became a headline: 'Need for shells: British attacks checked: Limited supply the cause: A lesson from France'.

Repington went on: 'We had not sufficient high explosives to lower the enemy's parapets to the ground . . . The want of an unlimited supply of high explosives was a fatal bar to our success.'

Immense pressure was brought to bear, much of it orchestrated by the owner of *The Times* and the *Daily Mail*, Lord Northcliffe, and by David Lloyd George, the Chancellor of the Exchequeur in the wartime coalition government led by H. H. Asquith. The prime minister was in turn very reluctant to criticise his Secretary of State for War, Lord Kitchener. His reputation had to be protected. A Boer War hero, Kitchener's was the face that launched the huge recruitment campaign for the British army on its famous, much-imitated poster. The extravagantly mustachioed general stared out sternly, pointing a finger at young British men, saying not, as is often assumed, 'Your Country Needs You!' but 'Britons, Lord Kitchener Wants You. Join Your Country's Army. God Save the King!'. The prime minister's wife, Margot Asquith, remarked tartly, 'He is not a great man, he is a great poster.' Her husband's problem was that Kitchener was the face of the war.

Nevertheless, intense pressure from Northcliffe's *Times* and the *Daily Mail*, coupled with Lloyd George's plotting behind the scenes, forced Asquith to act.

A new Ministry of Munitions was created, with Lloyd George in charge. One of his first acts was to have built the largest factory ever seen in Britain, and it was constructed across the southern half of the old Debatable Land. The site was far from any major population centres and it was thought that sea-mists might hide it from reconnaissance. The dimensions are staggering. HM Factory, Gretna, stretched for nine miles from near Longtown on the English side of the border to Eastriggs in Scotland. Covering nine thousand acres, it was serviced by one hundred and twenty-five miles of railway that linked four production sites (the danger of explosion demanded a low density of buildings), its electricity was supplied by the factory's own coal-fired power station and its water taken from the River Esk. More than eleven thousand women (the Munitionettes) and five thousand men worked in this vast complex and Gretna grew into the first government-sponsored new town in Britain. Thousands of workers also lived at Eastriggs.

The great factory made cordite – what Arthur Conan Doyle called 'devil's porridge'. He wrote:

> The nitroglycerin on the one side and the gun-cotton on the other are kneaded into a sort of devil's porridge; which is the next stage of manufacture . . . those smiling khaki-clad girls who are swirling the stuff round in their hands would be blown to atoms in an instant if certain small changes occurred.

Cordite had replaced gunpowder as a means of propelling a shell to its target. At its peak HM Factory, Gretna, produced eight hundred tons of cordite a week, enough to ensure that the British army's artillery would never run out of ammunition and that the catastrophe at Aubers would not be repeated.

After the end of the First World War (a phrase coined, incidentally, by Charles à Court Repington in his reports to *The Times*) much of HM Factory, Gretna, was decommissioned and the land sold off. At Longtown the site became the Central Ammunition Depot, storage for a huge volume of ordnance and explosives. There exists a leaflet local people should read. It details what to do if there is a major incident and it is updated regularly.

Once I'd passed the piers of the old railway bridge, I looked for somewhere to sit down on the shoreline as near to the outfall of the Sark as possible, where England and Scotland dissolve into the sea. It had been a long and eventful day and I was glad to find a grassy shelf above a small beach. The early evening sun behind them made a small herd of cattle grazing on Rockcliffe Marsh seem much closer. A man and his collie walked along the English bank of the river and we waved at each other.

At journey's end I felt I should try to arrive at some conclusions, but any that occurred to me seemed too pat, too tidy, like tying string around a neatly wrapped parcel, and not like the scrappy, messy, incomplete stories that history actually tells us. I'd discovered a great deal I didn't know or didn't fully understand. My morning on the Scots Dyke and its barbed wire had settled, and I was consoled by the notion that I rarely discovered anything new or worthwhile by walking down well-trodden paths.

War had been a constant theme along the border, from the blizzard of arrows on Halidon Hill to the firing ranges at Otterburn, and on to the vast quantities of cordite for the shells and bombs of HM Factory, Gretna. That is a legacy no one wishes to inherit. Too much blood was spilled at Flodden and a string of a hundred other battles. Hard borders harden attitudes and can entrench prejudices.

And yet nationalism, both English and Scottish, is a perfectly valid and understandable reaction to global-isation, to forces few can comprehend, far less control. We now live in a fast-moving society that is intimately and constantly connected, and at the same time we transact much of the business of our lives in a series of faceless exchanges. Instead of having the grocer in St Mary Mead wrap our purchases in brown paper and put them in our wicker baskets, we fill online baskets and have them delivered to our door. Instead of discussing matters with Mr Mainwaring at his bank in Walmington-on-Sea, we no longer have bank managers but instead type in our customer numbers and pins and shift money about. A great deal has been lost in the name of convenience.

Economic globalisation is now an irresistible reality, as the rows of flickering digits of the twenty-four-hour markets fluctuate, sending prices up and sometimes down, making governments react rather than initiate. But where unity of purpose across the world is essential is in the face of the greatest crisis humanity has ever faced, the climate emergency. The fields of flowers I found on the English side of the border at Carham need to send their windblown seeds across it.

But equally the globalisation of identity must be resisted. Our sense of ourselves is precious and it cannot be suppressed by a uniformity forced on us by either economics or politics. In Scotland, the tide of tartan must be made to recede; it is not a harmless or amusing cultural quirk but the cause of real damage. The matter of the flags at Lamberton Toll is a minor symptom of a major issue. Let local identity flourish, but let us all unite. I am not the only Borderer who contains multitudes. We all do. On both sides of the Tweed.

Evening clouds began to gather over the Solway, as the tide turned. A westerly wind rippled over the water and the cows had been moved off Rockcliffe Marsh as its pools began to fill. In the distance, echoing behind me, I heard a train sound its whistle as it raced across the border.

Acknowledgements

I want to thank Simon Thorogood for all his editorial skills, his excellent judgement and most of all for his faith in this book. It started life as something very different, and on every step of this long walk Simon supported me and I am more than grateful.

For all his steadfast kindness, I also want to thank my agent, David Godwin. His comments and commitment were both invaluable.

I am blessed with tolerant friends, people who read my manuscripts and point out blunders, infelicities and make helpful suggestions. Thank you to Gordon Brown, Walter Elliot and George Rosie for all your help and encouragement.

This book is dedicated to my sisters, Barbara and Marjie Moffat, with thanks for a lifetime of love, and a lot of tolerance.

Further Reading

Barrow, G. W. S., *Kingship and Unity: Scotland 1000–1306*, Edinburgh University Press, Edinburgh, 2015

Crofton, Ian, *Walking the Border: A Journey Between Scotland and England*, Birlinn Publishing Ltd, Edinburgh 2015

Grassic Gibbon, Lewis, *A Scots Quair*, Birlinn Publishing Ltd, Edinburgh, 2006

Moffat, Alistair, *The Borders: A History of the Borders from Earliest Times*, Birlinn Publishing Ltd, Edinburgh, 2002

Moffat, Alistair, *The Scots: A Genetic Journey*, Birlinn Publishing Ltd, Edinburgh, 2012

Smyth, Alfred, *Warlords and Holy Men: Scotland AD 80–1000*, Edinburgh University Press, Edinburgh, 1989

Sprott, Gavin, *Farming*, National Museums Scotland, Edinburgh, 1995

Watson, W. J., *The Celtic Place-Names of Scotland*, John Donald, Edinburgh, 2011